INTRODUCTION TO TH

It all started in the treasure room. OK, it was really the archive room in the New York Public Library. A friend of mine who oversees the library's extensive archives had called me in. Knowing I have always been fascinated with the history of the domestic arts, she said, "You HAVE to see this."

I hurried right over and was not disappointed. Laid out upon an old mahogany table was a treasure trove of dusty old books, pamphlets and other artifacts, speaking to a bygone era. Spread upon the table were early clippings from vintage magazines to several books, pages tattered and yellowed with age, with content ranging from recipes to etiquette to childcare to house plans.

As a homemaker and history buff, no other topic is as fascinating to me then to read about the ladies of yesteryear, how they lived, and their habits. I knew I'd have a lot of reading ahead of me. I also knew that if I was interested in these vintage treasures, that surely others would be too. From that day forward, a new hobby was born. I would bring these artifacts to a modern-day audience through the Vintage Homemaking series. This particular issue is the second volume in the series.

What follows is an advanced course in homemaking dating from 1937, painstakingly transcribed into this modern format. It details the practicalities of managing a home in that era as well as advice on how to conduct oneself socially. Truly, a trip back in time that offers a fascinating glimpse into the personal interests of a young woman living in the United States in the mid-to-late 1930s prior to embarking on her role as household manager.

We each have our own interests in reading from the days of old. For me, the moments in this specific course that remain my favorites are the intriguing, and often amusing, passages that suggest just how different life was back then. While much of the advice in this course can stand the test of time, many things will not. I would think that tipping a hotel porter of today only ten cents, as suggested in the book, might get your luggage angrily thrown from the hotel's rooftop! All joking aside, be sure to use caution regarding some of the first aid and home cleaning tips. I think it's safe to say that one would no longer want to use gasoline as a home cleaning aid and a modern-day physician should be consulted before resorting to some of the outdated and potentially harmful first aid remedies mentioned within this volume.

Despite the differences, in many ways, things are still the same. Numerous habits have gone the way of the wind, either due to modern innovation or simply to an increase in knowledge and newer technology. Though today's skilled housekeeper is not too different from one many decades ago. She plans carefully and executes her plans in the manner best calculated to save time, energy and money. She can use her skills to truly make a house a home.

Topics covered in this course include healthy habits, diet and nutrition, meal planning, food selection and preservation, meal presentation and entertaining, wardrobe selection, fabric care, beauty tips, household layout, selecting furnishings, decor and utensils, cleaning and sanitation, and keeping within a sensible budget by properly selecting items that will provide durability. Other topics include manners and etiquette as well as suggestions for leisure and recreation. Guidelines given many decades ago – many of which are still useful in household management today.

So sit back, relax with a cup of tea, and take a trip back in time. Class is now in session.

What follows is the exact Advanced Course in Homemaking, presented in Atlanta, Georgia in the year 1937:

Dedicated to co-workers in the field of education for home and family life, in tribute to the unselfishness and nobility of their service.

TABLE OF CONTENTS

Unit 1

HEALTH

CHAPTER 1

PERSONAL HEALTH

For Women, Beauty
For Men, Strength

The Webster Dictionary defines health as "freedom from bodily pain or disease." But that definition is insufficient. We think of health today as meaning more than the absence of disease and a condition of immunity built up to resist or arrest disease.

Mental, emotional, and physical health, and are so closely related that it is difficult to draw a distinguishing line. It implies keeping the body and the mind at the highest level, living at one's best, and not being satisfied with mere absence from the hospital and sick room. "To live most and to serve best" is a universal challenge and the possessor of good health is best able to meet it successfully and happily.

Essentials of Personal Health.

It is easy to learn the essentials of personal hygiene, but putting such knowledge into practice, although most worthwhile, is very difficult. There are four important phases of personal health — physical, which depends upon the right food and clothing habits, fresh air and sunshine, rest, sleep, and proper care of the body; mental, which depends upon good straight thinking and a cheerful attitude towards life; spiritual, which depends upon a satisfying philosophy of life and the cultivation of spiritual interests; and emotional, which depends upon self-control.

Physical Health.

Wholesome activity is one of the essentials of good physical health. Taking an active part in some kind of outdoor exercise or play, such as athletic games, hiking in the country, skating, swimming, playing tennis, golf, hockey, and other games, which give real exercise and which use the large muscles of the body, keeps our vital organs at their best. Indoor exercises, too, are valuable, but always should be supplemented by much wholesome outdoor exercise. A good system of "setting up exercises" should be in the hands of every individual and should be practiced daily.

Physical exercise also helps toward acquiring a good posture, which, by the way, is essential not only to physical health but to mental health. The correct posture is an erect body, with the head poised on top of the chest, the abdomen flat and contracted, and the weight so placed that the body can be moved readily in any direction. It is difficult to remain mentally depressed when you practice walking with a light, elastic step, your head up, and an expression of cheerfulness on your face.

Right food and clothing habits.

To maintain health we must have an adequate diet. Many people have ill health as a result of improper dietary habits. Food gives strength and energy to perform our duties. Food builds tissue, produces energy, and regulates the body processes. We hear much almost every day about someone with a food-deficiency disease, which usually means that the invalid's food lacks balance in vitamins and minerals. The importance of a balanced diet with generous servings of fresh, raw fruit and green vegetables, whole cereals, and milk cannot be over-emphasized. Sunshine and cod liver oil are all important for children and others whose diets are low in Vitamin D.

The manner of eating is also important. Eating meals hurriedly and eating when tired are among the chief causes of indigestion. Meal time should also be a happy hour, because cheerfulness aids digestion.

It is not enough merely to say that ill-fitting clothes retard the circular movement of the blood and by so doing hamper the other tissues and organs of the body in the performance of their natural functions. Clothes such as wraps, cloaks, and raincoats protect the body from exposure to sudden extremes of cold weather, and the clothes of everyday wear, if properly chosen, assist in keeping the body at its normal temperature by excluding heat or cold, according to the needs of the wearer. Various other health services are rendered by clothing, but these will be discussed in other connections.

It is desired here to emphasize the aspects of cleanliness and neatness in clothing. Self-respect and the respect of others have an important bearing upon the health of the individual. In the absence of either self-respect or the respect of others the individual suffers mentally and mental suffering affects the most vital parts of the body. Clothing that is neat and clean contributes to a feeling of personal pride and wins the good opinion of others. Pride in one thing leads to pride in another—work, play, personal popularity, and leadership. Therefore, too much care cannot be given to the cleanliness and neatness of one's clothing.

Good air another essential.

Good ventilation means fresh air with the complete absence of carbon dioxide, the right amount of moisture, the right temperature, and some motion. Indoor air should be as nearly like the air outdoors as possible. Common faults in ventilation are overheated rooms, lack of circulation, and insufficient moisture.

The temperature indoors should be between 65 and 68 degrees Fahrenheit, never more than 70 degrees in the warmest part of the room. A good thermometer is essential in determining when a room is at the right temperature. We should always see that our sleeping rooms are thoroughly aired. During the day, the living room and work room should be well aired by opening the windows on opposite sides of the room. This will provide a slight draft and renew the air. It is easier to keep the rooms warm and ventilated than to maintain the proper humidity. The amount of moisture varies a great deal in different sections of the country. An easy way to maintain moisture in the air is to keep a teakettle of water boiling in the room or to set a pan of water on the stove or in front of the fireplace.

Regular systematic breathing exercises which will increase the working capacity of the lungs should be practiced by everyone who is not engaged daily in some physical activity.

Rest and sleep.

Rest and sleep are necessary in order to keep the body in a perfect physical condition. When you use any part of the body too long, certain poisonous substances form in the body and cause a feeling of fatigue. Sometimes this is noticed in soreness or stiffness after we have worked a long time. When we have either physical or mental fatigue, the way to restore energy in our bodies and to the nervous system is to rest. Sometimes a change in work is all that is necessary.

Occasionally, we find people who suffer from insomnia. Insomnia may be caused by lack of exercise in fresh air, by drinking strong tea or coffee, by worrying, overeating, over-exercising, or by doing strenuous mental work just before preparing for sleep. In order to go to sleep quickly, the body muscles must relax. Sleep can usually be induced by walking in the open air or by taking a warm bath. As a rule, people who exercise in the open air are ready for sleep without further preparation. Who ever heard of a farmer or an athlete who had difficulty in sleeping?

Care of the body.

Consideration for our associates is one reason why we should be as clean as possible when we work and play. The cleaner we are, the better we look. It is agreeable to stand or sit near a person who bathes frequently, for no unpleasant odors come from the skin of such a person. We ourselves are not only more comfortable and happy when we are clean, but we are making others happy and comfortable.

Personal daintiness and cleanliness are important factors in winning and keeping friends. Armpits, particularly, perspire freely and not only give off an unpleasant odor but spot the sleeves of shirts and dresses. There are numerous preparations on the market that are simple and easy to apply, which, if used, assure both boys and girls of clean, odorless bodies and clothes. Fortunately, the well-groomed man of today and the well-groomed woman are using deodorants and are unwilling to appear in shirts or blouses whose arm-holes are circled with perspiration.

It used to be thought that during the menstrual period, bathing was harmful, but we know now that it is just as important to keep the body clean and healthy during this time as any other time. Although menstruation is often referred to as "illness," it is a perfectly normal function and during its period a girl should lead her usual life, with the exception that she should not indulge in strenuous exercise and should avoid undue fatigue or strain. Since the pores of the skin are more open during menstruation, colds are more easily taken. The girl who is menstruating should not take baths in cold water or in a cold room, and she should avoid sitting in drafts. Hot baths, too, should be avoided. It is best to use tepid water or water about the same temperature as the body. Occasionally a girl feels depressed during menstruation but this is the result of emotional disturbance rather than a physical condition. Fresh air and moderate exercise usually act as correctives.

Elimination.

Proper elimination is necessary to good health. A regular time for the bowel movement each day, preferably just after breakfast, should be made a habit. The muscular action of the intestines is rhythmic and there are certain times when this rhythmic action is more pronounced than at other times. Usually these rhythmic impulses are more pronounced in the morning after food has been taken into the body. Since the waste material in the intestines is made up of unabsorbed and indigestible portions of the food intake and many of the toxic poisons of disease, it is important that this waste be eliminated regularly. When the rhythmic impulses are disregarded, constipation results. Poor elimination causes the skin to be oily, rough, and muddy looking and also causes many illnesses.

The habit of taking cathartics should be avoided. The habitual taking of cathartics irritates the intestines and relieves constipation only temporarily. Proper food habits such as eating plenty of green vegetables and fruit, exercise in the fresh air, and a regular time of going to the toilet each day, will effect a permanent cure.

Mental Health.

The signs of mental health are many. They are fully as obvious to the observer as those signs which distinguish a state of perfect physical health from its abnormal opposite of illness and impaired vitality. And just as physical health results from the observance of habits, carefully planned and developed through undeviating practice, so, too, a healthy mind results from mental training persisted in until its product is habit.

Mental capacity is inherited but the brain cannot sustain its inherited powers without much effort to keep its growth and development under careful direction. To keep the brain normal, wholesome habits in its use must be formulated and unswervingly followed. Such habits would embrace the following as well as many others: weighing the consequences of an act before acting, forming accurate judgments, making truthful statements, resisting wrongful impulses, heeding the warnings of conscience, exercising tolerance, keeping an open mind, guarding against self-deception, keeping intellectually honest, controlling the emotional forces of the mind, cultivating a spirit of sportsmanship and fair play, keeping cheerful, and being respectful of others' opinions.

The above catalog of desirable mental habits seems tiresome if considered merely from the viewpoint of their number. But if viewed as essential characteristics of a healthy mind, each assumes at once an aspect of serious importance. What have you in a mind devoid of judgment? Conscience? Emotional Control? What kind of mind is that which lacks judgment, conscience, and control over the emotions? It will take the records of our criminal courts to supply a fitting answer to the last question. The possessor of such a mind might be a murderer, a sneak thief, an idiot, or merely a reckless driver. To keep the mind functioning at its best and to overcome obstacles to its health and growth, it is well to remember the important values mentioned in the following admonition:

"Learn the value of putting important things first; of facing difficulties squarely; of controlling the nervous system (control comes by degrees and requires much patience). Never hold grudges or criticize others in an unkindly spirit. Cultivate a pleasing disposition, and do not deceive yourself by believing a bad disposition is inherited. Use more intelligence than emotion in making decisions. Work faithfully and do not postpone important work. Have confidence in yourself and persevere in your efforts."

One with a too restricted view of life often has a mind that refuses to view new things with favor. New ideas cause revolt in the mind of such a person. His mind, when a new idea is held up to it, is closed to the appeals of reason. This type of mind could be termed "muscle bound" were it not for the fact that it has too little exercise instead of too much. Its possessor is generally called "narrow-minded." An open mind, on the other hand, sees new relationships, new ideas, and new values. It brings variety, interest, and health. Open-mindedness, together with confidence in self and faith in the goodness of the world, adds greatly to one's mental stature.

Spiritual Health.

Spirituality is the heart conviction, while morality is the social expression of it; morality may be practiced as a matter of habit without the inner urge, but when pressure comes, morality alone will fail. It must be supported by the spiritual. "Religion is a way of living. It is a two-way reach; out toward man, up toward God."

In the charm courses which have attained a wide measure of popularity, spiritual health is given as a helpful factor in winning friends and in making people want to be with you. These courses emphasize the importance of emotional control and the necessity of developing a satisfying philosophy of life in order to attain spiritual health.

If one has spiritual health it shows itself in love, joy, peace, unselfishness, honesty, and other attitudes. What sort of attitude do you have toward your fellowmen, your classmates, your brothers and sisters, your own self? This is all tied up with your spiritual health. A person who is spiritually healthy sees things in their relative importance; we say of him that he has "a good sense of values."

If we have faith in the goodness of life, we will not consider as lasting blights upon civilization such evils as devastating war and serious disease. We will view them as obstacles to the progress of the race that have yet to be surmounted and supplanted with institutions of service to mankind. Perhaps that is what Tennyson meant when he said:

"That nothing walks with aimless feet,
That not one life shall be destroyed
Or cast as rubbish to the void
Til God hath made the pile complete."

We cannot have the right faith in the goodness of life and be pessimistic. We must be able to see beyond the unpleasant, hard, or bitter realities of experience. If we have the right vision, play, laughter, and the joys of real living will come naturally to us. Joy is a tonic and is as needful to younger people and grown-ups as play is to children.

Some people are governed in their moods by the weather. Don't let the weather worry you or dampen your enthusiasm. You have enough sunshine inside if you know how to use it ; having this knowledge, you will not care whether there is rain or sunshine.

A poem by John Kendrick Bangs tells us:

"I do not sorrow when there's snow,
Or rain, or fog, or sleet,
There are more toys at home, yon know,
Than out there on the street.
So whether we have bright sunshine,
Or clouds all through the day,
I never sorrow or repine,
But play, and play, and play."

If people have faith in the goodness of life, the ordinary, everyday duties seem less monotonous and of deeper importance. Someone has expressed this thought as "The Glory of the Commonplace." Faith in life and commonplace things is the theme of the following poem by Don Blanding:

"I try to live each day
In such a way
That when tomorrow makes today a yesterday
I will have woven into the fabric of my life
Some gay design,
Some patch of color,
Bright to please the eye,
So that, in the graying years to come,
When all the quick, responsive senses dull,
I may look back across the patterns of my past,
And, in my memory.
Live the joys and pains
Of all my yesterdays."

Emotional Health.

Social and emotional health are closely related with mental and spiritual health. To develop a satisfying philosophy of life and to understand why we behave as we do, we need to study our emotions. A person who is physically seventeen years old is often emotionally very much a child; he demands shelter from every form of unpleasantness. In trying to run away from reality and in being unwilling to face life's situations, he not only injures his own health but makes an unpleasant associate for everyone else.

Many of the nervous breakdowns suffered by adults are really the result of a childish desire to be the center of attention. An emotionally healthy person, that is, one who is socially adjusted, realizes that he is a very small part of the world, and that while other people irritate him, he in turn irritates other people. In a world where each of us is a descendant of generations of people with widely diversified characteristics, emotions, natures, and interests, we each have developed peculiarities of disposition that are agreeable to some, disagreeable to others. We cannot live in a world of our own making, other people are necessary to our life and happiness; so it behooves us not only to make our own lives pleasant but to do the best we can to make life pleasant for those who necessarily come in contact with us.

In running away from unpleasantness, we often miss out on pleasant things as well. Others cannot shield us from pain or from our own share of hurts and unpleasantness. The more quickly we learn to make emotional adjustments in our lives, the happier we will be ourselves and the easier we will make life for those around us.

CHAPTER 2

HOME NURSING AND FIRST AID

Maintaining the health of the home is the most important problem we have. All of us are interested in our own health and in the health of our families, but few of us want to take the time or care that such a problem deserves. Those of us who are healthy too often neglect our bodies until they become diseased.

How Disease is Spread.

Many diseases are caused by harmful bacteria which enter the body, causing pain and suffering and producing poisons. These bacteria are passed from one person to another in various ways. Some of the most common means of passage are through drinking and eating "after other people"; visiting the sick who have communicable or contagious diseases; the refusal of some people to go to bed or to isolate themselves when ill with colds, sore throats, and other "contagious" diseases not under quarantine regulations; the refusal of others to obey the quarantine regulations; disregard for community health measures such as pure food and sanitary regulations; carelessness in handling clothing, dishes, and other articles used by the sick; and, finally, by unclean personal habits, such as coughing, sneezing, spitting without the use of a handkerchief, picking the nose, licking the fingers, depositing chewing gum on walls and furniture, and carelessness in using the bathroom at home and elsewhere.

Neglect of good health habits lowers resistance to disease. Worry and unhappiness interfere with digestion, rest, and sleep and prevent cheerfulness, which are all essential to good health. Overwork weakens the body. Wet feet and too much exposure to the cold lower resistance, thus giving disease germs a chance to grow. The use of alcohol and tobacco and all unclean personal habits leave the body weak and unprepared to "fight" disease germs. Rats, mice, mosquitoes, flies, "stray" cats, and dirt and filth of all kinds are carriers of disease.

The best way to prevent disease is to stop the spread of harmful bacteria. This requires the cooperation of every member of the family and every family in the community.

Choosing a Family Physician.

Your family physician should be one of the best in the community. The recommendation of friends and neighbors whose judgment you can trust is one helpful way of choosing, but even that has its drawbacks, as the one recommended may not be suitable for you! It is well to choose a physician carefully and not wait until an emergency arises when you have to take anyone you can get or one someone else recommends. Choose a physician in whom you can confide, whom you can treat as a friend, and do not forget that he will not betray your confidence. It is well to find out if the physician you are considering is in good standing with the American Medical Association and its branches in your community. Usually the better doctors in your community are continually studying in order to keep up with the new discoveries which are being made almost daily. One should be proud of having a family physician who frequently goes away to study. It is not only your doctor's duty, but his wish, to keep or make your body healthy, useful, active, and efficient.

After you have selected a physician you can trust, obey his instructions and do not allow the corner druggist, your neighbors, or yourself, to diagnose your case or prescribe remedies. It is wise to avoid the use of all patent medicines unless used upon the recommendation of a physician.

The Specialist and the Family Physician.

This is an age of specialization. A medical specialist is a person who has chosen some special phase of disease as his study and gives practically all his attention to that one thing. Doubtless he knows more about his specialty than your family physician. But no one can take the place of a family physician who knows each member of the family and has judgment that can be trusted in emergencies. He will not hesitate to send you to a specialist should his diagnosis show your need for one.

Some of the occasions when the advice of a trusted family physician will be appreciated are as follows: when some member of the family is seriously ill and needs the attention of specialists; when it is necessary to call a trained nurse or go to the hospital; when advice is needed concerning the use of vaccines, serums, and anti-toxins; when major health problems arise.

"An Ounce of Prevention."

The life of a machine depends upon keeping all parts in good repair. The human machine is no exception. It is therefore a good precaution to take a health inventory when some part sounds a warning.

A pain is nature's way of telling you that something is wrong with your body. Go to a reliable doctor at least once each year for a thorough examination. An examination often leads to the correction of physical defects and harmful health habits. It is better to go to a doctor though nothing is wrong than to fail to call him until some need is acute.

Visit the dentist every six months to have your teeth cleaned and examined. Having the dentist fill small cavities will keep them from growing larger and causing you pain or severe illness in later life. Have your eyes tested every few years. An oculist can tell whether or not you need glasses and can prescribe the type you need.

Usually the home is equipped to take care of minor illnesses and convalescent patients. But sometimes people become seriously ill very suddenly and must be cared for in the home until other arrangements can be made. Provision for such an event should be added to those for the treatment of minor illness and the care of convalescents. Statistics show that two percent of the people are sick all the time and that only ten per cent of the sick are cared for in hospitals. Ninety per cent then must be cared for in the homes and nursing must be done mostly by members of the family. For these reasons, simple rules for the care of the sick and for giving first aid should be learned by every member of the family.

The doctor does not mind leaving his patient at home when he can be assured of the interested and intelligent cooperation of some member of the family who will act as home nurse. He likes to have this person around when he visits the patient, in order that he may give her instructions and directions and also that she may help him by sterilizing instruments and moving the patient. If he cannot depend upon the proper cooperation, he will likely insist upon moving the patient to the hospital, when otherwise it would not be necessary.

The Personality of the Home Nurse.

Would you make a good home nurse? Cheerfulness, cleanliness, neatness, and tidiness in personal appearance are never more to be desired than when one is caring for the sick or convalescent. Personal cleanliness means a clean body, clean clothes, neatly combed hair, well-kept teeth, hands, and finger nails, feet well cared for and simply made cotton dresses, freshly laundered. Poise, good judgment, and self-control, as well as a cheerful, sunny disposition are much desired in the ideal home nurse. Personal charm, ease, and self-confidence are more appreciated in the sick room than elsewhere.

What the Home Nurse Should Know.

The home nurse should be able to understand and interpret the doctor's orders and should be in full sympathy with his instructions. She should be particularly careful in following the doctor's orders in giving medicine. She should read the directions carefully several times and should never change the amount of medicine to be given or the time of giving the medicine. If the directions say, "one teaspoonful after each meal," that does not mean before each meal or be- tween meals. If the directions say, "one capsule every four hours," the nurse should find out when to begin giving the medicine, whether to waken the patient if asleep during the day, and if the medicine is to be given during the night as well as during the day. The home nurse should not only be willing to follow the directions, but she should be able to understand the directions and should follow them intelligently.

The home nurse should know what furniture is needed in the sick room, how to keep the room clean and neat, how to give such personal attention as bathing the patient's face and hands, brushing the hair, adjusting the pillows, and doing other things that make the patient comfortable. The home nurse should know how to take the temperature of the patient and should keep an accurate chart for the doctor's information and convenience. She should also know enough about invalid cookery to prepare the food prescribed by the doctor and to serve it in an attractive way.

Something Else to Consider.

Nursing is a profession that requires one to study, just as one studies to be a doctor, a lawyer, or a teacher. Homemaking is a composite vocation, requiring the homemaker to learn to do many things and to meet many emergencies. First aid and the home care of the sick are among the skills she must acquire in order to be prepared for her responsibilities.
No one should expect the home nurse, for example, to be able to give a bath to the patient in bed, or to change the linen with the patient in bed, as well as the trained nurse could perform these services but she should know how.

When You Visit the Sick.

Whether you are acting in the capacity of home nurse or are visiting a sick person as a friend, there are certain rules that you should follow. Be pleasant, courteous, and thoughtful when you visit the sick room. Talk in a low tone of voice, but do not whisper. Walk quietly but do not tiptoe. Do not look sad or mournful. Cheerfulness is a good tonic. Tell your friend you hope to see him well soon. Have ready a jolly story or a good joke. Never tell a sick person sad or disagreeable news. Take a few fresh flowers, a magazine, or an interesting book with you when you can.

Do not stay long. Find out from the nurse or the one in charge of the patient how long you should stay. Usually a few minutes is long enough. A visit too much prolonged is worse than none. If someone else comes to visit your friend while you are there, you should shorten your visit but should not seem to hurry away. Ask if there are any errands that you can do or messages that you can send. Promise to come again soon.

People who are sick and those who are "just getting well" should be extremely careful about obeying the laws of health. Plenty of rest and sleep and quiet relaxation should be had before visitors are made welcome in the sick room. Fresh air, sunshine, and simple nourishing food should be allowed to help in the restoration of health.

A Cheerful, Well Ventilated Room is Needed.

The room in which a sick person must stay should be cheery, scrupulously clean, and kept in good order. Good ventilation is most essential as fresh air is even more necessary in sickness than in health.

The temperature should never be above 70 degrees Fahrenheit and a temperature of five or six degrees lower is usually better. The air in the room should be kept fresh by opening at least one window at both top and bottom. A sick room may be ventilated by placing a board at the bottom of the window so that the sash may be raised the width of the board. When possible, the sun should shine in the sick room some time during the day. Under all conditions, cheerfulness and cleanliness as well as good ventilation with plenty of fresh air and sunshine are essentials of the ideal sick room.

What Furniture is Necessary?

Remove all unnecessary furniture and use only that which can be easily cleaned. It is best to leave only such articles of furniture and other equipment as will add to the comfort of the patient or to the convenience of the nurse. A bed, a small table by the bedside, and a dresser for clothing and personal belongings are all that the patient needs. A chair and a closet or part of the dresser for her clothing and personal effects are all that the nurse needs, except that a cot is needed when the patient is so ill that the nurse must sleep in the same room.

Select Simple and Sanitary Furnishings.

The furniture and all the bedding used in the sick room should be of the type which can be easily cleaned and kept in a sanitary condition. Iron beds are better for the sick room than wooden ones because they can be washed with soap and water and a disinfectant when necessary. The mattress pad should be washable. The mattress should be firm and have a level surface. Pillows of medium size are usually more comfortable than large ones. The sheets should be two and three-fourths yard in length, long enough to tuck in well at the foot of the bed and to fold back at the head twelve inches or more to keep the blankets, quilts, and comforts clean. Blankets are better for covering than comforts because they are lighter and more easily cleaned. Sheets and pillow cases should be changed daily if possible. The washable bedspread should be changed often enough to keep it clean and neat.

Keep the Room Neat and Orderly.

The sick room should have a clean, sweet odor, and should be kept neat and orderly. Do not allow food and medicine, soiled dishes, tumblers of drinking water, soiled linen, or wilted flowers to remain in the patient's room. The floor should be swept with a brush or broom covered with a dampened cloth, or better, with a vacuum cleaner. Do not scatter the dust. Do you know why? Go over the walls carefully with a vacuum cleaner or with a broom covered with a clean, soft cloth. Begin at the top and brush toward the floor. Wipe the tops of doors and windows with a dampened cloth, and don't forget to clean and dust the window sills, the mirrors, and everywhere else that collects dust. Dust the furniture with an oiled cloth or dustless duster. Rugs are unnecessary in the sick room. In contagious diseases, no rugs should be permitted in the room that cannot be burned or easily fumigated.

Insofar as is practical, use the same methods in cleaning the sick room as those used in cleaning your own bedroom but give first consideration to the comfort and convenience of the patient. If the floor has been cleaned with hot water and soap, it should be allowed to dry thoroughly before the room is occupied by the patient.

Making the Bed.

Immaculately clean linen and bedding add much to the attractiveness of the sick room and to the comfort and happiness of the sick. Unless the patient is very ill or the doctor has given orders against it, the patient will prefer to sit up during the short time it takes to make the bed. When the patient is seriously ill, the sheets and other linen should be changed so that the patient will be disturbed as little as possible. Work quickly but quietly and gently.

Changing the linen and the bedding when the patient is in bed is usually considered a very difficult problem. Do you want to learn how to do it? Really, the hardest part is changing the under sheet, and this is merely a matter of making up one-half of the bed with the other half of the under sheet folded in the center in a long straight fold, then helping the patient to the clean side of the bed and completing the change. Now finish the bed just as you learned to make your own bed. It is important to keep the bottom sheet straight and smooth and tucked in securely on all sides of the mattress to prevent wrinkles.

Shake up the pillow, put on a clean slip, and place it gently under the patient's head. Additional pillows in the room add to the comfort of the patient, as it is restful to change pillows frequently. Often a pillow at the back or. under the knees makes the patient more comfortable. See that the bed is placed so that the sunshine and strong light will not shine directly in the patient's eyes.

Taking the Temperature.

No home should be without a clinical thermometer and every member of the family above twelve years of age should learn how to read one. Shake the thermometer down below 95 degrees. Hold the wrist loose and give the hand a quick jerk to force the mercury down in the bulb. Many thermometers are broken accidentally by shaking toward furniture or other objects in the room. After the thermometer is shaken until it registers 95 degrees or below, place the tube under the tongue and allow it to remain there at least three minutes.
The patient's lips should be closed firmly about the thermometer to hold it in place. The thermometer should then be read and the reading recorded. After each use, clean the thermometer by washing it in a weak solution of alcohol or carbolic acid and just before using it again, wash it thoroughly in warm water. Normal

temperature in the mouth is 98.6; in the rectum, 99.1; under the arm 98.1. Do not take the temperature immediately after giving a hot or cold drink.

The Pulse Beat.

The average pulse beat of the adult man is between sixty and sixty-five beats per minute; of the adult woman between seventy and eighty per minute; a baby's pulse rate is between one hundred twenty-four and one hundred forty-four beats at birth. Young children have a more rapid pulse than do older children, the rate gradually decreasing as they grow older. Use the finger, not the thumb, in counting the pulse for one minute at the wrist. The rate of an adult's respiration is from sixteen to twenty per minute. The respiration of children is more rapid than in adults.

Keeping a Record.

The home nurse should know how to carry out the doctor's directions. The doctor always wants to know how the patient has been since his last call. This requires keeping a record of the temperature, the pulse beat, and the medicine and food given, as well as the general condition of the patient. Some doctors want a more detailed record than others. Ask the doctor in charge to tell you how he wishes you to record what he desires to know.

Records usually show the day and hour of giving medicine and food; the readings of the thermometer; the count of the pulse beat; and the condition of the bowels and kidneys. It may also show the appearance of the tongue, the number of hours the patient slept during the day and night; the patient's reaction to company; and many more minor things which doubtless indicate more to the doctor than to the nurse.

Keep the room quiet by not allowing doors to slam, window shades to rattle, and other unnecessary noises to intrude upon the patient's hearing. Move quietly. Do not sit or lean on the bed. It is better to sit still in the chair and not rock. Speak quietly but do not whisper. Shade glaring lights so that they will not shine in the patient's eyes. Do not repeatedly ask the patient how he feels. Give the patient plenty of fresh water to drink unless the doctor has forbidden it. Keep the patient's feet warm. If necessary, keep a hot water bottle at the feet or place an extra blanket at the foot of the bed. Never enter a sick room in untidy apparel, and above all, be bright, cheerful, and smiling.

Bathing the patient's face and hands in cold water, brushing back the hair, shaking up the pillows and changing their positions, straightening the sheets and bedding, and rubbing the back with alcohol or talcum powder are little things usually appreciated. What else can you do to add to the comfort and happiness of the patient?

In cases of colds, sore throat, and other communicable diseases, keep the dishes separate from the rest of the family's. Wash them with a separate dish cloth or mop. It is just as essential to boil the dishes separately when one member of the family has a cold as when scarlet fever and measles are in the family. In boiling dishes, place them in a large kettle of cold water and let the water come slowly to the boiling point. The dishes should be left in the hot water until the water has cooled enough to handle the dishes.

Always wash your hands carefully with soap and warm water after handling anything that the patient has touched. Most diseases find their way into the body by way of the mouth. Wear clothing that can be boiled. Take time to follow the precautions given by the doctor, especially in boiling dishes and the bed clothing. Such precautions may be the means of saving the life of a member of the family. Flies and other insects should be kept out of the sick room on account of the comfort of the patient and because they spread disease germs.

Food for the Sick.

When serious illness comes into the family circle, all thoughts are directed towards providing the best possible care for the patient. The right amount of suitable food served at the right time and in an attractive manner is very important. Tempting and appetizing dishes are usually in demand, for sick people often think they do not want food. To be able to plan, prepare, and serve meals for the sick and convalescent in an attractive manner is an art.

Get your doctor to give you a list of foods which may be served to the patient, and from this list plan regular meals, giving as much variety as possible. If the patient asks for a certain food, first get permission from the doctor and then serve it at the next meal. Certain diseases require special diets, and in such cases the doctor prescribes the food as carefully as he prescribes the medicine.

In minor illnesses, the home nurse is told to serve well balanced meals, which means that the patient can have almost any kind of good wholesome food, but the home nurse should know how to select a good quality of food at the market, how to plan balanced meals, the best methods of cooking these foods, and how to serve them attractively.

Thus, it is seen that a knowledge of foods and cookery, or at least knowledge of the nutritive value of food and its digestibility, is necessary in order to carry out intelligently the doctor's instructions in regard to the patient's diet.

Planning the Meals.

A thorough knowledge of food and cookery is even more valuable when cooking for the sick and convalescent than when cooking for healthy, robust people. In long continued illness, the energy requirement must be met, to prevent the body tissues from being used as fuel. And so we have the problem of planning meals that stimulate the appetite, that are easily digested, and that furnish the right number of calories. In some types of diet, this becomes a rather difficult task, but the home nurse with the interest of her patient at heart, by careful, intelligent selection of food, usually solves the problem.

Too often hit-and-miss dishes are served to the sick with no thought of their peculiar and individual likes and dislikes. Do not overlook individual tastes. On the other hand, do not serve a patient food that the doctor has forbidden. Do not ask the patient to plan his own menu but try to find out what the patient wants without asking many questions. Watching the expression of the patient when the tray is received is one way to find out if the food is pleasing. Surprise dishes, attractively garnished, are usually appreciated.

Variety in color and texture and in methods of preparation add interest. Sometimes it is necessary to give foods that the patient thinks he does not like. That can be done by adding eggs, milk, and cereals to soups, or cooking cereals and vegetables in milk instead of water.

Diet for the sick is usually classified as liquid, soft , and light. A liquid diet includes such foods as broth, clear soups, beef tea, fruit juices mixed with water, milk and milk drinks, egg-nog, and cereal gruels. It is quite often necessary to feed patients who are on a liquid diet every two hours. In such cases vary the food. Do not give the same food twice in succession. Tea and coffee may be given to adult patients with the permission of the physician.

A soft diet includes all liquid foods, milk, creamed toast, strained cereals, vegetable pulp, soft cooked eggs, custards, junkets, cornstarch pudding, ices, and ice cream. It is sometimes necessary to serve a soft diet as often as every two and one-half hours.

A light diet includes the foods mentioned in liquid and soft diets as well as chicken, lean beef roasted or boiled, fish, oysters, fruits and vegetables, bread toast, and simple desserts.

Serving the Tray.

While the doctor prescribes the diet, it is left for the nurse to see that the food is properly prepared and served. Too many dishes on a tray give it a crowded appearance. Try serving the food in courses part of the time. "Serve hot foods hot, and cold foods cold," is an admonition never more appropriate than when serving food to the sick. Straws may be used when the patient is not able to sit up. Serve small portions of food. Do not fill cups and glasses or other dishes too full. A sprig of parsley or a single flower helps to make the tray more attractive. An attractively arranged tray with its spotless linen will often give zest to a jaded appetite and induce a patient to take the amount of nourishment needed to hasten recovery.

Knowing how to prepare simple, easily digested foods in a variety of ways will help; knowing how to garnish food attractively adds a pleasing touch and takes away the ordinary everyday look. Suggestions for cooking and serving invalid trays may be gathered from almost all cook books. Homemakers' sections of newspapers, magazines, and other publications also offer valuable suggestions. A "scrap book" of such suggestions would be useful and interesting.

First Aid

Often sickness comes at times when trained nurses and hospitals are not available. Imagine yourself in a situation in which someone dear to you is seriously ill under those conditions. Once a famous doctor was in a position to render aid in like circumstances, but he admitted that he was needed elsewhere. Before leaving, however, this doctor took time to remark that he would welcome the day when all such practical things were included in the school curriculum.

Prepare for Emergencies.

Study devoted to problems of the sick and convalescent will enable one to be more helpful when an emergency arises, more intelligent in asking the doctor questions about the patient, and more efficient in caring for the patient when the doctor is away. Very serious illness may often be avoided by giving preventive treatment quickly and taking prompt action when an accident makes first aid a necessity. Prolonged illness and much suffering can also be averted by knowing when to call a physician and what to do until he comes. Knowing where to find information is also helpful. Having a few supplies on hand for first aid is a wise provision. Then it is well to familiarize one's self with a few reliable books and bulletins on the care of the sick and first aid as well as to learn what supplies and equipment should be in the home medicine cabinet.

Fainting.

Fainting is probably the most common emergency which calls for first aid treatment. It is caused by a lack of blood in the brain. Place the patient on his back. Do not raise the head, but put a pillow under the feet so that the head is lower than the rest of the body. Loosen the clothing, sprinkle the face with cold water, and raise the windows. A stimulant may be given, such as aromatic spirits of ammonia, or a small amount of ammonia or camphor may be poured on a handkerchief and applied to the patient's nose. Coffee and tea are also good stimulants. Alcohol or whiskey should not be given to a person who has fainted or lost consciousness.

Shock.

Every injury is accompanied by more or less shock. The treatment is to stimulate the body. Lay the patient on his back, cover warmly, and give a half teaspoonful of aromatic spirits of ammonia in a half glass of water, then hot tea or coffee. Always send for the doctor unless the shock is very slight.

Burns.

Burns are caused by dry heat and scalds by moist heat. Stop the pain by excluding the burn from the air. Put a paste of baking soda and water or vaseline on the burned part and bandage lightly. In bums where the skin is broken or destroyed, there is always danger of infection. A boric acid dressing made of one teaspoonful' of boric acid dissolved in a cup of boiling water, or an ointment made with boric acid should be used.

Wounds.

Injuries in which there is a break in the skin are called wounds. In every wound, there is danger of infection. If sure no bacteria entered when the wound was made, simply apply a sterile dressing of surgical gauze, or a piece of cloth that has been boiled in water or dipped in an antiseptic solution. If dirt has entered the wound, it must be washed out with an antiseptic solution.

A good dressing for small wounds where there is an infection may be made by dipping cloths into a hot boric acid solution and applying them to the wounds, wetting the cloths as often as they dry out or become cold. If a wound shows inflammation, no time should be lost before a doctor is consulted.

Hemorrhage or Bleeding.

To understand better the nature of a hemorrhage, you should remember that the blood flows from the heart through the arteries and back toward the heart through the veins. If the bleeding is from an artery, the blood is likely to come in spurts, each spurt corresponding to a heartbeat. The blood from an artery is also a brighter red than that coming from a vein.

When an artery is cut, pressure on the side of the artery toward the heart will stop bleeding. For instance, if the blood is from an artery in the wrist, place the bandage around the arm to stop the bleeding.

In case the blood is coming from a vein and is coming freely, place a towel or handkerchief around the part away from the heart as tightly as it can be drawn. For example, if the bleeding is from a vein on the arm, put the bandage below the wound toward the hand.

In a small capillary that is bleeding, it is sufficient to make pressure with a piece of gauze or clean cloth directly on the wound for a few minutes. Pressure controls the bleeding and allows the blood time to clot.

Bleeding is the least dangerous part of a wound and is serious only in a few cases. The greatest danger is in infection. Remember, everything that touches a wound must be sterile or aseptic, in other words, surgically clean.

In cases of hemorrhage, it is dangerous to give a stimulant because the stimulant makes the blood flow with greater force and therefore increases the bleeding.

Drowning.

In the case of drowning, the lungs are filled with water. The first thing to do is to get the water out of the lungs in order that breathing may start again. To do this, turn the patient with face downward and one arm extended straight forward above the head and the other bent at the elbow to allow the head to rest on the hand or forearm. Keep the face of the patient turned to the side, leaving the nose and mouth free for breathing. Place your hands under his abdomen and lift him up, allowing the water to run out.

To start the resumption of breathing, kneel with one knee on each side of the patient's body. Be careful not to let the weight of your body rest on the patient. Place the palms of your hands on the small of the patient's back with the fingers resting on the lower ribs and the little finger just touching the lowest rib. Then, with arms held straight, swing your body forward slowly from the waist so that its weight is gradually brought to bear upon the patient. This movement takes about two seconds and decreases the size of the chest and helps to force the air out of the lungs. Now swing back to remove the pressure and the patient's chest will expand to its former size, drawing air into the lungs. Wait two seconds and swing forward again. Keep this movement going regularly until respiration is restored. Do not work too fast. From twelve to sixteen times a minute is a natural rate of breathing. Time your movements by a watch when possible. Keep working steadily for several hours, or as long as it takes to restore natural respiration.

While this artificial respiration is going on, let someone remove the wet clothing and cover the patient with warm blankets. Put hot water bottles or hot bricks at his feet. Rub the arms and feet toward the heart to start circulation. Don't get discouraged. Many lives have been lost because artificial respiration was not continued long enough. If the doctor does not arrive by the time the patient revives, give some stimulant, such as one-half teaspoon of aromatic spirits of ammonia in a small glass of water, or a cup of coffee or tea. Do not give liquids until the patient is fully conscious. After normal respiration is established, keep the patient quiet. Do not allow him to sit or stand up for several hours in order to avoid strain on his heart. Keep the patient warm while you await the doctor's arrival.

Practice the method of giving artificial respiration on members of your class who pretend to be drowned until you are familiar with every detail.

Insect Stings (Bees, Mosquitoes, Chiggers, and Ants)

When you can see the sting in the flesh, pull it out. Apply ammonia water, soda, salt, or camphor. Apply wet cloths if the affected part gives much pain.

Snake Bite.

Snake bite should be treated by thoroughly cleaning the wound and allowing it to bleed freely. When bleeding stops, a clean cloth saturated with a solution of boric acid should be applied warm. It is also well to tie a tight bandage above the bite to prevent the poison from going into the general circulation. If there are no sores in your mouth or on your lips, suck the wound when it does not bleed freely.

Dog Bite.

Dog bite should be treated in the same way as snake bite. Unless the dog is known to be rabid, he should not be killed at once, but placed where he cannot bite anyone else and held under observation until the doc- tor may know whether to administer the treatment for preventing hydrophobia.

Bandages.

The general purposes of a bandage are to retain a dressing in place, to prevent bleeding by exerting pressure, to protect the injured part from outside air and germs, and to lend support. The three general types of bandages are roller, triangular, and tailed.

CHAPTER 3

COMMUNITY HEALTH

In order to protect our own health and the health of others in our homes, we must be concerned about the health of our immediate community.

What is your responsibility in keeping your community clean and sanitary? One careless person may set at naught the efforts of the other family members to keep the home clean and sanitary. Likewise one insanitary home in a community may bring flies, mosquitoes, rats and mice to plague the entire neighborhood. Communities are made healthful places by the cooperation of their entire citizenry. The cooperation of each individual not only is necessary in working for the health of the community but is imperatively demanded.

Our state laws require healthful and sanitary conditions in industrial establishments and impose quarantine regulations, healthful housing conditions, and inspection of public rest and recreation rooms, parks, and playgrounds. Community governments pass laws and regulations to protect their citizens and the well modeled home provides sanitary and healthful conditions to protect the health of its members. The home that is lax in these respects is a menace to its neighbors.

We too often demand service from our community without expecting to give anything in return. It has given us service so long that we take it for granted, just as we take for granted that our fathers and mothers will clothe and feed us while we go to school. When the community furnishes a medical association to give us advice, a hospital to relieve suffering, and laws to protect our health, it has a right to expect its individual families to observe its safety laws and quarantine and isolation regulations, to comply with sanitary measures, and to immunize against communicable diseases.

The boy or girl who goes to school when he has a cold, instead of staying at home resting, is not only endangering his own health but the health of the entire community. We have heard thoughtless young people say, when afflicted with colds, "It won't hurt me to go to school; I just don't give in to colds." Even if that is true, it is a very selfish attitude to take, for while you might come home without seeming any worse physically, you have no way of knowing how many people you came in contact with and left with cold germs. You may not be punished in terms of money fines or imprisonment for such an offense against the health laws of the community as you would for disobeying its social and moral laws, nevertheless the offense is just as heinous. The community belongs to you, and your best interests obligate you to show respect for its laws and regulations.

That individual lives best who best knows and obeys the health laws that insure personal health, health in the home, and health to the community. What happiness is possible to him who attains business or professional success if he makes a poor inmate of the home and a poor neighbor of himself?

Professor John Dewey said, "What the best and wisest parent wants for his child, that must the community want for all of its children." More and more the community is becoming concerned with educating its citizens to understand and appreciate health. More and more, society is talking about health topics that formerly were taboo in public conversation, because people realize that it is only through education that the health problem can be solved.

Many diseases are caused by the growth of tiny micro- organisms called bacteria, commonly referred to as germs, which produce toxins or poisons. There are two types of diseases; communicable, those which are contagious; and non-communicable, those which arise from diseased organs.
Of the former, the most com- mon are measles, whooping cough, diphtheria, smallpox, chicken pox, scarlet fever, mumps, and colds.

Microorganisms enter the body through food, water, and air, hence it is important that we know and obey the health laws relating to their control. The habit of putting fingers, in the mouth, of using public drinking cups, and of eating after people would be more easily broken if we could visualize the thousands of micro- organisms which are carried to the mouth in these ways.

Prevention of Disease.

Through practicing right habits of daily living, our bodies can build up a resistance to disease in general. Healthful conditions of the body tissues help to protect our systems against the invasion of disease germs. We realize how much the general condition of our bodies influences our resistance to disease when we hear someone say he caught a cold because he was "all tired out." It is generally recognized that body fatigue lowers our resistance to disease. We should make it a point to get plenty of rest and sleep, to exercise in the fresh air and to form good food and clothing habits that we may increase our physical resistance to disease germs.

The body defends itself against disease poisons by means of the white corpuscles, antitoxins, and other germ- killing substances found in the blood. White corpuscles destroy disease germs by wrapping themselves around the germs, then absorbing and digesting them. When the germs begin to produce toxins in the blood stream, the body starts the manufacture of antitoxins, which it uses in stopping the poisonous effects of the toxins.

Another method by which disease is prevented is called immunization — natural and artificial. When we have an attack from certain diseases, substances are developed in the blood during the progress of the illness which have the power to counteract the germs of these diseases should they attack our body at another time. We call this natural immunization. Artificial immunity is effected by the use of serums or vaccines which are injected into the body by means of a hypodermic needle.

One of the oldest methods of prevention employed against a communicable disease is isolation of the patient from the public until he is entirely well. No one except those caring for him should enter his room. All dishes for the patient should be washed in soapy water and thoroughly rinsed in boiling water. All towels, bed linens and other clothing which the patient uses should be washed separately from the other clothes.

One of the most important ways an individual can show his appreciation of the community in which he lives, is by taking as much care as possible to avoid the spreading of contagious diseases.

The Venereal Diseases.

One of the latest ways the community has of protecting its families is through education, by bringing out into the open the discussion of causes, effects, and cures of the social or venereal diseases.

Hitherto, one of the reasons these diseases have been so prevalent and so hard to eradicate has been due to the attitude of society which banned their discussion before the public, in print or oral lectures.

The American Social Hygiene Association estimates that ten percent of the American population have some form of venereal disease. One of these diseases can be contracted quite innocently through contact with toilet seats or infected articles of clothing, which come in contact with the mucous membrane of the body. Such an infection is particularly dangerous to women, as it often extends into the reproductive organs and causes sterility.

One of the things that makes a venereal disease so serious is that the symptoms may disappear, even without treatment, and an infected person may think he is all right, while the germs continue to spread. The symptoms usually reappear after a time, even months or years later. Even in the arrested stages, the venereal diseases are communicable to others, so it is particularly important that proper medical care be given not only in the earliest stages, but continuously until the victims are pronounced cured by competent physicians.

Prevention of Venereal Diseases.

One of the ways that individuals can help to combat these diseases is to insist that society make laws to protect its homes and families. Laws making it illegal for marriage licenses to be granted to persons who cannot show a certificate of health would do much. Laws are also needed for the regulation and operation of such public places as restaurants, grocery stores, or any industrial center where employees come in contact with the food we eat or the clothes we wear. Employees in our homes, particularly maids and cooks should be required to show a health certificate, stating that they are free from the infection of any venereal disease.

The venereal diseases present no "class" problem. They are so widespread as to make demands upon the attention of society and the world at large. It is only by insisting upon examinations for all groups of people and all individuals that those who are not infected may continue to avoid infection and those who are found to be infected may take treatment for cure. In no other way can we hope to stamp out these social scourges.

Unit 2

FOOD AND NUTRITION

CHAPTER 4

ADEQUATE DIETS

"It is often as helpful to be reminded of something we have already learned as it is to gain new information." With the foregoing words a national Girl Scout leader opened a conference. This leader might well have been thinking about the food knowledge which many people have but never use through indifference to its value. Her statement justifies the use of facts here, that you have previously studied.

Does food really make a difference in our health; will the food we habitually eat actually influence the achievement of our deeper ambitions? Science answers this question in the affirmative. If you are skeptical, ask some breeder about his experience in feeding poultry and livestock or ask a physician about feeding tests with rats and mice.

Health is that condition of life which brings inner peace, joyful activities, and right attitudes; it is that state of physical, mental, emotional and spiritual fitness which gives individual happiness and brings happiness to others. Health is the result of doing things in the right way. Health does not come by accident or by chance, but by consistent and continuous training in food and other worthy habits. Practically everything in life that is worthwhile must be worked for. It takes years to grow a good oak tree. If health is worthwhile, it is worth working for and worth the time used in achieving it. Memorizing rules, which is but the mere repetition of words, will not bring health and its concomitants of beauty, vitality, and happiness to anyone. Health rules are helpful only in proportion to their use. The challenge of today is somehow to devise methods of making health practices consistent with health teaching.

Interdependence of Health and Nutrition.

Human health is dependent to a large extent upon the correct ap- plication of the science of nutrition. Likewise, all good health habits contribute towards providing good nutrition. It is true that the scientific selection of food is a controlling factor in nutrition, but other health practices influence the use that the body can make of food. Fresh air, plenty of sunshine and outdoor exercise, sleep, good work and study habits, and the right mental attitudes are other factors which play a vital part in the processes of nutrition.

Sometimes all these other requirements are met without achieving good results because the wrong foods are eaten. An eminent dietetic authority said that at least seventy-five percent of all sickness in the world today is caused directly or indirectly by inadequate diets. The aim of everyone of youthful age should be to select meals at home and elsewhere that furnish the essentials for body building that are required to make girls attractive, well poised, and radiant and to impart the qualities of strong, virile manhood to boys and younger men.

Almost everyone could give from personal experience examples of food habits which were discontinued because newer and better knowledge was made accessible. Little children are told, "Milk is good for you," without being given reasons. "Eat this for mother," or father, or teacher. These earlier appeals to children must give way to scientific knowledge in the case of older people. If older boys and girls are to practice good eating habits, they must be given those facts within their comprehension which science has revealed concerning nutrition. The adjurations: "Eat nourishing food," "Eat wholesome food," "Select a well-balanced diet" are too indefinite. Specific knowledge, right attitudes, and wholesome ideals, strong enough to influence and establish habits, are necessary.

Health and happiness depend to a large extent upon the application of the science of nutrition. Obviously then, the chief aim in teaching nutrition is to secure better health and greater happiness for everyone. The everyday use of a few essential foods should serve as the basis in meal planning. Food studies can be made interesting through disclosing the chemical composition of these essential foods and the relation of such composition to our bodies. Knowledge gained from these studies will prove to be a real nutritional safeguard.

Adequate and Inadequate Diets.

What is an adequate diet and by what means do we determine that a person is adequately or inadequately fed? Very quickly we may answer that one has an adequate diet when his food adequately provides growth, maintenance, repair for the body, and energy for its activities. On the other hand, malnutrition arises when the tissues of the body do not receive enough food to build them up and furnish energy and vitality for their functioning. Malnutrition is not a disease like measles or mumps, but a low condition of health and body resistance that makes one either susceptible to disease or defenseless against disease when it is contracted.

During the last forty years nutrition as a science has made rapid progress. Definite knowledge has been acquired by experimenting on white rats, guinea pigs, and even on human beings. Everyone needs to study nutrition and then be guided by a sensible combination of scientific knowledge and good judgment. Individual leaders with a large following among the masses are becoming more and more interested as science shows the importance of the study of foods and nutrition. They see, as we have, that these not only affect physical health but influence mental and emotional health, which we all know are closely related to the physical. The evolution of food study is most interesting. One by one, science has discovered the essentials of an adequate diet. One by one, science has proved beyond a doubt how each of these essentials affects one's health and how the lack of these essentials, or an inadequate diet, brings weakened vitality and actual disease, such as scurvy, beriberi, rickets, etc. Adequate diets give the body the best possible functioning capacity, as the chief purposes of food are to furnish energy, regulate the body functions, and build or repair tissue which is constantly being worn out.

Energy Needs.

Our bodies have often been called human machines because in numerous ways they are comparable to an engine or a furnace. Yet we are inclined to misuse them much more than we do our other machines. The surprising thing is that they seemingly do not get out of order so easily as other machines. This is because our bodies and the food we eat are composed of the same materials, so our bodies use up some of their own tissues when they are not fed regularly and properly.

As long as life exists we are burning fuel to give energy for work, for warmth, and for body activities. Every movement of the body — turning the head, raising the arms, and all internal and involuntary processes call for the use of more fuel for energy. Every muscular movement requires a certain amount of energy. Digestion, respiration, and circulation use energy; the eating of food itself increases our fuel needs. Deep breathing, rapid breathing, and vigorous heart action all cause increased activity of the muscles concerned and greater use of energy. Even when we are completely relaxed, breathing continues, the heart still beats, and all internal organs continue their functions through the use of energy.

Amount of Energy Needed.

The amount of energy needed each day depends mostly upon one's age, size, and activity. During growth, the energy requirement is greater in proportion than when full growth is attained. Generally, a large person uses up more energy than a small one, and the greater the activity in work or play, the more energy is needed.

Muscular work is the most important factor in raising the energy food requirement of adults. The minimum amount of energy is used during sleep, the maximum during great physical activity. The amount of energy saved during sleep depends upon the ability of the person to relax completely while sleeping. Other factors which influence the energy requirement are climate, season, housing, and clothing; they help to regulate the temperature of the air surrounding the body. An extra amount of heat is produced when we exercise or work, and extra energy food is needed to produce this heat. This explains why we be- come so warm when we are working hard, running, or walking rapidly and why such activity often makes us hungry.

Body fat acts like a woolen garment. The fat prevents loss of heat by radiation. At a low temperature of the air a layer of fat is valuable in preventing rapid loss of body heat and saves the body from burning fuel merely to keep warm. With a rising temperature, fat hinders heat loss. That is why a fat person is more susceptible to heat prostration than a thin person. A fat person suffers severely in hot, humid weather and works with difficulty as each movement adds heat which coupled with the humidity brings general discomfort.

The presence of a layer of adipose tissue under the skin as well as the custom of covering the greater part of the surface of the body with clothing tends to keep down the loss of heat. Therefore, healthy people warmly clothed and living in houses which are heated in winter, do not burn any considerable amount of material merely for the production of heat. If extra heat beyond the amount supplied by the food intake is required in cold weather to keep the body warm, it is obtained by exercising the muscles. One naturally exercises the muscles more vigorously in cold than in warm weather, and if one attempts to endure too much cold, without muscular exercise, the result is evidenced by shivering. Any muscular exercise required to keep warm demands more energy and this energy is produced by the foods just eaten, from a reserve stored in the body as fat, or from the tissues themselves.

When the tissues are burned to produce energy, there is loss of weight, and loss of weight may lead to a weakened condition and less resistance to disease. Too thin clothing in cold weather increases our need for food unnecessarily or uses our reserve energy.

How Much Food to Eat.

The amount of the various kinds of food to eat to keep the body fit is an important question to be discussed in relation to wise food selection and properly balanced meals. Sufficient food must be eaten to furnish enough energy to keep the body at its greatest degree of efficiency. We ordinarily depend upon our appetites to tell us how much food to eat. When a young person makes healthy, steady gains during his period of growth and when adults maintain uniform normal weight from year to year, in all probability they are eating the right kind as well as the right amount of food. But not all young people grow normally and not all adults maintain normal weight and thus it becomes necessary to substitute intelligent food selection for appetite, which is not always a safe guide.

Calories.

The unit in measuring the energy stored in the food we eat is called a calorie. When we speak of the caloric value of certain foods, we mean the power of those foods to produce units of heat in the body. A calorie is the amount of heat required to raise one kilogram of water one degree centigrade, or approximately two cups of water (a pound) four degrees Fahrenheit.

A special apparatus called a calorimeter is used to measure the energy value of food. The food under test is burned in an atmosphere of pure oxygen in a gastight chamber and the heat is taken up by water surrounding the chamber; the change in the temperature of the water shows the amount of heat produced. The calorimeter has been called a "food thermometer."

What Foods Yield Energy.

Proteins, fats, and carbohydrates can be burned and measured by calories. Water, vitamins, and minerals cannot be measured in this way. Food materials differ in the amount of protein, fat, and carbohydrate which they contain. From very many digestive experiments, food specialists have learned that an ounce of pure carbohydrate or pure protein yields 113 calories to the body while an ounce of pure fat yields 255 calories. If we wish to express the weight in grams, we say one gram of protein or carbohydrate yields four calories, one gram of fat yields nine calories. In an ordinary meal, we do not eat pure protein, carbohydrate, or fat.

Articles of food are usually combinations of the six food-stuffs. Cellulose is a form of carbohydrate which the body uses mostly for bulk. The more water and cellulose found in food, the lower the energy value, while the more fat a food contains, the higher its energy value.

The 100 Calorie Portion.

Since eating the right proportion of food is essential to good health, it is necessary
that we learn how to count the calories in the food we eat.
This would require a great deal of work if we had to
calculate the food eaten each meal in terms of protein,
carbohydrate, fats, water, and vitamins, but it is possible
to learn the relative value of these foods and thus choose
wisely with only a little thought.

Energy Requirements for Adults.

The United States Department of Agriculture estimates that the following amounts of energy are necessary for the average man or woman of average size. Less is allowed for women than for men, because they usually weigh less.

Man doing hard muscular work: 4,150 calories

Man doing moderately active work: 3,400 calories

Man at sedentary work or a woman at moderately active work: 2,700 calories

Man without muscular exercise or woman at light or moderate work: 2,450 calories

Getting the correct number of calories by no means solves the problem of what we should eat. We could eat pure sugar, protein, or fat, and easily get enough calories if we considered only the caloric requirement. But all our calories from any one — carbohydrate, fat, or protein — would not satisfy all the needs of the body.

The Fuel Foods.

Wherever work is to be done, fuel is required. The fuel for the human body is supplied as food. The first requisite in good nutrition is an adequate supply of fuel for all body activities. Carbohydrates, fats, and proteins all burn to produce energy. Protein also serves as material for growth and repair of body tissues. Of the fifteen or more chemical elements essential to the functions of the body, protein furnishes only five; carbohydrates and fats only three; water two; the other elements are found in the ash of the food and are known as minerals or ash constituents. All these essentials of the balanced diet must be included in the foods we eat. The only practical way of getting them is to learn how to select foods that will furnish the correct number of calories and at the same time include the necessary protein, minerals, and vitamins. Remember that the four chief constituents in a balanced diet are energy foods, proteins, minerals, and vitamins.

How Much Carbohydrate and Fat are Needed?

While protein may furnish the body with energy it should never be the chief source of fuel. The essential function of protein is to build and repair the body. Sufficient carbohydrates and fats should be present with the protein to allow it to be used chiefly for body building. A normal amount of foods rich in protein should be used with a generous supply of foods rich in carbohydrates, fats, minerals, vitamins, and bulk.

The correct number of calories for one's age, size, and occupation should be supplied by the requisite amount of protein, carbohydrates, and fats that are needed by the body. Sufficient protein should be eaten to furnish from ten to fifteen per cent of the calories. In general, two or three times as much starch as fat and just enough sugar to add flavor to the diet should be eaten.

Both carbohydrates and fats are composed of carbon, hydrogen, and fats. Hence they both act as fuel foods and to some extent one can replace the other. But we need some of both in our diet. Fat is valuable for "staying qualities" because it keeps one from becoming hungry at once ; sugar for flavor; cellulose for roughage or bulk; and starch for energy as well as because it is our most economical food.

Growth, Regulating, and Protecting Foods.

The body needs food to promote growth and foods that will help the organs of the body to do their best work. This regulating group includes vitamins, minerals, water and cellulose (bulky foods). The chief foods in this group are fresh fruits, green vegetables, milk, milk products, eggs, whole grain cereals, and water.

You will learn more about these important foods as you continue the study of foods. In the meantime, see that you drink plenty of water and that your diet includes an abundance of fresh fruit, green or bulky vegetables, milk, eggs, and whole grain cereals.

Basal Metabolism.

The basal metabolism test is used to show bow fast your body is burning up fuel and turning it into energy when you are at rest. This test is usually conducted by measuring the amount of oxygen that is taken in and the amount of carbon dioxide given off by the body. A basal metabolism test shows the number of calories a day which the food intake must supply when the body is completely inactive. The day's activities account for all other energy needs.

Body Building Foods.

Since the body is constantly being worn out even while we sleep and rest, this loss must be replaced by food. New tissues must be formed for growth. Proteins, mineral matter, and water supply the chief needs of the body for tissue building.

The proteins, because they contain nitrogen, are used in building muscles, nerves, blood, and even bone, and they are essential to every animal and plant cell. The cells of our bodies are largely protein, although they also contain all the other foodstuffs.

Carbohydrate is the chief body fuel and is found stored in the cells, particularly in the liver and blood. Carbohydrates in the living body are used not only as a source of energy but as constituents of proteins and other compounds found in the brain and nerves.

Fat not only provides fuel but furnishes protective coatings for the organs of the body and for the nerves. A small portion of fat is found in the composition of nerve tissue. The rest of the fat is stored as adipose tissue.

Proteins, fats, and carbohydrates pass from the intestines into the blood stream after we digest them and material for building and other purposes is withdrawn as needed by the cells of the body.

All tissues contain water. Water which flows constantly through the body is an essential part of the body structure and constitutes about three-fourths of the body weight in the new-born baby and about two-thirds in adults.

In addition to proteins, fats, carbohydrates, and water, we find that minerals occur in all body tissue and fluids. These minerals are calcium, phosphorus, iron, iodine, chlorine, fluorine, magnesium, manganese, potassium, silicon, sodium, and sulphur. The supply of each mineral in the amount needed is equally as important as the supply of energy. Shortage of any one of them will interfere with normal nutrition. Since protein, minerals, and water are so essential to the building of body tissue, they are spoken of as the body building foods.

Proteins are used for both body building and fuel. They are the only foodstuffs that contain nitrogen and are essential for the building and repairing of the body tissues which also contain nitrogen. Protein also contains carbon, hydrogen, oxygen and other elements, such as sulphur and phosphorus, in small quantities.

Proteins which do not furnish these amino acids are called incomplete because they do not support life and growth. Proteins which maintain life but lack some amino acid essential to growth are called partially complete. Since proteins are many and varied in kinds and amounts of amino acids, it is wise to use a good variety in the diet, that all needed substances may be included. One good reason for using milk is that casein, the chief protein in milk, is in itself a complete protein, or one which sustains life and promotes growth.

Foods very rich in protein include eggs, milk, cheese, nuts, and lean meats of all kinds. Cereals are not very rich in protein, but because we eat a large amount of cereals, the protein becomes of importance. Legumes, particularly peas, beans, and peanuts are comparatively high in protein. In animal foods, the proteins are all complete, while in vegetable foods, often an incomplete and a complete protein are both found, as in navy beans. Thus, the supplementing value of one protein for another must be kept in mind. It is well to know that the protein deficiencies of cereal grains and legumes can be made good by a liberal use of milk in the diet.

Daily Protein Need.

Since protein cannot be stored in the body for future use, we must learn how to select foods to meet our daily needs. The amount of protein needed will not vary with the kind of work being done. Two children of the same weight and age will use the same amount of protein, even though one is studious and the other is not. An athlete will require more energy but not necessarily more protein. The younger the child, the larger the proportion of calories from protein sources that is needed.

Amount of Energy from Protein Needed Daily Per Pound of Body Weight:

Adults: 2 calories
Young people from 12 to 17: 3 calories
Children from 3 to 12: 3 to 4 calories
Children from 1 to 2: 4 calories

Water and Body Tissue.

We can go without food for weeks if we have water, but no one has yet gone many days without water. Water is needed to build body tissue. In fact, two-thirds of the adult human body is water. No cell in the body will function when absolutely dry and most cells must be constantly bathed with fluid to do their best work. Food must be carried to the cells by the blood, which is mostly water. The surface of the lungs must be kept moist else we could not take in oxygen or get rid of carbon dioxide. We get water in food — even the driest bread or cracker is not absolutely free from water. Water is also produced in the body by the combustion of fuel foods. In addition to the water we drink, there are three other important sources for getting water: (1) water taken in beverages or in other liquids; (2) water contained in foods, particularly fruits and vegetables; (3) water formed in the tissues by the combustion of fuel foods.

Water and Digestion.

Recent experiments have shown that digestion takes place more quickly when water has been taken during the meal; it stimulates digestion rather than hinders it.

The average person should drink about eight glasses of liquid a day. Some of this should be taken in milk, and fruit drinks, but from four to six glasses of pure water should be taken by the average adult. As long as we re- member to chew our food and not wash it down with water, it is not harmful to drink water with meals.

Water is equally essential to the infant, the growing child, and the adult. The adult body loses about four and one-half pints of water daily through the skin, lungs, kidneys, and bowels. When we do not drink enough water to make good this loss, the body ceases to function properly.

Minerals and Body Building.

Minerals are used in the body to build tissue and to regulate the vital processes such as digestion, assimilation, respiration, and muscular control. We depend upon food to supply all the necessary mineral elements just as we depend upon it for the necessary amino acids which make protein in the body.

Minerals are found in every tissue and every fluid in our bodies. They are necessary for building bones and teeth, they are present in the digestive juices, and they assist in the digestion and absorption of food. By being dissolved in the blood they regulate its specific gravity and its alkalinity. Minerals are found in all body secretions; tears and perspiration are distinctly salty. Although they occur in very small amounts, minerals are a vital necessity; life would cease to exist without them. Each day a comparatively large amount of mineral matter is lost through excretions and this must be replaced by the selection of the right kind of food.

Mineral Starvation.

We sometimes speak of starvation when we are thinking of being deprived of practically all food. It is possible however to eat a large amount of food and still suffer from real starvation — such as iron starvation when one is anemic or calcium and phosphorus starvation when the bones, teeth, and blood are deprived of these minerals to the extent that rickets develop, or growth is retarded and general weakness and lack of resistance to disease result.

Calcium and Phosphorus.

The largest amount of mineral elements in the body are calcium and phosphorus, which give rigidity to the bones and teeth. Ninety-nine percent of the total calcium and ninety percent of the phosphorus are in the framework of our bodies. Phosphorus is also a necessary element in brain tissue; and calcium helps to regulate the body by making the contraction and relaxation of muscles possible, by helping to determine the steadiness of nerves, and by assisting in the coagulation of the blood. Phosphorus helps in keeping the blood neutral and in using the carbohydrates for fuel. Dr. Sherman, who has done much research concerning phosphorus, says that the body needs from one-fortieth to one-fiftieth as much phosphorus as protein each day. Phosphorus leaves the body through the kidneys and bowels.

Iron.

Iron is necessary for growth, for good nutrition, for reproduction, and for life itself. It is necessary for the formation of the red blood corpuscles which carry the oxygen from our lungs to all parts of our bodies, where we use it in the oxidation (burning) of food for the tissues. Iron and phosphorus are both present in every active cell of the body.

The amount of iron contained in the body is small, about .004 per cent, or one part in 25,000 in weight, but its functions are very important. There is little of reserve storage present in different food sources is also very small, so it is important that we learn to select foods that will give us an adequate daily supply.

In calculating the iron requirement for a family, increased allowances must be made for women and children. Women need a more liberal supply during menstruation, pregnancy, and the period of lactation. Growth and development in children affect the demand for iron to a greater extent than they affect the total requirement for food.

Foods rich in iron include green and leafy vegetables, fruits, eggs, lean meat, liver, and milk. Since a liberal supply of calcium is favorable to the effective use of iron, the liberal use of milk is desirable.

Iodine.

Iodine is important because it is needed in a very, very small amount to prevent goiter; it is also essential for normal growth and health. When the iodine in ordinary food is lacking, the small amount needed to prevent goiter can be supplied by adding iodine to the drinking water or table salt or by taking some form of iodine compound in tablets prescribed by a physician. Sea salts and sea water are good sources of iodine; iodized salt is now being used in many homes. Sea foods contain iodine, and milk, and especially milk fat, furnish iodine in significant quantities.

Sulphur.

Sulphur is needed for the assimilation of protein substances in the body. It is an essential regulatory agent being considered an important factor in the control of the oxidation processes in the body. The protein foods vary in their sulphur content but in the ordinary diet, when the protein requirement is met, sufficient sulphur will also be supplied.

Other Minerals.

The other mineral elements are found distributed in the body in various ways. Chlorine occurs chiefly in the gastric juice; sodium in the blood, and in other fluids combined with chlorine; potassium in the protoplasm of the muscles and brain tissue; magnesium in the bones, muscles, brain, and blood; and fluorine in the bones and teeth.

Minerals, although required in comparatively small quantities, are just as essential to the body's wellbeing as protein, carbohydrates, and fats. All losses of minerals through the intestines and kidneys must be replaced daily by food so that their work may go on in the body. Like the amount of protein required for the body, the required amount of these minerals does not vary with occupations.

It is evident that one who lives largely on meat, potatoes, white bread, with butter, and sweet desserts, will not have a diet sufficient in these elements. Generous servings of milk, milk products, whole grain cereals, vegetables, fruits, eggs, and lean meat, are necessary to give the requisite minerals. Sugars and fats are deficient in minerals. Whole grain cereals supply some mineral, but when the outer coats are lost in the milling we cannot depend on cereals for minerals. Rice loses half its mineral content when polished.

It is necessary to learn how to prepare foods so as not to lose their mineral content. Cooking our vegetables in a large amount of water and then throwing the water away, loses most of the mineral matter, because minerals are dissolved in the water during cooking.

The Regulating Foods.

In addition to the energy and building foods, the body requires foods that regulate or keep the body functioning smoothly. These foodstuffs are grouped in three main divisions: minerals, water, and vitamins. These regulating substances help the body to use the available fuel and building material to the best advantage. The regulating foods have also been called growth promoting, health, and protecting foods. It has been said that they have the same relation to the body that oil has to an engine. At least we know they are essential in regulating the body processes and are also essential to growth and health.

Minerals as Body Regulators.

Mineral elements help to determine the steadiness of the nerves. The right proportion of calcium, potassium, and sodium are necessary to the regulation and control of the nervous system. Mineral elements also control the movement of liquids in the body; the digested food must pass from the intestine into the blood without allowing blood to pass back into the intestines. Other liquids must pass from the blood into the various organs and tissues. It is the minerals that make possible the elimination of waste products which are taken into the blood from the cells and not carried away by the usual processes of elimination.

The various minerals keep the blood in good condition and are responsible to a large extent for the coagulation of the blood; they are vital factors in the digestion of food. In the stomach, the gastric juice owes its characteristic acidity to hydrochloric acid, which is necessary for the action of pepsin in digestion. In the small intestine other mineral salts make the secretions alkaline thus assisting the digestive processes there, especially the digestion of fat. Another important function of minerals is to keep the blood neutral, that is, neither acid nor alkaline. The minerals help to carry oxygen from the lungs to the tissues which enables the food to be burned for fuel and they carry carbon dioxide from the tissues back to the lungs. The power of the iron-bearing hemoglobin of the blood to com- bine with the oxygen and the carbon dioxide is essential to respiration. And thus, we see that minerals are essential to every live cell and to all essential fluids in the body. They influence all the vital processes of life itself. Without mineral elements or ash constituents life would cease to exist.

Water as a Regulator.

Water moistens the digestive tract, makes it possible to swallow food, softens the food itself, mixes with the digestive ferments, and helps them to act upon all parts of the food. It dissolves the food as it is digested and carries it through the lining of the digestive tract. Water dissolves and carries away the wastes of the body. It is possible that none of the chemical and physiological changes could go on in the body except in the presence of water. The body gives off water from the lungs, skin, kidneys, and bowels. As water is given off daily, it must be supplied daily.

Any decrease in the normal amount of water in the body interferes with processes essential to life and health. The seriousness of vomiting, diarrhea, or fever is partly due to the loss of water. Infants with nutritional disturbances may lose water so as to reduce the flow of the digestive juices and thus interfere with digestion and absorption.

When we do not drink enough water to make good the body loss, the body ceases to function properly. Drinking plenty of water stimulates the secretion of the digestive juices and aids in the digestion and absorption of food. It also retards the growth of bacteria in the intestines.

Bulky Foods as Regulators.

Our digestive system requires bulk for roughage, which, though taking little or no part in active nutrition, is useful in keeping the muscles of the intestines properly exercised. By kneading or churning the so-called indigestible material, the intestines move it onward. It is therefore wise to include green and watery vegetables, fresh and canned fruits, whole grain cereals and bran in the diet. By eating these foods we are adding minerals, vitamins, water, and cellulose — four factors which are necessary in a healthful diet.

Cellulose.

Indigestible matter called cellulose is found in the fiber and roots of vegetables and in the fibers of fruits and outer layers of cereal grains. Some of this indigestible material or bulk must be taken with the food to stimulate the intestines and to prevent constipation.

Cellulose has practically the same chemical composition as starch but is less easily dissolved. Tender cellulose, as found in the walls of such seeds as the cereals and young vegetables, is capable of being digested to some extent. However, we know that the less cellulose present in vegetables, the more digestible they are. Boiling in water does not change real cellulose but it stiffens the cell walls of plants and cereals, and by thorough cooking, the cell walls are ruptured by the swelling of the starch grains.

Cellulose is necessary as roughage to stimulate the intestines and hasten the passage of food through the intestines, through the peristaltic action. Cellulose aids in preventing constipation. The laxative action of food rich in cellulose may, however, be due to certain salts which occur in the husks of the cereals and not due to the large amount of cellulose found in them.

Fruits and Vegetables for Alkalinity.

It seems strange that we should eat fruits to prevent over-acidity when fruits are acid. Fruits contain sodium, potassium, calcium, and magnesium. The body is able to burn (oxidize) the acid part of these just as it burns sugar. The wastes left from burning, carbon dioxide and water, are sent out through the lungs. There is left an ash residue of sodium, potassium, calcium, and magnesium which combines with and neutralizes the mineral acid residues left by the burning of protein foods such as milk and meat. There are three fruits, plums, prunes, and cranberries, which retain their acid nature after absorption into the blood stream; but all the other fruits, so far as is known, lose their acid content as described above.

Fruit and vegetables help to keep the body alkaline by neutralizing the mineral acids in the body which are residues from the protein that we eat. These mineral acids will not bum and must be neutralized by such basic sub- stances as magnesium, calcium, potassium, and sodium. It is necessary to neutralize these mineral acids in order to keep the blood as alkaline as the normal condition of the blood demands. Fruits and vegetables are the chief foods in preserving this alkalinity.

Summary.

While most fruits are acid in taste, the sour- ness of fruit is due to the presence of organic salts. The acid part of these salts is converted into carbon dioxide and water, and the carbon dioxide and water are eliminated through the lungs. This conversion, or burning, leaves a residue of sodium, potassium, calcium, and magnesium which combine with and neutralize the mineral acids that are left from the burning (use by the cells) of protein. Plums, prunes, and cranberries contain a little acid which acts like a mineral acid. Practically all other fruits result in the end in an alkaline reaction. Fruits and vegetables are equally important in the diet in keeping the blood alkaline, and even though they seem expensive compared to the amount of energy and building material which they contain, they should not be omitted from the diet.

These foods will help in keeping the blood alkaline: Almonds, Apples, Asparagus, Bananas, Beans, Beets, Lima beans, Cabbage, Carrots, Cauliflower,

Celery, Chestnuts, Currants, Lemons, Lettuce, Pears, Muskmelon, Oranges, Turnips, Peaches, Milk (cow's), Potatoes, Radishes, and Raisins.

When the following acid producing foods are eaten to the exclusion of the alkali producing foods, the blood will become acid: eggs, meat (including fish, chicken, pork, veal, beef, oysters, oatmeal, bread, crackers, peanuts, rice, plums, prunes, and cranberries.

In general, fruits and vegetables are alkaline while meats, cereals, and nuts are acid.

Vitamins.

Vitamin is the name given to unseen substances occurring in natural foods which are essential to growth and health. They are called health protective and regulating foods because a sufficiency of these little-known substances protects the body from disease and helps it to grow strong and keep healthy. Vitamins exist in but small proportions in food materials, yet experiments have proved that they are just as essential as proteins, fats, carbohydrates, water or minerals. Although scientists have discovered that these vitamins exist and that without them we could not keep well or live long, much remains to be revealed of their nature and functions. A liberal supply of at least five vitamins is essential to proper growth in childhood and in keeping the body in good repair and in health during adult life. Young people show the bad effects of a diet low in vitamins more quickly than do adults. Some of the results of diets lacking in vitamins are beriberi, scurvy, rickets, pellagra, eye diseases, imperfect development of teeth and bones, habitual susceptibility to colds, and low resistance to all diseases.

Today six vitamins are recognized as essentials in our diet. They are designated by the letters of the alphabet: A, B, C, D, E, and G. For a while it was thought that a Vitamin F had been discovered but upon thorough investigation, it was discovered to be a fractional part of Vitamin B. Deficiency of Vitamin A results in a dry inflammation of the eye : of vitamin B in an inflammation of the nerves ; of vitamin C in scurvy; of vitamin D in rickets; of vitamin E in sterility; and vitamin G in pellagra. When one of these important vitamins is omitted from the diet, the type of deficiency disease appears which results when this particular vitamin is lacking in the food. The functions of the known vitamins are broader than the prevention of the deficiency diseases. They also have functions in normal nutrition.

Vitamin A.

Animal fats, butter, egg yolks, cod-liver oil, cabbage, spinach, lettuce, green peas and beans, and milk are especially rich in Vitamin A. Tomatoes, bananas, oranges, lemons, and carrots are also comparatively rich. While Vitamin A does not hold a direct relationship to some specific disease as does Vitamin B to beri-beri, or Vitamin C to scurvy, it is probable that Vitamin A is the factor of greatest importance in nutrition and health. It will protect young people from susceptibility to lung disease which so often develops in young men and women, at the age when they should be in the prime of life. It is not only needed during growth but in adult life to insure good nutrition and a high degree of health and vigor.

Vitamin A is a fat soluble and therefore not dissolvable in water, but food chemists have found that the vitamin A in animal fats gradually loses some of its vitality when exposed to air. This loss is greater when the temperature is raised. It seems wise, therefore, to use animal fats such as butter and cream without subjecting them to the heat of cooking. Vitamin A in plants does not seem to be so easily oxidized. Hence drying and the ordinary cooking temperatures do not materially decrease the amount of vitamin A in vegetables and fruits.

Vitamin B.

Vitamin B stimulates the appetite and promotes better digestion, thus resulting in growth and better health. A liberal supply of Vitamin B in the diet results in more successful reproduction and lactation. This fact is partly due to the stimulation of the appetite which causes the eating of more food and partly due to the influence of Vitamin B in directly nourishing the glands and organs concerned in reproduction.

Vitamin B is found in almost all foods, except such foods as white flour, white rice, starch, fats, and sugars. The healthy adult who eats a varied diet including fruits and vegetables need not be concerned as to the amount of vitamin B in his daily diet. There is little danger of a deficiency except in diets consisting too largely of artificially refined foods.

Since Vitamin B is a water soluble, care should be taken in cooking our vegetables. When we throw away the water in which vegetables are cooked, this vitamin is lost. Whenever possible save the water from the vegetables and use it in soups and gravies. Heating does not readily destroy this vitamin until the temperature is raised above the boiling point. The addition of soda greatly increases the rate of destruction and should be avoided. Those measures are best which accomplish the cooking most quickly and with the least loss of the juices.

Vitamin C.

Vitamin C is the third vitamin necessary for growth in the young and good health in all. It also prevents scurvy and was discovered when a cure for scurvy was in demand. Human scurvy usually follows serious food shortages, when the diet is lacking in fresh fruits and vegetables or when only the refined cereals, meat, fish, etc. are available.

A tired, worn-out, so called lazy feeling may be due to too little Vitamin C. Some of the common symptoms of such a condition are the loss of energy, pains in the joints and limbs which are often mistaken for rheumatism, and a muddy, sallow complexion. More vitality and more resistance to disease frequently follow a liberal supply of foods containing Vitamin C.

Tomatoes, oranges, lemons, potatoes, cabbage, carrots, dandelions, and other fresh vegetables are among the best sources of Vitamin C. In fact, all green vegetables and fresh fruits supply it in relatively large quantities.

Vitamin C is irregularly distributed in foods and very easily destroyed. Heating, drying, and aging have all been known to be factors in decreasing the amount in different foods. For practical convenience, it is wise to establish the habit of eating regularly the foods known to be rich in Vitamin C, such as fresh raw fruits, vegetables, and canned tomatoes, in addition to potatoes. Cooking of vegetables should be done quickly and the juices retained when possible.

Vitamin D.

Vitamin D is essential to the proper development of the growing child and to the maintenance of health in adults. When this vitamin was found to prevent rickets, that fact was ranked as one of the most important discoveries made by modern nutritional science. A lack of balance in calcium and phosphorus in the blood produces rickets. Although rickets affects the whole body, the chief characteristic is failure of the bones to calcify properly, causing deformities. When the diet lacks the proper balance of calcium and phosphorus, rickets can be prevented by taking cod liver oil, eating egg yolk, milk, and green vegetables, and exposing the patient to the direct rays of the sun or to the rays of the mercury vapor lamp which provides artificial sunlight. The ultra-violet rays of the sun fail to go through window glass or clothing; direct exposure therefore is necessary. The use of the mercury vapor lamp in providing artificial sunlight is of inestimable value, during the winter months especially, for babies or invalids who for any reason cannot be exposed to the direct rays of the sun.

Window glass which allows both the visible and the ultra-violet rays to penetrate is now being manufactured. When the price is not prohibitive, at least one window pane of this kind should be in every home. Hospitals, schools, and other public buildings will doubtless make more general use of this wonderful discovery in the near future.

Cod liver oil is higher in Vitamin D than most any other source. For babies and young children, it is wise to add from one to three teaspoonfuls of pure cod liver oil to the diet at least during the winter months. All others, including adults, should have daily exposure to the sun or should take their dose of cod liver oil or its equivalent daily. Of all foods except fish oils, egg yolk seems to have the greatest anti-rachitic value. Butter fat, green vegetables, and milk all contain Vitamin D but sufficient quantities of these foods are not ordinarily eaten to give complete protection against rickets, especially during the winter months. Milk is essential to the diet for many reasons but too much emphasis cannot be placed on its use as a protection against rickets because of its liberal supply of calcium. Green vegetables assist materially in the assimilation of calcium in the child's diet.

Vitamin E.

An adequate diet should include all the elements necessary to maximum health, growth, and all the normal activities of the human body. It is probable that Vitamin E is not only necessary to reproduction but that it assists materially in the assimilation of iron. The oil of the wheat germ contains Vitamin E in abundance. Seeds and green leaves are also very rich in this vitamin. Raw fresh milk contains all the vitamins but the amount present varies with the diet of the lactating animal.

Food Groups.

When we go marketing, we do not buy calories, proteins, minerals, and vitamins, as such, but we buy articles of food, such as milk, eggs, fruits, vegetables, and cereals. For the convenience of those who select their own food or who prepare food for others, foods have been grouped according to their nutritive value. Perhaps the most useful classification of foods is that prepared by the United

States Department of Agriculture in which all foods are grouped into five general classes:

Group 1. Fruits and Vegetables.

Group 2. Milk and other efficient proteins: eggs, fish, meat, cheese, soybeans, and peanuts.

Group 3. Cereals and cereal preparations: wheat, oats, corn, barley, etc., breakfast foods, flour, macaroni, spaghetti, etc., breads, cakes, pies, etc.

Group 4. Sugar and sugary foods: sugar, honey, syrups, jellies, preserves, etc., candy.

Group 5. Fat and fat food: butter, cream, bacon, vegetable oils, oleo, lard, salt pork, pork sausage, chocolate, all common nuts except chestnuts.

Fruits and Vegetables.

The chief reason for eating fresh raw fruit and green leafy vegetables is their richness in minerals and vitamins. The green leafy vegetables are important sources of iron and all known vitamins; the richest source of Vitamin A is the thin green leaves of any vegetable; vitamin B is found distributed rather plentifully in all vegetables; vitamin G is obtained almost exclusively from fresh fruits and vegetables; Vitamin D, as well as Vitamin E, is found in thin green leaves such as lettuce and dandelion greens.

Canned fruits and vegetables are convenient and economical, but they should never be used to the exclusion of green leafy vegetables and fresh fruits, since their vitamin content is lowered by cooking. Peas, beans, tomatoes, and spinach are among the commercially canned vegetables commonly used. Fresh fruits are best but when necessary the following dried fruits may be purchased: peaches, apricots, apples, raisins, prunes, dates, and figs. Fruit is usually dried in trays either in the sun or by artificial heat. Some of the canned fruits that are available are peaches, pineapples, apricots, pears, cherries, and berries of all kinds.

The mineral elements in vegetables and fruits occupy a place of great importance. The minerals in fruits and vegetables help in maintaining the normal neutrality of the blood. Spinach is perhaps the best source of vegetable iron, although lettuce, green cabbage, and other leafy vegetables such as dandelions, turnip greens, mustard, and beet tops yield a large percentage. Fruits richest in iron include cranberries, huckleberries, pineapples, strawberries, blackberries, prunes, and plums.

Milk and Other Efficient Proteins.

Eggs, milk, cheese, and meats (including lean, medium, and fat meats, poultry, game, fish and other seafoods), nuts, and soybeans are called efficient protein foods. They are grouped together because the proteins are of the best quality and all support growth. The body must be supplied with complete proteins to replace the daily nitrogen loss and to furnish all the amino acids necessary to growth and health.

Milk is the best source of calcium for the growing child, and for the calcium of their diets adults should depend more upon milk than any other food. Milk also contains a liberal supply of phosphorus and all the vitamins. As to the amount of milk to drink, a good rule to follow is: One quart a day for children and at least one pint for each adult.

Eggs are rich in protein, minerals, and vitamins all of which are needed in the growth and repair of the body. In fact, all substances necessary to growth are abundant in the egg with the exception of calcium and Vitamin C.

Cheese is another valuable protein food but it takes a gallon of milk to make a pound of cheese. One-fourth of the calories yielded by cheese come from protein and the other three-fourths from fat. The sugar in milk is lost in the whey or changed to lactic acid in the ripening process of cheese making. However, most of the calcium, phosphorus, and iron of milk are retained in the cheese; also, in large part, the effectiveness of Vitamin A is retained. Cheese is usually thought of as a meat substitute because of its high protein and fat content. It is especially valuable when used to give flavor to such bland foods as macaroni, rice, bread, and hominy.

Meats and Other Flesh Foods.

Meats usually include beef, veal, mutton, lamb, pork, poultry, game, fish and other seafoods. The main contribution of meat to the diet is protein. The proteins of meat contain all the essential amino acids; hence they support growth, but they are not superior to the protein of milk and eggs. They also supplement the protein of cereal grains as do milk and eggs. The chief advantage of meat is its palatability, ease of digestion, and ease of preparation for the table. It should never displace eggs, milk, fruits, and vegetables in the diet.

Nuts.

Nuts are often accused of disturbing digestion but this disturbance is usually caused by eating nuts between courses at dinner or between meals, such as at afternoon teas, when there is little need for food. Nuts are very rich in protein and fat; hence they digest very slowly and their fuel value is very high. Nuts are rather poor sources of minerals and also are poor in Vitamin A. They are effective in supplying Vitamin B, but are lacking in Vitamin C. Because of their texture, nuts should be thoroughly chewed or finely ground in order to be thoroughly mixed with the digestive juices and easily digested. Nuts should be combined with foods low in fat when they are eaten in large quantities.

Cereals and Cereal Preparations.

This group is depended upon chiefly for energy. They also supply protein but since they do not contain complete proteins, the diet must be supplemented with milk and other complete proteins. Cereals are easily digested.

Starch should be the chief source of energy after the first year of life. It is present in large quantities in all grain products, such as flour, barley, rice, and macaroni. Usually starch furnishes about one-third of the energy of growing children after the second year. Potatoes, both white and sweet, corn, dried peas, and dried beans are rich in starch. The banana is the richest source of starch among the fruits.

Vitamin B is generally found in cereals; E is especially abundant in the germ of wheat, while A, C, and D seem to be lacking in these foods. Hence, no cereal alone makes a satisfactory diet.

Sugary Foods.

Sugars and sweet foods are valuable chiefly as fuel foods. Pure sugars contribute nothing else to the diet; they lack vitamins, minerals, and proteins. Sweets dull the appetite and are harmful to the digestive system when eaten between meals.

Cane sugar, maple sugar, molasses, and honey are important sources for sugar for older children and adults. There is also a valuable supply in dates, raisins, prunes, among the fruits; and in beets, green peas, carrots, sweet corn, sweet potatoes, and squash among the vegetables. Sugars are soluble in water and cannot be seen in moist fruits and vegetables; however, when fruits are dried sugar can frequently be seen in small lumps as, for example, in raisins. All starches and sugars are changed during the digestive process into glucose in which form they are absorbed into the blood.

Fats and Fat Foods.

Fats are sources of energy in the most concentrated form. They include butter, lard, fat meat, oils, egg yolk, bacon, sausages, and cream. Cheese, milk, oatmeal, olives, and nuts are also rich in fat. Some fats carry vitamins A and D, which, as you recall, are soluble in fat. Some of these fats are cod liver oil, butter, and cream. Milk fat is rich in Vitamin A and is more desirable than any other fat food. Fat retards digestion but, because it digests slowly, it gives a feeling of satisfaction after eating. From two to three ounces a day is as much fat as should be consumed by the average adult.

Fat acts as a pad and protects the nerves and vital organs. We therefore need a certain amount of fatty tissue, not only for the sake of appearance but to protect the tissues, nerves, muscles, and vital organs. Too much fat, however, accumulating around the heart and other organs, throws an extra amount of work on the heart which results in discomfort, waste of energy, and general inefficiency.

Fats are the most concentrated form of body fuel. An ounce, or one tablespoonful, of butter fat or any other fat will give 100 calories. Ordinarily, butter and milk should supply most of the fat used in the daily diet.

The problem of supplying adequate food in everyday life is rather difficult. In every normal family, there are people of different food likes and dislikes and different food requirements. With a baby, a preschool child, a high school boy or girl, father, mother, and grandparents in the family, the problem becomes more and more complex.

It is possible to construct an adequate diet from two or three foods, provided they are carefully and intelligently selected, but this requires definite knowledge concerning the food needs of the body as well as the composition of the foods we use in everyday life. Instinct is a poor guide in food selection and is by no means a substitute for intelligence.

Hunger and appetite ordinarily can be depended upon to take care of the energy requirement but not for the selection of the necessary protein, mineral elements, and vitamins. Whether or not hunger and appetite are used as guides as to the amount of food that is being consumed, we can usually judge by the fatness of the person, since an excess of fuel food, of whatever kind, is stored in the body as fat. If year after year the body keeps in good condition, with a fairly constant weight, it is reasonably certain that sufficient energy food is being eaten. If, however, by following the appetite, we become too stout or too thin, develop a lack of energy or resistance to dis- ease, or become annoyed by digestive disturbances, it is certain that the appetite is not a perfect standard. We know, too, that the individual appetite often proves in- adequate in selecting a well-balanced combination of all the essential foodstuffs.

The more scientific knowledge we have concerning food values, the less apt are we to select an inadequate meal, even though rigid economy is necessary. The science of nutrition has demonstrated beyond doubt that simple meals are more healthful than those of elaborate type. It is therefore rather superfluous and a waste of effort to spend much time on fancy cookery and highly refined edibles when there are simpler foods that serve the purposes of nutrition in a better way.

CHAPTER 5

DIGESTION

Properly selected food and intelligent habits of eating and living are essential to good digestion. The digestive system receives the food and puts it into a form that is available for use in the body. As food passes through the mouth, stomach, and intestines, it is finely divided and brought into solution through the action of the digestive juices. Most of the nutrient material contained in food requires more or less change to bring it into forms most useful in nutrition. These changes take place in the digestive tract and we call them digestion.

Water Assists Digestion.

The regular drinking of water helps the food to digest. It keeps the digestive tract clean and the action of the intestines regular. Water is found in every food that we eat and in every part of the body. It does not change during the process of digestion, as do other foods, but is used as a medium for carrying the other five foodstuffs through the body and holding them in solution until they can be absorbed and used in the proper way. Plenty of water in the diet moistens the tissues, stimulates the flow of the digestive juices, promotes circulation, and aids in digestion, absorption, and excretion.
Plenty of water will flush the system and help get rid of waste material before it poisons the body. Drink water between meals and at mealtime, but do not wash the food down with the water. With an average amount of activity, about eight glasses of liquid should be taken every day in the form of milk, fruit juice, and pure water. Take one glass of pure water before breakfast, one glass with each meal, one glass about two hours after breakfast and lunch, and another after dinner unless you are going early to bed.

Ventilation.

Good ventilation in the living rooms and sleeping rooms aids digestion. Fresh air must be provided to replace the air that has been made impure by breathing. When we take cold because we are not getting enough fresh air, the digestive processes are seriously impeded. If special means of ventilation are not provided, the room can be ventilated by opening the windows at both top and bottom to allow the lighter hot air to rise and pass out when the cold air comes in at the bottom. The air should always be about as moist as the outdoor air. Dry air causes one to be irritable and nervous and may cause colds, catarrh, adenoids, and enlarged tonsils. A room is well ventilated when the air is sufficiently moist, cool, and in motion.

Rest, Sleep, Exercise, and Sunshine.

Rest and sleep are necessary factors in providing good nutrition. Sleep provides the most perfect rest for the body and the most thorough relaxation of the nervous system. Waking up sleepy and tired in the morning is a sign either of insufficient sleep or of a diseased condition of the body. Ordinarily eight hours of sleep, eight hours of work, and eight hours of recreation and attention to the daily routines of life are an excellent division of the twenty-four hours of the day.

Outdoor exercise does much to aid digestion. Exercise in the open air and sunshine sharpens the appetite, develops the muscles, and stimulates every organ of the body, thus aiding respiration, circulation, digestion, and elimination. Under the stimulus of exercise, the blood carries food and oxygen to every cell of the body. Boys and girls who play outdoors grow faster, keep healthier, have more graceful bodies and make better progress in their studies than those who spend too much time indoors.

Sunshine has been called "Nature's insurance policy" because it not only helps to prevent disease but will actually assist materially in curing those who are sick.

Good Elimination Necessary.

Waste products are eliminated through the skin, lungs, kidneys, and intestines. Headaches, bad complexions, and tired, worn-out, stupid feelings are often caused by poor elimination. The digestive tract should be freed from waste at least once daily, preferably immediately after breakfast, when the automatic muscular action of the digestive system is best. Too much sugar and highly seasoned food irritate the digestive tract and interrupt this automatic muscular action which is so necessary to good health.

Constipation can usually be cured by adopting corrective food habits. Corrective practices would include generous amounts of water and bulky foods such as vegetables, fruits, and whole grain cereals in the diet; regular meals, a regular hour for bowel elimination; and suitable exercise. Cathartics do not cure constipation and should be taken only on the advice of a physician. Drugs of any kind provide only temporary relief and do not effect a permanent cure. Water assists elimination by keeping the food in a semi-liquid state; it not only serves to prevent congestion of food in the intestines but helps to carry away poisonous products through the kidneys.

Two generous servings of green or bulky vegetables should be eaten daily. The skin of vegetables, especially the skin of baked potatoes, should be eaten. Eat large servings of asparagus, string beans, beets, broccoli, Brussels sprouts, cabbage, carrots, cauliflower, celery, corn, greens, chard, dandelion greens, kale, lettuce, spinach, onions, green peas, potatoes, squash, tomatoes, and turnips.

A Happy Mealtime.

Good digestion is the key to good nutrition, and good nutrition is the equivalent of good health. A happy atmosphere at mealtime aids digestion. One who is happy and good humored is practically always well nourished. Digestion is retarded when one is worried, angry, or in a bad humor. It is best not to eat when one is tired or in too much of a hurry to eat calmly and deliberately. Talking about interesting things, in pleasant anticipation of mealtime and during meals stimulates the digestive juices and increases their effectiveness in the digestion of food. Well-balanced meals, served at regular hours, in an attractive manner, with all the family present, do much not only to aid digestion but to keep the family well and healthy.

Sharing responsibilities often changes the whole atmosphere of the meal. Many mothers are too tired to enjoy their meals. By waiting on the table during the meal in regular turns, boys and girls can give their mothers sufficient rest and time to eat with benefit to their health.

Disagreeable arguments, cross words, and fault finding are especially out of place at meal time. Likewise, the discussion of petty topics, repulsions, or any unpleasant matter should be avoided at the table. Many digestive disorders have their origin in unpleasant conditions brought about by disregard of the niceties and distinctions that mark the well-bred from the churlish.

How the Body Handles Excess Foods.

In the well-nourished human body, some fat is distributed generally over the body. This fat helps to protect the body from cold, serves as padding for the internal organs, the muscles, etc., protects against jars and blows, and is a storehouse of energy for emergencies. The amount of fuel burned in the body depends upon the energy used in muscular activity and not upon the amount that is eaten.

Carbohydrate foods (sugar and starch) are stored as glycogen in the liver and to some extent in the muscles. When no more glycogen can be stored, the carbohydrates, if not needed, will be stored as fat. Fat eaten as such is stored in the body practically unaltered if not required as fuel at once. Protein, when eaten in too large quantities, is either used for fuel or eliminated along with other wastes. It cannot be stored for future use.

Overweight and Underweight.

A condition of overweight or underweight shows that nutrition has been badly neglected. A diet of high fuel content is intended primarily for those who do a large amount of muscular work; therefore, when this work is not done and the same amount of fuel food continues to be eaten and digested, it is stored in the body chiefly as fat. The amount of fat which a person carries is an indication of whether too few or too many calories are being eaten habitually.

Authorities differ as to the proportion of weight in relation to height that one should carry. As a rule, men and women keep themselves slightly too thin while young and allow themselves to grow slightly too stout as they grow older. Underweight before the age of twenty-five is unfavorable and is often associated with low resistance to disease. After the age of thirty, underweight unless extreme is not considered unfavorable. Life insurance companies report that the lowest mortality at middle life is found among those who are a few pounds underweight.

Usually people who are proportionately underweight for their height show signs of both mental and physical fatigue and are subject to indigestion and nervous disorders. Likewise, they are susceptible to colds and other respiratory diseases such as bronchitis, pneumonia, and tuberculosis. The disadvantages and dangers of overweight are also very serious. In this condition, the tissues are not nourished to the extent they can resist infectious diseases. Functional disorders of the heart and kidneys are prevalent where overweight is excessive.

The best way to decide whether you are overweight or underweight is to have a complete medical examination. You can determine to some extent by a comparison of your own weight with standard weight tables whether or not you are the average weight for your height and age. Variations of a few pounds in either direction are not likely to be significant, but it is best to have an examination to disclose the effect upon your health and efficiency the variation may be having.

Overweight is generally caused by too much food, the wrong selection of food, physical defects, glandular disturbances, and the lack of exercise. Eating too much food from the energy food groups causes overweight, as the body, being unable to burn up all the energy it produces, stores the surplus for future use in the form of fat. Overweight persons should choose their food from groups containing plenty of minerals, vitamins, proteins, water, and cellulose. Using too much time in inactive diversions such as riding in automobiles, sitting in parks, playing bridge, etc. reduces the energy requirements below normal. Those who lead sedentary lives should observe this fact and eat less.

To correct overweight, be sure that your diet is balanced; reduce the consumption of fuel foods; avoid overeating; practice proper exercise and right living; and correct physical defects. Reducing should be done only under the direction of a physician. The use of patent medicines that are advertised as a quick method of making one "slender and youthful" might injure your health for life. Make an effort to increase the amount of lettuce, asparagus, spinach, Brussels sprouts, string beans, and all kinds of greens in your diet. Eat raw apples, oranges, grapefruit, berries, etc. for desserts. These fruits provide minerals, vitamins, water, and cellulose which are necessary for all the internal activities of the body.

If you are habitually tired physically and mentally, are susceptible to diseases, and lack the vigor and strength to enjoy life, it probably means that you are not getting enough calories in your daily diet and have become underweight.

Deficient nutrition in children is more serious than in adults because it interferes with the normal growth and development of the body. A few calories short in the daily diet often causes a child to be undernourished. Children must eat steadily day by day if they want to grow properly.

How to Overcome Underweight.

If you are underweight for your height and age, it does not necessarily indicate that you are in poor health for weight is not the only standard by which we judge good health. Yet it is a good plan to watch one's weight since this is the best single standard for checking the physical condition. The following suggestions will help you in increasing your weight:

1. Be examined by a doctor to be sure there are no physical defects which interfere with your health and growth, such as bad teeth or enlarged tonsils.

2. Drink as least three or preferably four glasses of whole milk each day.

3. Eat concentrated foods such as eggs, cheese, and butter, plenty of cereals and potatoes, and at least one green vegetable and one serving of fruit every day. The vitamins, minerals, and cellulose contained in the green vegetables are necessary for growth and health.

4. Go to bed early and sleep with the windows wide open.

5. Practice regular habits. Follow a regular schedule each day, resting at regular times, going to bed and eating meals regularly.

6. Avoid excitement, worry, and violent exercise. Learn to rest and relax completely.

7. Pure, fresh air, sunshine, and suitable exercise will develop the muscles and get them ready to carry the extra weight you gain.

The United States Department of Agriculture gives the following requirements for a well-balanced liberal diet for each person:

Milk — 1 quart daily for each child, to drink or in food. 1 pint daily for each adult, to drink or in food.

Vegetables and Fruits — 6 to 7 servings daily: 1 serving daily of potatoes or sweet potatoes. 1 serving daily of tomatoes or citrus fruits. 2Y2-3 servings daily of vegetables, at least one- half of which are leafy, green, or yellow. 9-10 servings a week of fruit (once a day, sometimes twice).

Eggs — 4-6 times a week, also some in cooking.

Meat, Fish, or Poultry — Once a day; sometimes twice.

Butter — At every meal.

Bread, Cereals, and Desserts — As needed to meet calorie requirements or as desired so long as they do not displace the protective, foods.

What is Malnutrition?

Bad nutrition has been given the general name of malnutrition, which means a low condition of health and body resistance. A healthy, well-nourished high school boy or girl meas- ures approximately up to the average in height and weight for his age, has a good color, bright eyes without blue circles or dark hollows under them, smooth glossy hair, erect posture, elastic step, firm flesh, and well-developed muscles. He is usually happy, good natured, full of life, sleeps soundly, has a good appetite, good digestion, regular bowel movements, and from every standpoint is a picture of health.

Portrait of a Malnourished Boy or Girl.

A malnourished boy or girl may lack one or all of the characteristics of a healthy boy or girl. He is usually thin (although he may be fat and flabby); his skin is pale, delicate, sallow or muddy; his eyelids are pale and colorless with blue circles or dark hollows under the eyes. His hair may be rough; his tongue coated; his bowels constipated; and his muscles undeveloped. Usually his shoulders are rounded and his shoulder blades stand out, while his chest is flat and narrow, and his abdomen protrudes. Also his teeth may be decayed and he may have enlarged, diseased tonsils and adenoids. An extremely malnourished person cares little to play with others, tires easily, and is sometimes called lazy. Malnutrition will cause one to become a restless, fretful, nervous, and fidgety person who sleeps lightly and eats little.

Causes of Malnutrition.

Too often we hear the remark, "This child will never be fat, he is just like his father." On the other hand, when overweight is evident, fatness may be said to "run in the family." Too much is blamed on heredity. Bad health habits are largely responsible for underweight or overweight. A child may be "thin like his family" because all his family have low resistance and a weakened physical condition induced by unwise eating and other bad health habits. Fatness may "run in the family" because it is a family characteristic to indulge the appetite for the richer foods.

On the other hand, we know that we have slender and stout types in the human family just as we have greyhounds and bulldogs in the dog family. Slenderness should not be confused with malnutrition. Neither should a child of stout type be put in the overweight class by simple comparison with the child whose slenderness is characteristic of her family. While standard weight-height-age tables are perhaps the best criterion of good health, other conditions should always be taken into consideration. It is sensible to take it for granted that every child is capable of maximum health and growth and the least sign of poor nutrition should be viewed with concern.

The chief causes of malnutrition are an insufficient diet, wrong food habits, insufficient sleep, enlarged or diseased tonsils and adenoids which make swallowing and breathing difficult, decayed teeth which interfere with proper mastication of food, poor posture, eating between meals, drinking coffee or tea.

Effects of Malnutrition.

One of the most serious results of malnutrition is an increased susceptibility to disease and a lack of resistance. When a malnourished child contracts a disease, especially if he has bad teeth, diseased tonsils or adenoids, he recovers with great difficulty. The effects of malnutrition on mental capacity are also evident. Malnourished children are not always dull and backward in their work; neither do mentally retarded children always improve their work materially by improving their nutrition, but every child's mental powers are lowered by extreme malnutrition.

Treatment of Malnutrition.

The treatment of malnutrition should begin with finding the causes by means of a careful investigation into the methods of the child's living and a thorough physical examination. When the causes are discovered, remedial work should begin at once. Tonsils and adenoids may need to be removed, bad teeth cared for, the diet regulated, and in general, all health habits improved. When children are eating cold lunches at noon, provision for at least one hot dish should be made; and if sufficient time is not allowed for meals, the lunch period should be extended.

Interesting those afflicted by malnutrition in the improvement of their own health habits is the only means by which to affect a permanent cure. The chief factors in the correction of malnutrition are: (1) correction of physical defects such as bad tonsils or adenoids; (2) good food and health habits; (3) prevention of over-fatigue; (4) proper food and taken at sufficiently frequent intervals; (5) fresh air by day and by night.

Diet for Abnormal Conditions.

Sooner or later in almost every family there comes the problem of changing the diet of a normally healthy individual to suit the needs of some special condition due to illness. Although it is desirable to serve the most suitable and easily digested foods in every type of sickness, there are diseases in which the diet of afflicted persons is more important than drugs and medicines. These are the so-called "diet diseases," such as diabetes, gout, tuberculosis, and excessive overweight. If the diet were controlled from the time the first symptoms appear, the acute stages of the disease, or the setting in of other diseases, might be avoided.

Constipation and its resulting ill effects might very frequently be entirely prevented by a well-chosen diet.

The principles involved in food selection should become familiar not only to those who plan and prepare meals, but to those who buy their meals in public dining places. Moreover, it is but exercising common sense to take insurance in the protection of one's health when all it will cost is the use of time and patience in becoming intelligent about what to eat and what not to eat.

CHAPTER 6

FOOD SELECTION AND MENU PLANNING

To be well fed is as important as to be well dressed. The scent of flowers, the song of birds, and all pleasures follow in the order of their enjoyment after the elemental satisfaction that is derived from eating a good meal.

Hunger is the teacher of the arts and the parent of invention. He who gives a cup of cold water to a thirsty man has done an act of divine charity, but he who serves an appetizing dish of wholesome food has, in his way, done even more, for he has heightened the primitive pleasure of eating by satisfying the cultivated desire of the soul. He has delighted the imagination as well as the palate.

To feed a man is to feed his spirit as well as his body. For that reason, the Culinary stands at the pinnacle of the utilitarian arts. This service is elevated into an art because it is more necessary than music and nearer to the everyday life of man than poetry and painting.

Meal Time Psychology.

Meal time should be one of the happiest hours in the daily life of the family. It usually provides the only opportunity during the day for an assemblage of all members of the family in one group; therefore, it should be a pleasant, enjoyable meeting. If meal time in your home is not an occasion of camaraderie and good cheer, try as an experiment for one week, to turn discussion away from any disagreeable topic or circumstance that is likely to create unpleasant feelings or associations. Perhaps, it would be unwise to acquaint the other members of the family with your plan. Let them match purposes with yours in subconscious response to your efforts at being agreeable. Cheerfulness and good nature are infectious psychic forces that move spontaneously from one individual to another. Attitudes of cheerfulness and good nature have but to be sincere, unforced expressions of inner feeling in order to infect others with their influence. Therefore, if you try sincerely, you can become the center from which happiness will spread to every other member of the family group.

Try to eat some of everything that is put on the table. If you do not like certain dishes, create a taste for them through their substitution for foods that you like. As you grow older and go out in public more, you will find it increasingly necessary to adjust yourself to the likes and dislikes of others. If you cultivate a taste for the various kinds of food while you are still young, it will spare you from annoyance when dining out with friends. Occasionally there are foods to which certain people are allergic but such cases are rare. Ordinarily, good, wholesome food can be eaten in all the various ways of preparing it without causing discomfort or illness.

The after dinner period should be used at the table in the quiet enjoyment of friendly conversation about topics of mutual interest. After eating, the body needs rest and the mind needs relaxation in order that the processes of digestion may function thoroughly. The "eat and run" habit of many people becomes a serious impediment to their physical well being and mental health. Activity of mind or body while the stomach is full draws blood away from the centers of digestion. The most important nerves connect with the digestive system. Interruptions of their functions bring other nerves into distress and finally throw out of gear the entire mechanism of the body.

There should be a scheduled time for serving meals that is suited to the activities of the family. The time for breakfast and lunch should be adjustable, letting the irregular members serve themselves.

The appearance of the table has a great psychological effect on the members of the family. All things that help the appearance of the table stimulate the appetite and aid in the digestion of food. The linen should be simple and clean. There should be an orderly arrangement of dishes as well as linen. It is well to have a centerpiece, no matter how simple. Small ferns, ivy, available flowers from the garden, and even sweet potato vines make attractive center- pieces.

Planning Family Meals.

Do you help in planning menus for your family? The selection of food in the right proportion as to kind, amount, and balance is essential to the health of every member of the family. You can assist in the solution of this important problem by a study of your own body needs.

Those who have made a special study of nutrition tell us that for maximum health and growth, three whole meals each day eaten at regular intervals give the best result for the average individual. You have learned that ordinarily people who are underweight should increase the amount of food and those who are overweight should eat less food. Estimating the calories on the basis of the energy needed in the natural metabolism and that required for activity is the best method of finding out how much we should eat. A more practical way is to consult the calorie tables and make your estimate from these on the basis of your age.

Counting Calories at the Family Table.

It is convenient to be able to estimate ordinary servings in relation to 100 calorie portions. You have learned that in discussing the amount of food for a day or a week, we often speak of the number of 100 calorie portions, just as we speak of a dollar representing 100 cents. No one needs to memorize calorie tables. Learning to recognize the approximate number of calories in average servings of the common foods can be done with little effort.

Calories, of course, tell only the energy or fuel value of foods. We should remember that obtaining the correct number of calories is only part of this important food problem. To select food intelligently, we must learn how many calories we need and then see how, by careful choice of food, we can get them with all the necessary food essentials. Of the total number of calories needed during the day, about fifteen percent should come from efficient protein in order to supply the daily nitrogen loss. Other foods should supply the essential minerals, vitamins, and bulk so necessary to perfect health.

There are two important rules to remember in estimating the amount and kind of food to be eaten by each individual or by the family. The first has to do with the division of calories in the accustomed three meals a day. Simply stated, it is as follows: Generally, the total number of calories for one day should be divided approximately as follows: one- fourth or more for breakfast, one- fourth for lunch or supper, and one-half for dinner. The other rule has to do with the division of calories in accordance with the need for each of the various types of food, proportioned as follows:

Fruits and Vegetables 20% or 1/5 the total calories.

Efficient Protein Foods 25% or "1/4 "

Cereals and Starchy Foods 25% or "1/4 "

Fat and Fat Foods ...20% or "1/5 "

Sugar and Sweet Foods 10% or "1/10"

Guide to Balanced Family Meals.

The following seven essentials of balanced meals should be remembered in purchasing food for the family table from the market as well as in making menus for the home and selecting meals in public places. Daily needs are:

1. A quart of milk for everyone who is still growing and at least a pint for adults. These quotas may be used in cooking, eaten with cereals, or drunk as a beverage.

2. One complete protein, such as meat, fish, poultry, or cheese for each member of the family, and an egg or at least an egg yolk for a growing boy or girl. A second protein dish, such as nuts of the various kinds, kidney, lima, or navy beans, peas, and lentils may also be used. Milk may be used for additional protein. The egg also furnishes iron and Vitamin D, as well as other minerals and vitamins.

3. Three vegetables, including a raw leafy vegetable and one other besides potato. Potatoes are valuable for minerals and vitamins and when digested give an alkaline reaction; the peelings of vegetables are valuable for their minerals and bulk which help to regulate the digestive system.

4. Two fruits, including tomato, canned or fresh, or one of the citrus fruits (orange, grapefruit, and lemon) and one other fruit, fresh, dried, or canned. Tomatoes and the citrus fruits supply Vitamin C, which is believed to be destroyed in most cooked food.

5. At least one whole grain cereal or whole grain bread.

6. Sufficient fats and sweet foods to add calories and flavor to the other foods. The habit of eating sweets between meals should be discouraged as it destroys the appetite for more wholesome foods. Butter, cream, cod liver oil, and cheese are valuable for vitamins and minerals. Cheese is also valuable for the protein it contains. Nuts are rich in protein. Dates, figs, raisins, and ripe bananas are valuable sources of vitamins and minerals; molasses of calcium and iron; honey of vitamins and minerals.

7. From four to eight glasses of water or other liquid. Water is a necessary body substance and is also necessary for the body's regulation.

Making Menus for the Family

Pleasing, attractive, and wholesome menus at home, at school, and elsewhere are all based on the same fundamental principles. To select one's tray at a school cafeteria intelligently requires knowledge of food values, body needs, and pleasing food combinations. This same information should be applied in planning family meals.

Intelligent menu making means and implies knowledge of how to combine the necessary foods into wholesome, attractive meals. Specifically, it implies (1) knowing food values and body needs; (2) it means training the appetite; (3) it means selecting food combinations that can be digested with comparative ease; (4) it means giving attention to the temperature, flavor, texture, color, and cost of food.

Food values and body needs have been discussed in relation to your own diet; you have learned why the body needs food and how food meets this need; you know that for practical purposes, food should be thought of in the following groups: milk, fruit and vegetables, complete proteins, and the foods rich in starch, fats, and sugars. Knowing how to combine these foods in the right proportions in the planning of wholesome, attractive family meals is now the problem before you. Good food habits formed early in life usually carry over into adult life. It would constitute a real achievement in self-development for you to be able to say that you had learned to like all kinds of simple, nourishing foods.

The temperature of food is another factor to be taken into consideration in planning as well as in serving food. The adage "Serve hot foods hot and cold foods cold" loses no force because it is often repeated. A meal consisting altogether of hot foods or one consisting altogether of cold foods is to be avoided. Even in summer, one hot dish is desirable. Too much cold food retards the flow of digestive juices. Iced tea and iced water should be used sparingly. Too much hot food is bad as it relaxes the muscles of the stomach and interferes with digestion.

Climate and season have much to do with the temperature of our food. In hot weather, low calorie dishes and but few hot dishes are desired, while in cold weather, hot soup and rich foods are needed to keep the body warm. In general, it is wise to use less meat, fat, and sugar in summer than in winter. Milk, fruit, vegetables, and cereals are better hot weather dishes. Fresh fruit and vegetables should be used abundantly when in season.

The flavor of the foods combined makes or mars the meal. One strong vegetable, such as onions or cabbage, in a meal is sufficient. Repetition of the same flavor, such as potato soup and mashed potatoes should be avoided. Generally speaking, foods of strong flavors, such as ham, cheese, cabbage, onions, turnips, should be combined with mild flavors, such as potatoes, rice, and macaroni, while mildly flavored food, such as cauliflower, fresh green peas, and young chicken should be served with foods that are not too highly flavored or their mild distinctive flavor will not be appreciated.

Combinations of food which are generally liked include broiled steak with baked potato and a green salad; apples with pork; tomatoes with fish; cheese with crackers.

The texture of foods should receive serious consideration. Some foods of hard texture should be used each day to give exercise for the teeth and gums. Two or three different kinds of creamed dishes are not appetizing because there is no contrast of textures. Some soft and some hard food should appear in every meal. Too much liquid in even a child's diet will exclude needed calories. When you planned your lunch, you learned that something substantial, something hot, something crisp or juicy, and something sweet made a pleasing combination. Thus you discovered through personal experience that foods of different textures should be combined in the same meals; some foods juicy, some crisp, some hard, and some soft.

The colors of foods should be varied so as to make a pleasing color combination. Foods of the same color are unattractive, just as those of the same flavor are monotonous. A sprig of green parsley with a slice of red tomato is an example of contrasting colors, which, added to dishes, give interest and variety. Foods that are attractive and pleasing in appearance stimulate the appetite, while unattractive combinations have just the opposite effect.

Menu building is a fascinating study. Here are some rules to follow to make yourself a good "menu builder."

1. Variety is the keynote. There is no food or menu so good it cannot be used to excess.

2. Avoid repetition or sameness, whether of food, preparation, color, or flavor in the same meal — sometimes even in the same day or succeeding days.

3. Strive for contrasts, such as hot soup and cold dessert, soft macaroni and cheese with crisp lettuce salad, bland spaghetti and high flavored tomatoes, a tart salad course and a sweet dessert, crackers with soup.

4. Use flavors that naturally go together, as chipped beef and rice, horseradish and beef pot roast, liver and onions, apple sauce and pork, corned beef and cabbage, cranberries with poultry, mint with lamb or mutton.

5. Use highly seasoned foods sparingly for adults — not at all for children.

6. Avoid serving more than one "heavy" food at a meal, such as pork and mince pie.

7. Serve only one jelly, jam, or marmalade, and only one relish at a meal; choose this to add contrast of flavor and color.

8. Plan to have no left-overs or to use them the next day in appetizing ways.

The following suggestions for preparing food will help to retain and develop flavor.

1. To tempt the appetite and please the palate — food should taste even better than it looks; serve hot foods hot, cold foods cold. Never sacrifice good food to so-called attraction, as for example, serving warm or cold potato roses instead of plain hot, boiled, or mashed potatoes.

2. For flavor — bake potatoes or cook in skin; steam carrots or boil in skin; cook strongly flavored vegetables, as cabbage, uncovered in much water.

3. To be digestible — cook cabbage, onions, etc. only until tender; cereals long enough to soften fiber and cook starch; eggs and cheese at low temperature; avoid overheating fat.

4. To obtain and retain minerals and vitamins — use orange pulp as well as juice; steam spinach or cook quickly in boiling water; cook carrots in little water having no liquor left; heat milk quickly to prevent sediment from forming on bottom of

pan. If sediment forms, scrape and stir into milk again as this contains the valuable calcium.

These suggestions will help you to serve attractive meals.

1. Avoid overcrowding the table.

2. Set the table so it is balanced and harmonious. Avoid diagonals.

3. Place food and all service in convenient positions.

4. Use a centerpiece low enough to allow persons to see each other easily.

5. Use simple, edible garnishes.

To encourage hospitality and good fellowship:

1. Plan the kind of meals that can be prepared and served easily and correctly, with family alone, or with guests.

2. Organize work to avoid last minute hurry and confusion.

3. The mother is hostess and should remain at the table when possible. Children should help both before and during the meal.

4. Happy meal time is essential for good digestion.

5. Manners, service, and conversation should be the same whether guests are present or not. A simple meal, well prepared, which enables the hostess to enjoy both the food and her guest is more appreciated than an elaborate meal presided over by a tired- out hostess.

6. A thoughtful woman will not ask her husband to serve meats or fowl to guests without his having had the opportunity to be- come skilled in carving and serving when the family is alone. She can help by not overloading dishes, by arranging all food conveniently, and by providing a sharp carving knife.

7. Avoid strongly flavored foods and dishes unless the likes and dislikes of the persons to be served are known.

There are so many current misconceptions with regard to foods and their values, few of them containing a scintilla of truth, that it seems wise to reproduce here from Food and Nutrition Leaflet No. 4, Oklahoma State Department of Education, Vocational Home Economics Division: Fifty Superstitions About Food.

Some people believe — do you?

1. Carrots and bread crusts make the hair curly.

2. Water should not be taken with meals.

3. In accepting without question grandparent's ideas of food and food combinations.

4. Fish is brain food; it increases reproductive capacity.

5. Onions in soup are good for weak digestion; taken raw at bedtime are an insomnia remedy.

6. Dental decay is due to excess candy and sweets.

7. Lemons and oranges aid digestion; oranges cure dyspepsia if taken the first thing in the morning; oranges cause acid-stomach; acid fruits cause acidosis.

8. Prunes are a cure-all for constipation.

9. Everyone needs raisins for iron.

10. Figs, currants, strawberries are purifying; lettuce and cucumbers are cooling.

11. Eating lettuce makes one sleep.

12. Spinach directly affects the kidneys.

13. Nuts have special curative properties.

14. Beet sugar injures chest, causes apoplexy.

15. Olives are harmful to children.

16. Nuts, bananas, and cheese are hard to digest and should not be eaten.

17. Certain foods combined in the stomach with other foods react and explode.

18. Pickles and ice cream should not be eaten at the same meal; poisons are formed when lobster and ice cream are eaten together.

19. It is dangerous to eat fish and milk or cherries and milk together.

20. Milk will curdle if drunk after eating oranges.

21. Children should not drink milk at the same meal with tomatoes.

22. Oysters should be eaten only during months with R in their names.

23. Fruit should be eaten with meals only at breakfast.

24. Cucumbers should be soaked in salt water to remove the poison.

25. Liquid of canned food is harmful, it must be poured off when can is opened.

26. Highly milled grains should never be used.

27. Everyone should use bran and yeast.

28. Nature did not intend milk to be used after teeth are in ; is not suitable food for adults; is fattening, constipating, its curd in stomach causes indigestion.

29. All foods should be eaten raw, its natural state, because cooking kills nutritive substances. All vitamins are destroyed by heat.

30. Extremely hot and cold foods are good for the stomach.

31. Tomatoes clear the brain; cause cancer.

32. Each bite should be chewed fifty times.

33. One should never eat when there is no appetite.

34. Eating when ill feeds the disease.

35. Starve a fever; feed a cold.

36. Diseases disappear if one starves long enough to free system of toxins.

37. Craving for food means system needs food craved; dire results follow if cravings are not satisfied.

38. Nature intended foods to be eaten in season, or those native to residence.

39. Adequate diet is impossible without meat; it develops strong, active, brave, venturesome personalities; it is needed for muscle and red blood; it produces physical and mental energy; it has a rejuvenating effect; it makes people fierce and warlike.

40. A vegetarian diet leads to anemia, muscular weakness, lack of vigor; people on it lack courage, stamina; talented or handsome persons are rarely developed on it as preponderance of cereals deteriorate mind and body.

41. Those who do a great deal of work need a heavy protein diet.

42. Meat eating is injurious, nature intended us to be herbivorous, eat natural foods from the soil; high meat diet necessarily leads to intestinal putrefaction by which toxins are developed which poison the system, result in disease; freedom from meat poisons lead to higher state of health, greater endurance; meat is dangerous because of parasites or bacteria contained.

43. Eat starches for breakfast, vegetables for luncheon, proteins for dinner.

44. Aluminum cooking utensils are harmful to food.

45. All fried foods and all hot breads are detrimental to health.

46. Food should be emptied from can immediately after opening.

47. Veal is more dangerous to health than beef.

48. Greens and spring remedies purify the blood.

49. When reducing, eat no potatoes.

50. Digestion is aided by standing 15 minutes after eating; sleeping after eating.

Eating Away From Home.

The selection of food for oneself when away from home is just as important as for the family as a whole. There is the advantage when a person is eating at a restaurant that he may select more foods that he likes, provided, of course, that he keeps in mind the essentials of a well-balanced meal and remembers that good health depends to a large extent upon well-chosen food. Today there are so many first-class restaurants, cafeterias, and tea rooms, that eating out is no excuse for making poor selections.

Search for a place that is clean, where there is good service, reasonably priced first-class food, and freedom from noise. The location of a restaurant often determines what must be charged the patron for his food. The rent, wages of employees, overhead expenses, etc. are factors in all calculations. Where these costs are high, the patron pays more.

The menus at a restaurant are usually classified as "table d'hote," "a la carte," and "carte de jour." The first signifies that the meal is given at a set or fixed price, although there are probably several choices of combinations at that particular price. In ordering a la carte, each article of the luncheon is listed and priced separately, and the servings are larger than in the meal given at a set or fixed price. If one does not desire a full meal, he may order as many single items as he chooses from the a la carte menu. The waiter may have to help you with the French terms, if you order a la carte in order that you may select the variety of foods adequate to a balanced diet. The items under the carte de jour list are already cooked and ready to serve to those who do not care for a full meal and cannot wait for the a la carte items to be cooked.

When girls are eating out as guests of boys, the boy consults her wishes and then orders for her. While she should not deliberately select the cheapest thing on the menu merely because it is cheap, she should not go to the other extreme of selecting the most expensive things, particularly if she wishes to be invited again.

In restaurants where there is a head waiter, the girl follows the waiter to the table and the boy follows the girl. The waiter will pull out the most desirable seat for the girl. Usually this is the seat facing the street or the point of interest in the room. If there is no waiter, the boy takes the lead to the table and gives the most desirable seat to the girl. Where one seat is a couch or wall seat, the girl takes that, with the boy seated opposite her.

The boy helps the girl with her wraps. She places her gloves and purse on a vacant or nearby chair, not on the tablecloth. The hair or other matters of toilet, such as applying lipstick and powder, should not be attended to in the restaurant.

When couples are dining together, the two girls face each other, and the two boys face each other.

Bad table manners will show up anywhere, but of course in public they are more apparent. The impression others receive from an exhibition of bad manners is a lack of background and poor training at home. It is necessary to avoid every unpleasantness in a public eating place and to refrain from exhibiting manners that would offend. If it is necessary to send back any food, do so without comment and allow the waiter to remove it and bring other food. The waiter will furnish extra silver in place of that dropped by accident on the floor.

The boy should stand and remain standing in case a friend stops at his table to speak with the girl he is with. An introduction is not necessary, but a visit should not be prolonged.

It is not good taste to linger if the restaurant is crowded; others may be waiting to obtain seats. Boisterous or loud talking or anything that approaches loud or vulgar display is of course taboo. If fingerbowls are used at the close of the meal, the fingers should be dried on the napkin after which the napkin, unfolded, should be returned to the table. The boy is expected to attend to the check, and the well-bred girl will show no curiosity in regard to it. A tip of ten percent is customary. Some dining places have rules in regard to tipping, which of course should be observed.

The girl should allow the boy to assist her with her wraps after which she should wait quietly until he has paid the bill. Toothpicks are not used by people who understand etiquette except as a toilet accessory in the bath room. It is not permissible to walk arm in arm either in entering or leaving the restaurant.

When girls dine out together, they frequently share costs, each paying for her own check; or preferably, the check may be paid by one, the other paying her part later. Any argument about paying the check is obviously out of place, and in poor taste.

Marketing.

Feeding a family on a small income requires careful planning based upon knowledge of food values and body needs. The less money a family has to expend on food the more it is necessary to have thorough knowledge of nutrition. On the other hand, when money is too plentiful, the same knowledge is needed to keep meals from being too rich with fats and sweets. Overeating not only wastes food but overworks the body. Irregular eating, especially of rich food, is another bad habit too often noted when finances are not at all limited. Simple, well balanced meals, wholesomely prepared, attractively served, and eaten in a leisurely manner at regular intervals, represent the essentials of good nutrition for rich and poor alike.

Since going to the store is a frequent home activity of boys and girls, it should be as rich and as educational as possible. Do you ever go to market to select the family's food supply? Many families do their marketing once a week, which necessitates only a few emergency calls to the grocery store during the week.

Choosing a Market.

The two most commonly known markets are the cash-and-carry and the credit-and-delivery stores. The cash-and-carry stores usually sell food cheaper, as there is neither the wages of a delivery boy nor a bookkeeping entry to consider.

The credit-and-delivery store will give you more personal service. Marketing may be done by telephone or personally by going to the store.

One of the most important things to consider in selecting a market for your food supply is the matter of sanitation. Everyone who handles the food should be scrupulously clean and free from disease. The proper selection of food means little if that selection comes from a store with unsanitary surroundings.

Suggestions for Buying Economically.

While still maintaining or even increasing nutritional values, the following suggestions can be used to reduce the cost of food for the family:

1. Buy food in season. Storage and transportation increase costs.

2. Buy less expensive foods. Food costs depend upon the costs of labor and risk in production, care in handling, and perishability. Apples cost less than peaches, pears, or cherries, which are more perishable; cabbage costs less than cauliflower; winter carrots less than new ones. Use cheaper cuts of meat, they are nutritious and well flavored. Smaller, thin skinned oranges, heavy for their size, yield more juice than some large ones.

3. Buy more economical, substantial quality. When satisfactory, buy standard and sub-standard grades instead of fancy or choice. Buy large peas for soup; buy broken sliced pineapple.

4. Buy in the most economical quantity. The quantity to buy depends upon storage facilities in the home, amount of each kind of food needed, amount that can be used before spoiling, and fluctuation of prices. Dozens and cases usually cost less than single articles. Be as careful with a large supply as a small one or no saving will result. Even small families, with adequate refrigeration and storage facilities, planned use of leftovers, recanning and repacking contents of larger containers, can save by quantity buying.

5. Buy according to weight. Avoid purchasing 10^, 25^, or 50^ worth. Watch net weight of all packages, cans, and car- tons. A carton of butter may weigh 14 oz. instead of 16 oz.; a No. 2 can of pineapple may contain six instead of eight slices; a No. 2 can of peas, weighing 20 ounces, may still contain a variable proportion of peas and liquid. There are three sizes of cans between No. 1 and No. 2 sizes.

6. Produce and prepare food at home when possible and practicable. Ready-to-eat foods usually cost more than uncooked ones. Compare quantities of uncooked and ready prepared cereals of equal cost. For both saving of money and maximum food value, buy foods as nearly as possible in their natural form.

7. Canned foods are safe, often richer in food value, often cheaper than fresh foods; dried and frozen foods often cost less than fresh or canned.

8. Watch markets for prices; save when merchants are overstocked.

9. Have a few well selected cans in reserve and replenish staples before entirely out; last minute buying is almost always costly.

10. Determine relative time, energy, money advantages and disadvantages of cash-carry, credit-delivery, delicatessen, curb or roadside market, mail order buying.

Terms Used in Grading Canned Fruits and Vegetables: Fancy, Choice or Extra Standard, Standard, Sub-Standard, Waterpack.

Waterpack is wholesome food, unsweetened, may be irregular in size or have a few blemishes, therefore unsuitable for other grades.

A Federal regulation requires canned fruits and vegetables below standard to be labeled, "Below U. S. Standard." They are good foods, suitable for many uses, and economical.

Become informed on existing legislation about foods in order, individually and as a member of groups, to urge standardization, grade labeling, sanitation, and needed laws for enforcement.

Summary

Intelligent food selection means more than satisfying the appetite or eating for pleasure. Eating the right kind of food as well as the right amount of food is a physiological duty. The intelligent selection of food entails securing an adequate diet in the kind and amount suited to the needs of each individual. It entails selecting the right food from each class of foodstuffs so that we will have: (1) foods that give energy for warmth and activity; (2) foods that build muscle, bone, and teeth; (3) foods that regulate the body, make it grow, and keep it healthy.

It also implies eating a sufficient amount of food to yield the number of calories required by the individual body. To do this, we must learn how many calories we need; and then, by intelligent choice of food, obtain these calories from all the necessary food essentials in proportion to the need for each. Thus, determining the correct number of calories is only part of this important food problem since calories measure only the energy or fuel value of foods. Ascertaining the needed amount and kind of protein, minerals, and vitamins is the next important step. That we include plenty of water and bulk in our diet is also essential to good health and growth.

To do all this requires a special study of the individual foods. We should know what foods to select to supply the energy requirement for adults and children of various ages. We should know the kind and amount of protein needed for growth and health and should know how to select foods through which the necessary minerals and vitamins will be supplied.

The intelligent selection of food and the planning of meals is by no means a simple task, for in everyday life it involves such questions as cost, market conditions, food habits, palatability, the labor and time required in meal preparation, and the knowledge of how to prepare food so as to conserve the essential minerals and vitamins.

CHAPTER 7

CARE, PRESERVATION, AND STORAGE OF FOOD

Upon examination of statistics relating to the processing of food products, it will be found that the storage of food and the preservation of food are carried on more and more outside the home.

Commercially canned food is becoming less expensive and more satisfactory in every way. Canned fruit, vegetables, and meat can be used with only a partial sacrifice of value or flavor when fresh food is scarce or too expensive. Cold storage lengthens the season for many fresh products. In cold climates, many vegetables such as pumpkins, potatoes, and turnips can be kept in storage. Apples and pears are two of the fuits that can be stored in the home cellar. Modern methods of keeping food and transferring it from place to place make it possible for us to have fresh fruit, green vegetables, and fresh meat all the year around.

Canned Foods.

Do you like canned foods as well as fresh ones? As a rule, canned goods are not liked so well as fresh foods, but they add variety to the diet, making possible balanced meals throughout the year. Canned vegetables and fruits are especially helpful in communities where fresh food is not available and they have practically the same food value as the fresh foods.

Many minerals are soluble in water and for this reason the liquid in canned vegetables and fruits should be used. The water from canned vegetables can be utilized in making soups and vegetable stews.

Canned food sometimes spoils and when it does, it should never be eaten or even tasted. Bulged cans and any unusual odor indicates spoilage. The inside of a tin can should be clean and smooth. Dark or corroded spots should be sufficient reason for discarding the food. Reliable grocers will gladly replace all canned goods, as well as other food that shows signs of spoilage.

Why Foods Spoil.

Because food is so perishable various methods of food preservation have been used since the earliest time. Primitive man discovered that dried food would not spoil, hence drying was the first method used in preserving food. Later it was learned that food such as meat and fish would not spoil as quickly during cold weather and that food could be stored for later use during the winter months, hence the beginning of cold storage and refrigeration.

Napoleon offered a prize to anyone who could invent a practical method of preserving perishable food. Appert, a Frenchman, won the prize for inventing canning. Thus, food was preserved by drying, by cold storage, and by canning even before anyone knew why food spoils. It remained for Pasteur to show the world that food was spoiled by little microorganisms or germs. His discovery laid the foundation for all modern methods of preserving and storing food.

Bacteria, Yeast, and Molds.

These tiny vegetable plants are classified as yeast, bacteria, and mold. If you could look at yeast plants under the microscope you would see that they are tiny cells, oval in shape and somewhat resembling tiny seeds. Some bacteria are like little balls; some are short and straight; some are curved and bent, while a few look like a branching stem.

Molds are larger than either yeast or bacteria. Un- der a microscope they look like tangled threads or color- Yeast Plants under the Microscope less stems. When ripe, these threads or stems end in a head or pod which is a mass of spores. These will scatter and later develop into new mold plants.

How do "germs" get into our food? These germs or microorganisms that we have just been talking about are so small that they are blown about in the air. They are likely to be found on anything that is exposed to the open air. Did you ever see mold on a loaf of bread? Did you ever taste over-ripe fruit? Yeast is usually the cause of fermentation and spoiling of over-ripe fruit and vegetables. When vegetables and fruit ferment, the fiber or cellulose becomes soft; the juice bubbles and becomes sour.

When food is spoiled by bacteria and other microorganisms, certain poisons sometimes develop which are very harmful to our bodies. Did you ever hear of anyone having ptomaine poison? This is caused by eating spoiled fish, meat, and other protein foods. Bacteria develop and multiply rapidly in milk, meat, fish, etc., and for this reason these foods should be kept in the coldest part of the refrigerator, which is directly under the ice.

Yeast is killed by very low or very high temperature. Mold is killed by heat but will grow in a low temperature unless the air circulates freely. Mold cannot grow on dry food as moisture is necessary to its development. Yeast and mold are easily killed by boiling. Some kinds of bacteria are also killed by boiling, however, the bacteria that form spores are very difficult to kill by heat. The spore-forming bacteria are more likely to be found on vegetables than fruit. This accounts for the fact that it is much easier to can fruit than vegetables at home. A high temperature maintained for a long period of time will kill spores. Commercial canning factories are equipped to do this while the average home is not.

All microorganisms require food, moisture, and warmth for growth and development. It is evident then that eliminating any one of these factors retards or stops their growth. When we want to preserve food, we may (1) kill the bacteria present by heat as in canning; (2) prevent their growth by cold storage; (3) exclude the air, as for example, preserving eggs with waterglass; (4) add some preservative as vinegar or sugar; (5) remove all moisture as in drying.

Are all microorganisms harmful?

Many microorganisms serve a useful purpose. Yeast is rich in vitamins and makes bread light and porous. The delicious flavors of buttermilk, butter, and all kinds of cheese including cottage cheese result from bacterial action.

When bacteria cause vegetation to decay they are useful. What would happen if the ground was never enriched by decaying vegetation? If it were not for this fertilizer, the soil would become so poor it would not grow vegetables, fruits, and cereals for food. Some bacteria cause disease and of course they are harmful. Thus it has been the problem of science to discover how to make use of the helpful bacteria and how to destroy the harmful ones that come in contact with our food and our bodies.

While the most important cause of food spoilage is the action of yeast, mold, or bacteria, we should not overlook the action of the enzymes which bring about the natural ripening of fruits and vegetables. These enzymes change starch into sugar and otherwise prepare our food for use. Unless the action of these enzymes is stopped in food, it goes on into natural decay and spoilage. Someone has said that enzymes and microorganisms do nature's work in getting rid of food products when they are not used by man, bird, or other living organisms. The action of both enzymes and bacteria can be stopped by heat, hence the convenience of canning food. Milk is pasteurized to stop the action of enzymes and microorganisms. Cold storage and other methods of food preservation stop or arrest the action of these enzymes as well as the growth and development of bacteria, yeast, and molds.

Methods of Preserving Food.

Drying is nature s own method of preserving food and was the first method used by primitive man. All seeds are dry, hence seeds have good keeping qualities. Dried fruits, such as prunes, dates, figs and raisins; all kinds of nuts and cereals, beans, and peas are examples of the dried fruit and vegetable products used for food today. Dried beef and fish are examples of dried meat. Since moisture is necessary to the growth of microorganisms, the chief object in drying food is to extract the moisture. This removal deprives the microorganisms of one element necessary to their growth. Apples, pears, apricots, peaches, and corn are easily preserved by drying in the home.

Cold storage or refrigeration is another example of food preservation. We have learned that yeast will not grow at a low temperature. The use of refrigerator cars, cold storage plants, and the ice box at home, are all examples of preventing the growth of microorganisms by lowering the temperature. Fresh fruit, vegetables, meat, fish, poultry, and eggs are made available throughout the year, through the use of cold storage and refrigeration.

By excluding the air, the growth of all kinds of bacteria is prevented. This is true because air is necessary to the growth of all living cells, plant or animal. An example of this method of preservation is in the use of waterglass in preserving eggs. Air can pass through the porous egg shell and for this reason eggs spoil. Waterglass closes the pores of the shell, and thus prevents the entrance of bacteria. Eggs kept in waterglass for many weeks lose some of their valuable properties and taste stale. However, waterglass, vaseline, and paraffin are all useful for keeping eggs for a short time over a period of high prices. Apples and peaches and other fresh fruits can be kept for some time by clipping them in paraffin. By excluding the air, bacteria are kept out. However, if the bacteria are already present, the food will spoil anyway.

Food may be kept by preservatives such as vinegar, sugar, salt, and smoke. Pickles are made by adding vinegar to fruits and vegetables. Sugar is the chief preservative in jellies, jams, and marmalades. Spices are used as preservatives in making mince meat, and various pickle combinations. Salt is used in curing fish and meats.

Cured meats that we use every day are bacon, ham, and fish. Many years ago, when much home butchering was done, meats were cured in salt and smoked in a specially prepared building called a smoke house. Liquid smoke preparations are now in use, but people who have tasted the old-time smoked meat, prefer the delicious flavor imparted by wood smoke.

Harmful preservatives are sometimes used to prevent further bacterial action and to disguise the flavor of inferior food. The substances which are commonly used for this purpose are borax, benzoate of soda, salt peter, and alum. The Pure Food Laws of the Federal Government, known as the Food and Drug Acts, prohibit the use of harmful preservatives unless the percentage is stated on the container. Such food preservatives are injurious to health.

Canning is the most practical method of preserving food at home. The underlying principle in canning is to kill all microorganisms and to stop the action of enzymes by heat. By canning fruits and vegetables in season, for example, when there is an over supply, much saving may be made in the food budget. Many families can fresh fruits and vegetables during the canning season sufficient to last throughout the year. By canning food when it is inexpensive, much variety can be given to the menus during the winter months when fresh food is so expensive as to make its use prohibitive. Canned fruits and vegetables are partially lacking in some of the minerals and vitamins which are so abundant in fresh food.

Five methods of preserving foods are in common use. Each one of these methods is a means of preventing the growth of microorganisms by depriving them of some of the essentials to their growth. For example, in drying, the moisture is removed; and in cold storage, the temperature is kept below that which is required for favorable growth. Extreme heat kills bacteria, and chemicals of many kinds, including vinegar, spices and sugar, prevent their growth. In excluding the air, we also exclude bacteria as in coating an egg with vaseline, paraffin, or waterglass.

A study of the causes of spoilage in food only emphasizes the need for keeping food under sanitary conditions. People who handle food should be clean personally and free from all diseases. Germs and microorganisms which are responsible for the spoiling of food are so very small that they can be blown about in the air and for this reason are found practically everywhere. The importance of being immaculately clean and careful in handling food can scarcely be overestimated.

Successful food preservation depends upon the efficacy of the methods used in preventing the growth of micro-organisms and in killing those present. Food is preserved by (1) applying low temperature, (2) by applying high temperature, (3) by drying, (4) by excluding air, and (5) by preservatives.

Methods of Canning.

There are three methods of canning, namely the open-kettle method, the cold- pack method , and the hot- pack method.

In the open-kettle method, the food is sterilized by cooking it in an open vessel. It is then packed quickly in jars and sealed at once. If these jars are not thoroughly sterilized, bacteria will be present in the food, and will later multiply and develop, spoiling the food. The open-kettle method is used successfully for all kinds of jellies, preserves, marmalades, conserves, fruit butters, and fruit juices, as well as in the making of pickles, relishes, catsup, and in canning fruits and tomatoes.

In using the cold-pack method, the cold food is packed into the jars or cans, but the fruit and vegetables are previously shrunk by blanching which is done by dipping them into boiling water. Brine or hot syrup is added, and the container is partly sealed. The jar must then be heated in order to exhaust the air before the final sealing and sterilizing. In the cold-pack method, the container and the food are sterilized at the same time. Fruits, vegetables, and meats are canned by the cold-pack method.

The hot-pack method is a combination of the advantages of the cold-pack and the open-kettle methods of canning. In this method, a little water is added to the food and the food is heated thoroughly. It is then placed in the jars or cans and then heated to exclude all air. This preliminary cooking shrinks the food and makes it easier to pack. Practically all foods can be canned by this method.

Canned food that spoils does so because there are bacteria present. These bacteria may have been in the food in the form of spores or on the lids and cans which were not thoroughly sterilized. Foods to be canned should be clean and fresh and every effort should be made to keep germs out of the cans. A wash boiler or large kettle, with a rack for a false bottom, makes a splendid improvised or homemade water canner. Fruits and tomatoes can be canned by the open-kettle method. Some vegetables such as beans, peas, asparagus and corn have been successfully canned by the cold-pack method, using an improvised hot water canner, but for most vegetables and all meats, a pressure cooker or canner is necessary.

Steam cookers or pressure cookers are real labor-saving devices where much cooking or canning is to be done. Directions for using the pressure cooker should come with the cooker when purchased. Commercial concerns handling pressure cookers and canners will gladly demonstrate their use. Read the directions for their use carefully, even though you attended such a demonstration. Learning to follow directions from the printed page is certainly worthwhile. A special study of canning outfits will be profitable to the one who expects to do much home canning.

Learning How to Can.

Home canning is an economical thing to do when there is a surplus of fruits and vegetables and when they can be bought at a comparatively low price and used during a period of high prices.

In climates where the season for fresh fruit is short, home canning and home storage are more necessary than in the southern regions where fresh fruit and vegetables grow in the garden practically every month in the year. Canning for market may be used as the means of making money. Home canned food, especially jellies, jams, preserves, and marmalades are thought by many people to be superior to the commercially canned products.

Care of Food.

Nowhere are clean and sanitary habits more necessary than in handling food. Many diseases are carried to the stomach through the food we eat. Cleanliness is not only necessary at the grocery store, meat market, and all public places where food is handled, but in the home as well.

There are many tiny living plant and animal forms all about us. These tiny little plants are known as yeast, bacteria, and molds, while the tiny little animals are called protozoa. Millions and millions live in the air, water, and soil. The wind blows them around on dust. They float in rivers and streams. They even grow in the dirt and soil. Each single cell grows and multiplies very fast. Warmth, moisture, and darkness are necessary to their growth. Light and sunlight kill them. High temperatures destroy them if the heat is continued long enough. Cold prevents their growth but does not kill them. Hence, unclean food and water are not made safe by freezing.

Only the organisms which cause disease are to be feared, but since we cannot see them except under a microscope, the only safe thing to do is to keep our bodies, our food, and our water clean and sanitary. Coughing, sneezing, and spitting on the sidewalks and floors will cause the spread of disease. Wherever there is dust, disease germs are apt to be present. Flies spread disease germs as do mosquitoes, rats, and mice, and every effort should be made to get rid of them. Write to your state agricultural college or to the United States Department of Agriculture for bulletins on how to prevent and get rid of such filthy disease carriers.

Cooking helps in making our food safe. All fruits and green vegetables eaten raw should be washed thoroughly and should be bought only at clean, sanitary stores and markets.

A good refrigerator is a real economy. We have learned that a low temperature prevents the growth of microorganisms. The melting ice cools the refrigerator. For this reason, it is not wise to cover ice with paper or blankets; neither is it wise to put food in the ice chamber. As the ice melts, the cold air goes down, passing through the refrigerator and back up to the ice to be cooled again. The coldest part of the ice box is just beneath the ice. Prevent warm air from entering the ice box as much as possible. Leaving the ice box door open while carrying food from the kitchen table is one way that ice is wasted. Warm dishes placed in the ice box also waste ice.

The modern mechanical refrigerator is a real labor-saving device. By its use food can be kept over long periods with safety, thus making it possible to buy perishable food in large quantities and cut down the cost of food as well as the time required in marketing. Also, the larger sized cans of food may be purchased for a small family and the unused portion kept safely in the refrigerator until it is welcome again at the family table.

Milk and butter absorb odors of other foods and should be kept covered. Butter wrapped in oil paper may safely be placed in the ice box; it may also be kept in a covered jar made for the purpose.

The refrigerator, as well as all storage places for food, should be thoroughly cleaned with hot water, to which a little soda or ammonia has been added. The drain pipe should be flushed out with this hot water. A good refrigerator has pipes that can be taken apart for cleaning. Often the shelves are removable also. A long-handled brush, such as that used in cleaning bottles, will be helpful in cleaning the pipes.

No doubt you have heard of an iceless refrigerator, a cold air closet, a cellar, or even of a window box being used for storing food. A window box in a north room can often be utilized successfully during the cold months. Cold air closets are also useful and convenient.

Dishwashing.

Dishwashing becomes one of the most interesting tasks in the home when we understand how much difference it makes whether we do it properly or improperly and go about it systematically. Dishes which have been washed thoroughly with a clean dish cloth or mop in clear sudsy water, and then scalded and allowed to drain dry are much freer from bacteria than those which have been carelessly washed.

For efficiency and fun in dishwashing, decide upon some order for washing dishes, the kind of equipment needed, and have utensils and supplies arranged conveniently so that it will entail the least possible effort. It is a good idea to have at hand a plate scraper, sink strainer, dishpan, dish cloth or mop, drainer, and dish towel. There should be plenty of boiling water.

Dishes and utensils can be more quickly and efficiently washed if they are scraped free of food and rinsed in cold water. Greasy dishes should be wiped with paper before putting them into the water. Paper towels are inexpensive and very valuable for purposes of this sort.

Put only a few dishes at a time into the dishpan. Pick up one dish at a time, wash it thoroughly, and place it in the dish drainer. After they have all been washed and placed in the drainer, pour boiling water over them. They will dry quickly and, with the exception of glassware, silverware, and certain cooking utensils, will not need wiping.

After the dishes have been washed, the dishpan should be washed thoroughly with soap, scalded, and put away. Dish cloths or mops and towels should be boiled in soapy water and rinsed thoroughly to keep them fresh and clean.

Foods and Insects.

Food that is left around attracts insects, such as flies, ants, and other insects. The kitchen should be screened to keep out flies and if flies find their way into the house by passing through open doors, they should be killed. Flies are filthy and often carry disease germs. No one likes to think of flies crawling in dirty places and then crawling over food, yet this is just what happens wherever flies are found. Uncovered food, crumbs, and soiled dishes left scattered about may also attract ants and cockroaches. The sink should be thoroughly cleaned after each meal, and all waste food should be burned or placed in a garbage can. Some kinds of garbage can be fed to chickens and pigs. The garbage pail should be cleaned thoroughly once a week. Spilling garbage on the ground around the can is almost sure to attract flies and other insects. Garbage cans should have a firmly fitting lid and should be kept covered. A garbage can which can be opened by pressing the foot on a spring is a convenience.

Food and Dust.

Wherever dust and dirt are present, germs are also to be found. Foods kept on dirty shelves or in dirty boxes; foods handled by those with unclean hands and wearing dirty clothes are vicious examples of unsanitary food habits. How does it affect you to see some- one with unclean hands and dirty clothes handling food? Tasting food with the cooking spoon, putting fingers in food, and other habits of carelessness are not only repulsive but may be the means of spreading disease. Would you buy food that is kept in unsanitary stores? Would you eat food that is handled in unsanitary ways in your own home?

What are the sanitary regulations in your city or town? In almost every state, there are sanitary rules for handling food. Write to your state board of health for its dairy regulations. Why did the Federal Government pass laws to protect you from buying meat that is unfit for use? What laws govern the sale of milk in your community? These laws, rules, and regulations have been made to protect you from eating unclean food. Are you doing your part? Do you always wash your hands before eating food? Before handling food for others? Make a list of unsanitary habits that you have observed in other people who handle food. Find out all you can about the laws and regulations for the protection of food in your state and community.

Milk Regulations.

Since milk is the food of infants and invalids, it is guarded most rigidly by our laws. Skimmed milk and watered milk are prohibited. The milk must be clean. The highest grade is called A, but there is a special grade of milk for the use of infants called "certified" milk, although it is not commonly sold. Invalids also procure the certified milk when possible. In order to keep the milk clean, regulations are made in regard to the animals, the quarters, the workers, and the utensils. In cities, these are all scored and the dairies with the highest marks or scores naturally have their full quota of customers, while those that fall below fall off in their list of customers. The cows must be healthy; all utensils sterilized.

Pasteurized Milk.

In pasteurizing, the milk is heated to 145 F. for thirty minutes. Heating at this temperature changes the quality of the milk but little and is therefore better than boiling, since it destroys the disease bacteria
that are sometimes found in milk, such as typhoid, diphtheria, and tuberculosis. The milk should be cooled rapidly and bottled immediately. Many cities use the pasteurization plan altogether to secure pure milk.

Rules for having good milk:

1. Keep milk in a cool place.

2. Buy milk in bottles.

3. Place milk in the coolest part of the refrigerator as soon as received.

4. Wash the mouth of the bottle before pouring out the milk over the dirty edge. Keep milk in the bottle until used.

5. If new and old milk are mixed, the mixture will spoil.

6. Cleanse the refrigerator once a week.

7. As milk absorbs odors and spoils rapidly, be careful not to place it near articles with strong odors.

Care of Meat.

Meat should be unwrapped as soon as it is received, wiped, and put in the refrigerator in a clean, dry, uncovered dish. When cooked meat is stored in the refrigerator, it should be covered with waxed paper.

Care of Fish.

Fish should be kept in the refrigerator in a covered dish so that its strong odor will not be absorbed by the other foods.

Care of Eggs.

Eggs may be preserved in waterglass or kept in a covered container in the refrigerator. If they are preserved, only infertile eggs should be used as they do not spoil so easily. Since bacteria enter the eggs through their porous shells, the eggs which are to be kept some time should be submerged in the syrup-like liquid called waterglass, which may be bought at the drug store. One part of waterglass is required with nine parts of water that has been boiled and cooled. This mixture should be placed in a stone crock. Place the fresh eggs in this solution, a few at a time, taking care to see that they are at least two inches below the surface of the solution. The crock should be covered and kept in a cool place. Eggs should keep a year, if properly packed.

CHAPTER 8

PREPARING AND SERVING FOOD FOR SPECIAL OCCASIONS

The special occasions on which food or refreshments in some form are served have increased in number at a rate that is commensurate with the increase in leisure that has come about through social and economic changes in our national life. On some of these special occasions, the demand for food may be met with the simplest of refreshments; on others, the demand is for foods as substantial and nourishing as those served at a regular family meal. In either case, the hostess is most successful who knows exactly what to do in the preparation and serving of food or refreshments appropriate to the occasion. It is, however, not to be inferred that the successful hostess is bound slavishly to an undeviating procedure. She can show originality, inventiveness, and even make innovations in custom if the departures from custom are made in obedience to the principles of art that govern in cuisine and service.

The type of food or refreshments that may be served appropriately is very largely governed by the nature and purpose of the gathering. For instance, at a reception, where many people are invited in honor of some notable person, the most appropriate refreshments consist of something light and easy to serve; but at a buffet supper or luncheon, the menu is expected to contain foods as substantial as those the guests ordinarily eat at these meals. The occasions which call for special menus or refreshments include teas, receptions, open house occasions, at homes, morning coffee, after-theater parties, buffet meals, picnics, steak fries, barbecues, and many other outdoor parties.

Planning Special Menus.

The factors that should receive preliminary attention in making a special menu include the following:

1. The age and sex of the group — whether high school girls and boys, girls alone, or mixed ages and sexes.

2. Time of serving — before or after a regular meal, late supper, or in place of a regular meal.

3. Season of the year — spring, summer, fall, or winter.

4. Place of serving — indoors or outdoors.

5. Facilities for preparing and serving.

6. Cost of the food and service.

7. Color, flavor, and texture combinations.

Preparing and Cooking Special Menu Foods.

After planning the menu, the next thing to consider is the method of preparing, cooking, and serving each dish in the menu. The following aims and precautions should be faithfully observed:

1. To cook or prepare each food so as to preserve or accentuate its palatable qualities.

2. To serve each dish in an attractive form.

3. To serve each food in the condition that is dictated by the method of its preparation. For example, foods that are chilled become insipid if served in a lukewarm state.

4. To drain fruits and vegetables used in salads in order to prevent an unsightly excess of liquid from running over the plates.

5. To avoid serving lettuce and other raw foods that are not fresh, crisp, and free from spots or bruises.

6. To avoid profuseness in the garnishes used with food.

7. To avoid cutting or shaping food such as sandwiches, cookies, and molded dishes into so many fancy shapes as to give the appearance of grotesqueness.

8. If color is used, to use it sparingly and in a natural combination.

Teas.

Teas are friendly social affairs which no other form of entertainment excels in popularity during the high school period of life or in after years. They present an opportunity for young people to gain practical and cultural knowledge as well as the opportunity to overcome youthful diffidence and acquire social grace or poise. The politer amenities of social conduct may be better observed at teas, despite their informal nature, than at most social gatherings. Older people are then seen at their best — relaxed, friendly, and affable yet mindful at all times of the decorum that marks the well-bred. In such an atmosphere, the talent and capacity of the hostess are shown to greatest advantage through the ability she discloses in greeting her guests, making introductions, and putting everyone at ease.

The time set for afternoon teas should not be too near the hour at which people customarily go to their dinners lest the refreshments served interfere with the appetite. Nor should it be so soon after the midday meal that guests will have no desire for refreshments.

The tea menu should not consist of the richer foods that invariably cloy the appetite and upset regular schedules for eating, if eaten between meals. It should consist of simple foods that digest readily and leave the appetite for substantial foods unimpaired.

Tea Dances.

For many reasons, young people very much enjoy tea dances. Small groups of friends and school mates find in these affairs many advantages over other forms of entertainment. They are less expensive than dinner dances which usually must be given in hotels and clubs where food costs are high. Music may be provided at little cost by a small orchestra consisting of no more than two or three instruments. If no orchestra is available, good phonograph dance records may be used. Also, since these affairs are entirely informal, simple informal clothes are more appropriate than elaborate and costly costumes.

Tea dances are especially popular with high school students because it is more convenient for them to go direct from school, in groups or singly, than to come back to an evening party from their widely separated homes.

The menus may vary in consistency from the light simple foods appropriate for warm weather to those of a more substantial nature which are enjoyed when the weather is cold.

Tea Menus.

The refreshments served at formal or in- formal teas vary in different sections of the country and with the coming and going of fads. There being no hard and fast rules, the hostess may feel free to serve anything she chooses in her own home provided it is dainty and tasteful. The following menus are merely suggestive.

I - Tea Sandwiches or Small cakes or (Two kinds) cookies

II - Tea, chocolate, or coffee Sandwiches, cookies, or small cakes

III - Tea (coffee or chocolate) and Punch Sandwiches, cookies, small cakes Caramels and Fudge

Tea may be either hot or iced and served plain or with a slice of lemon or lemon and cloves, the clove being imbedded in the lemon. The spiced, sweetened tea, such as the Russian, requires neither lemon nor sugar on the tea table and may be kept hot and fresh with less attention to service than plain tea. Hot tea to be at its best should be kept hot.

Chocolate may be served plain or with whipped cream. When chocolate is well prepared and served hot, it is both delicious and nutritious.

Coffee is usually served hot but many people drink iced coffee in hot weather. Adults often prefer coffee to tea if a choice is offered between the two.

Punch is usually provided in addition to the hot beverage at large, formal teas. On hot summer days punch, lemonade, or a light iced drink is always appropriate and highly appreciated.

Sandwiches.

There are more opportunities for the creation of pleasing effects in the preparation and making of sandwiches than in any other food combination. There are many kinds of bread, and the many fillers that may be used are almost unlimited. Ingenuity, art, skill in cooking, and knowledge of nutrition may have the fullest sway in the use of colors, flavors, and textures in order to make pleasing combinations. Decorations may be employed to advantage if restraint is exercised in their use.

The decorations used on a sandwich should conform to its structural outline. For example, if the bread is cut into a round or triangular shape the decoration should follow that pattern. One must avoid using too many intense colors or the effect will be displeasing. A good plan to follow, when fancy shapes are used, is to leave off any other form of decoration; and if the bread is colored to cut it into simple shapes since one form of decoration is usually sufficient.

Sandwich Combinations.

The following combinations are suitable for teas and other occasions where the equivalent of the tea menu may be used:

Cheese

1. Cream cheese, moistened with cream or mayonnaise, and seasoned.

2. Cream cheese, grated pineapple, mayonnaise, and seasoning.

3. Cream cheese, chopped nuts, mayonnaise, and seasoning.

4. Cream cheese, chopped stuffed olives, mayonnaise, and seasoning.

5. Cream cheese, chopped dates, mayonnaise, seasoning.

6. Cream cheese, jam or jelly, mayonnaise, seasoning.

7. Cream cheese, green mint cherries, mayonnaise, seasoning.

8. Cheese, pimento, mayonnaise, seasoning.

9. Pimento cheese, olives, mayonnaise, seasoning.

Eggs

1. Eggs, hard cooked and chopped, mayonnaise, seasoning.

2. Chopped hard cooked eggs, chopped olives, mayonnaise, seasoning.

Fruit

1. Dates, chopped nuts, mayonnaise, seasoning.

2. Dates, raisins, chopped nuts, mayonnaise, seasoning.

3. Figs, chopped nuts, mayonnaise, seasoning.

4. Pineapple, dates, chopped nuts, mayonnaise, seasoning.

Nuts

1. Almonds, salted and crushed, tart jelly, mayonnaise.

2. Nut meats, currant jelly, creamed butter.

Hot Food Suggestions

1. Grated cheese well-seasoned on slice of bread, rolled, and toasted.

2. Small hot biscuits, with bacon or sausage inside.

3. Tiny patties (shells) filled with creamed chicken, and served hot.

Preparing Sandwiches.

Plain bread, nut bread, raisin bread, whole wheat bread, rye bread, salt rising bread, and brown bread are the kinds most often used in making sandwiches. Plain bread may be tinted in any desired color if an order is placed with the baker in advance of the day set for baking. Tinting is deprived of the pleasant effect it creates if the color used is too intense.

Cutters for shaping the bread may be purchased, although a biscuit cutter or the top of a small can may be used for cutting circular shapes. Sandwiches should be small and dainty when served at teas, but larger than those made with the so-called "appetizer cutter."

In making sandwiches, select fresh sandwich bread at the bakery, have it cut uniformly into slices % of an inch in thickness, place the bread on a flat surface one slice at a time, spread the filler evenly at the desired thickness, apply the cover slice of bread, trim the edges with a knife, and cut straight across or diagonally if a triangular shape is desired. If the sandwiches are to be round or have other shapes, the bread is cut into the desired shapes before the filler is applied.

To make a layer sandwich, slice bread the average thickness, spread the lower slice with almost an equal thickness of the filling, place on this another slice of bread and spread as before. Repeat until five slices are used. Cover with a slightly dampened cloth and leave in the refrigerator one hour before trimming the edges and slicing. If smaller sizes are preferred, the slices may be split in halves before serving.

If the same kind of bread is used in layer sandwiches, the fillings may be tinted in order to give variety. A cream cheese filler, if made somewhat stiff, may be used successfully for this purpose.

Bread sliced the length of the loaf, spread with the filling, rolled, wrapped in a cloth, chilled, and sliced before serving makes an attractive sandwich.

Unless one has servants or the means to assure the serving of layer and rolled sandwiches in perfect condition, it is better and far easier to prepare the simpler styles as the round, diamond, or triangular shapes.

Sweet Accompaniments of the Tea.

Small cakes, small pieces of cake, assorted cookies or wafers are a necessary part of any tea menu. In addition to these sweet foods, it is appropriate to serve ices, sherbet, ice cream, or orange or pineapple frappe. Fudge cut in squares, and caramels are also very often used although the tendency is away from the use of candy in most forms.

Receptions.

Receptions usually are formal affairs given in honor of some notable visitor or guest of more than local distinction. The guest list for a reception is large for the purpose of allowing the person in whose honor it is given to meet the local people who are interested in his career.

Invitations may be engraved or written and should be issued at least a week in advance. Acknowledgment of the invitation is unnecessary but no guest should prolong his stay beyond the conventional time of fifteen or twenty minutes within the hours set for the reception.

The procedure at a reception is about the same as that of the formal tea. In fact, the two atmospheres are almost identical and the refreshments served at one would be appropriate for the other.

Card Parties.

Within recent years, card parties have surpassed in frequency and number any other form of home entertainment. They are given either in the afternoon or evening.

The refreshments most appropriate to serve should be simple as most guests enjoy card games and like to use the conventional time, which is two or three hours, in play. Then too, the presence of the hostess is in constant demand and this she cannot meet while supervising the serving of elaborate refreshments.

Parties in the Garden.

In recent years the latent love of people for flowers has been awakened into activity by the growth of garden clubs and other movements designed to create interest in the propagation of flowers, shrubs, and other growths that beautify the home environments. More gardens are daily coming into existence, and they are being utilized as never before as places for the informal entertainment of friends.

In the summer, a spot more ideal than a beautiful garden cannot be found for serving tea and giving other informal parties. Refreshments, china, glassware, and all table decorations are chosen in conformity with the out-of-doors picture. Appropriate refreshments for these occasions are as a rule simple, consisting of iced beverages and very light accompaniments. Iced tea, punch, iced chocolate or iced coffee are suitable for the beverage, which is served with sandwiches, thin and simple in design, and simple cookies or small cakes.

At Home.

The trend in social affairs now seems definitely away from the formal and toward the informal types of entertainment. For that reason, many people prefer an "at home" over teas and other forms of entertainment that exact more effort on the part of the hostess and express less in the way of friendliness and hospitality.

Invitations for an at home should follow the style used in invitations to teas. Where visiting cards are used, if a daughter is co-hostess with her mother, her name is written under the mother's.

What to serve on these occasions is largely a matter of individual preference. As a rule, the refreshments are similar to those served at an informal tea.

Buffet Meals.

The necessity to serve a larger number of guests than the average home can provide with seats at tables probably accounts, more than any other factor, for the growing popularity of buffet meal service.

There are three types of buffet service — -the informal, the semi- formal, and the formal.

Where the informal type of service is used, the guests help themselves from the buffet or table. Where the service is semi-formal, a friend of the hostess sits at the table to serve the piece de resistance (main dish) and another friend may sit at the opposite end to serve the beverage. This form of service is very popular. If the service is formal, waiters pass the plates already served. This type of service is invoked in serving large groups because it is systematic and convenient as a procedure.

Invitations.

Since buffet meals are most often informal affairs, invitations may be extended orally or written across the face at the top of the host's and hostess' visiting cards.

Example:

Friday May Tenth
Buffet Supper at 7 o'clock

Mr. and Mrs. Harry Windsor

Acceptances or regrets may be delivered orally or written on a visiting card. Where a card is used for either purpose, it should state the date and hour and read "with pleasure" or "with regrets."

The Dining Table.

At any buffet meal, the dining table should be the center of interest through the capacity of its decorations and arrangement to attract favorable attention. To accomplish that effect, buffet service lends itself admirably both in the use of novel decorative schemes and in artistic arrangement. Bright colors, pottery of unusual design, pewter, copper, and chromium are not only not forbidden, but may be used very effectively, if their use is guided by good taste.

The dishes containing food should be arranged in a balanced effect. If the tea or coffee service is at one end of the table, the large platter of hot food, or the punch bowl, should be on balance at the opposite end. If the punch bowl is used to balance the coffee service, the larger dishes of food should be on opposite sides of the table.

Planning menus for buffet suppers, breakfasts, and luncheons requires serious thought because of the limitations that arise from having to serve a variety of foods on one plate. Agreement in flavor, color, and texture is an imperative requirement with regard to the food and garnishes. Also the decorations must not conflict with the principles of a harmonious effect. Foods that can be eaten easily with a fork should be provided, and those that slip easily or resist cutting with a fork should be relegated to the category of those that are too juicy or "soupy" to serve.

It is far better to have a few substantial foods ample in portions and well prepared than too great a variety. A few foods may be more easily served and served more in the manner dictated by their preparation, as hot or cold, than is possible with a multiplicity of different things.

The following list of suggestions contains only a few of the foods that may be appropriately served buffet style:

1. Hot Protein Dishes: meat pie, curry of lamb, hot roast, lobster or oyster Newburg, chicken a la king, meat loaf, Welsh rarebit, cheese soufflé, scrambled eggs and sausage, eggs scrambled with mushrooms.

2. Cold Protein Dishes: baked ham, boned chicken, stuffed eggs, aspics — tongue or boned chicken, salads — chicken, lobster, crab meat.

3. Sandwiches: butter, anchovy paste, mustard butter, canape.

4. Salads: stuffed tomatoes, fruit.

5. Bread: buttered rolls, hot biscuits.

6. Desserts: ice cream, tarts (individual), fruit cups, macedoine of fruit, cakes, maple mousse, maple eclairs.

7. Sweets: plain or chocolate peppermints, fudge, caramels.

8. Beverages: coffee, tea, punch, chocolate.

9. Nuts: pecans, walnuts, pistachio, mixed nuts.

The following menus are typical examples of the buffet style of service:

I - Smithfield Ham — cold, Creamed chicken patties, Tomatoes stuffed with fruit and celery, Parker House Rolls, Coffee, Fruit Macedoine

II - Meat Pie (chicken or steak), Chiffonade salad, Hot Biscuits, Coffee, Ice cream Cakes, Mixed nuts

The informality which is characteristic of buffet meal service relieves the host and hostess of the obligation to follow conventional patterns. On the other hand, the food that is served must meet all the demands of art in the methods of its preparation, cooking, and serving. Likewise, the decorations of the buffet or table and the arrangement of food and serving dishes must meet the same test.

Unit 3

CLOTHING

CHAPTER 9

YOUR CLOTHES AND YOUR PERSONALITY

Our personalities stage us, represent us, and advertise us to others. They tell the truth by stamping us with the individuality and distinction which character, intelligence, pride, honest thought, and high-held ideals impart; or they portray us in that partial or utter barrenness of interest which is signified by the absence of one or all of these characteristics.

Attractive, suitable apparel plays a conspicuous part in the presentation of a dignified and pleasing personality. To play this part well, the clothing should "proclaim the girl" by expressing and accentuating her individuality. This achievement, when successful, comes as the joint result of exercising good judgment in selecting becoming clothes and of giving careful attention to the details of grooming. Taste is a guiding factor in matters of dress, but taste must be cultivated and improved; hence, unless one keeps studying and improving there is little hope of her becoming intelligent in the appropriate selection of clothing and adept in the other arts of grooming.

Good grooming starts with our bodies. We must, first of all, possess the correct posture, that is, have an erect carriage with head and chest high, abdomen and hips pulled in. Our bodies should be kept clean with a daily bath. A shower each day with a warm tub bath once or twice a week, not only will keep our bodies radiant and clean but impart to us a feeling of health and vitality.

Well-groomed hands are represented by smooth skin, clean nails, and smooth cuticle. Hair and scalp should be clean, the hair glossy from daily brushing. Combs and brushes should be washed each week. The hair should be shampooed at least once every two weeks, and oftener if oily. The teeth should be white and clean from daily care. At least once a year the teeth should be cleaned by a dentist and examined for decay or needed repair.

High school girls should use cosmetics sparingly, if at all. A clean, healthy skin is much more attractive when it is free or almost free from make-up. Fortunate is the girl who does not have to resort to the excessive use of cosmetics to conceal skin defects.

To prevent body odors, a deodorant may be used on the skin or in the bath water. One of the most effective, as well as inexpensive deodorants, is a little baking soda dissolved in the bath water.

With our bodies the picture of clean, radiant health through care and cleansing, we may turn our attention to the selection of apparel which will make a suitable frame for that picture. How do you buy your clothes? Do you accidentally encounter some "tricky little number you simply must have," or does your entire wardrobe show the result of careful, thoughtful planning? You will never have suitable clothing if the procedure you follow in shopping is haphazard or dictated by sudden whims. To accomplish distinction in our grooming, we need a keen sense of color, line, and proportion.

It is relatively as important to consider suitable color schemes in selecting our clothes as it is to count the calories in our food.

The general background of life is neutral gray. Bright or pronounced colors worn against a neutral gray background emphasize the body outline. Small, well-proportioned figures can withstand unusual emphasis but those who wish to conceal size or unattractive lines should use gray or natural hues. Bright colors and warm colors make objects appear larger than they really are. Therefore, light or conspicuous colors should be avoided by large people.

There are few things in the world more attractive than color. Everybody loves color. Despite the many effects that may be achieved by the use of color, there are only four possible combinations of color, that is, four kinds of combinations. These are known as the monochromatic scheme of color — a light color getting darker and darker, different tones of one color; the analogous scheme of color; a complementary color scheme, such as blue and its complements, warm colors over cold; and the triadic color scheme, in which three colors are placed against themselves.

How Colors Are Made.

Blue, red, and yellow are the primary or fundamental hues and the only colors that cannot be made by mixing other hues. By mixing all three primary colors in equal parts, we have gray. By mixing any two primary colors in equal parts, we have the complementary color of the third. As an example, blue and yellow produce green, which is complementary to red; yellow and red produce orange, the complement of blue; red and blue produce violet, the complement of yellow. Orange, green, and violet are secondary colors. When primary and secondary colors are mixed, they produce inter- mediate hues: yellow-green, blue-green, blue-violet or blue-purple, red-purple or red-violet, red-orange, and yellow orange. All different hues, shades, and tints are made by various mixtures of these primary, secondary, and intermediate colors, and for this reason a study of the color circle is necessary to the intelligent use of colors.

Color harmony is a pleasing agreement of color tones used together. This may be produced either by contrast or by similarity. All colors are beautiful when used correctly, in the right place and proportion. Colors affect each other and produce different effects when used in different quantities and in varying degrees of lightness and brightness. There are three color harmonies: one-tone, or the variation in value and intensity of the same color; adjacent harmonies, or those which lie next to each other on the color circle; and complementary, or those directly across from each other on the color circle.

Balance.

Balance is one of the most important color problems. In a dress of dull green and bright red, the red must be used in small quantities, for balance between bright and dull colors may be secured only by using the bright color sparingly. Large spots of dark color may be balanced by small spots of light color.

Harmony with one's personal coloring is the first essential for making proper clothing selections. In planning your wardrobe, build it around one definite color to emphasize your best point. If your eyes are brown, your basic color could be one of the many shades of brown, ranging from buff to very dark brown. To select the color most becoming to you, hold material of different colors up to your face and have your classmates or others give their opinion of your most becoming color.

If the eyes are clear and bright, the dress must be chosen to repeat the color of the eyes, in order to give the eyes more depth and beauty. If the eyes are pale or not especially pretty and the hair is beautiful, the dress should be chosen to bring out the beauty of the hair. A person with auburn hair has many opportunities for beautiful effects in color harmony. Most girls have a good complexion and they should select colors which will show it off to its best advantage. A boy's strong point is usually his eyes, and his suits may be chosen with attention to that detail.

Clothes should harmonize in color with each other, with the wearer, and with the environment. Clothes that do not harmonize create a gaudy, cheap, and unattractive appearance. By studying carefully the color circle, together with your personal coloring, you should be able to select a color scheme for your wardrobe that will be both becoming and harmonious.

Every girl wants a well-planned wardrobe. The first thing to do in planning it is to distinguish between what we want and what we really need. Make a list of the things you need in your wardrobe. Then check the use each garment will serve. The material, color, design, and cost all hinge on the purpose of the garment. If it is a house- dress to be worn at home after school, it may be of gay gingham, simple in design, and small in cost. If it is to serve as a party dress, the material, design, color, and cost will all be different. It will not be worn so often as the housedress, and will not have so much hard wear, so it may be of less durable material and more elaborate in design.

No purchase should be made without keeping the background color in mind. Fill in all the articles you will need for the next two seasons. It is wise always to plan for spring and summer or for fall and winter at the same time.

Beauty and Design.

Good design is the harmonious and orderly arrangement of lines, shapes, and colors to create beauty. Order and beauty are the two chief aims of design. Beauty should be expressed in everything we do and in everything we buy for the quality of things chosen is more important than the cost. Too much design makes things gaudy and cheap looking while too little becomes monotonous and uninteresting. Knowing and applying the principles of design will enable one to show good taste in selecting clothing and all the things that go into home interiors and home surroundings. There are five fundamental principles of art which should be applied to one's clothes, home furnishings, and home environment. These principles are harmony, proportion, balance, rhythm, and emphasis. Good taste is molded, to a very large extent, by the constant application of these principles to one's clothes and everyday surroundings.

Kinds of Design.

Designs are of two kinds — structural and decorative. Structural design is the design made by the shape and size of an object. It includes the color and texture of an object as well as its shape. Decorative design refers to whatever is added to structural design to enrich its beauty. Structural design is beautiful when it is simple, well proportioned, suited to the material out of which it is made and to the purpose for which it was made. Good decorative design should in no way destroy the usefulness of the object being decorated but should help to strengthen the natural or structural shape of the object and therefore should be kept simple and dignified. All decorations should be used in moderation and should be suited to the material and to the original purpose of the thing being decorated. Good decorative designs also conform to the structural lines of the thing being decorated. The lines of a dress should harmonize with the lines of the human body and the decorative design or trimmings of the dress should be in harmony with the structural lines of the dress. In the same way, good structural design in furniture means that the furniture should be made to fit the purpose for which it will be used and that any decorative design which is added should be in harmony with the main lines of the furniture.

What is Harmony?

Harmony has to do with orderliness and "order is the first law of Heaven." Harmony, then, in design, means order and unity. A design that has harmony is one in which every part of the design contributes to the whole. We must have harmony in lines and shapes in order to produce a pleasing effect. When there is much difference between the foundation, shape of an article, and its decoration, the effect of unity can never be secured. Harmony, then, means that lines and designs should harmonize or be in accordance with the structural lines or main body of the thing being decorated. It means that there is a pleasing relationship between the elements of decoration and that the decoration is in keeping with the whole. For example, the decoration on collar and cuffs should be in harmony with the shape of the collar and cuffs, the collar and cuff set should be in harmony with the structural lines of the dress, and the dress itself should harmonize with the figure of the wearer.

What is Proportion?

Good proportion is a pleasing relationship of all parts of an object to the whole and to each part of the whole, giving an appearance of unity and harmony. For example, a dress must first be suited to the figure of the wearer and then the collar, cuffs, pockets, belt, and trimmings must be planned in accordance with the proportions of the dress, as well as with each other. Proportions must not be so much alike as to become monotonous. If a collar or curtain is trimmed with tucks, the effect is more pleasing if there is some variety either in the size of the tucks or in the spaces between the tucks. However, if every space and every tuck were of different sizes, the design would lack unity. The Greek artists believed an object was most pleasing when the proportions were not too obvious. The Greeks developed a very fine sense of appreciation for proportion, hence the Greek Law of proportion is used as a standard. Briefly, the Greek Law of proportion is stated in the ratios of three to five, four to seven, and five to eight, etc. It will be noted that these are of unequal division. This relationship of space is usually thought of in connection with margins in framing pictures, with rectangles, and doors, but it also applies very definitely to one's clothes and environment. The pleasing arrangement of lines is called good proportion or good spacing. No principle of design is more important or more adaptable to one's clothes, for it is this law of design that begs so hard for good lines in dress.

The normal human body is the most beautifully proportioned of all natural objects. For this reason, garments that conform to the natural lines of the body are beautiful and interesting while those that do not are apt to be ugly and in bad proportion.

Good proportion in dress demands that the lines conform to the natural lines of the figure unless the figure is out of proportion. For this reason, short, stout girls select designs that make them look taller and more slender, while tall, slender girls select clothes which make them look less slender and tall. In both cases, the girls are attempting to approach the proportions of the normal human body.

What is Meant by Balance? Balance is that essential of good design that produces a feeling of equilibrium, that is, one part does not outweigh or overbalance another part. The lack of balance is frequently seen in hats where one side is overbalanced with heavy trimmings. Another example is a dress with a side trim. When both sides are exactly alike, equal balance is the result. Equal or symmetrical balance is dignified, formal, and simple in its effect. Unequal balance is obtained when dissimilar articles are used, and the design as a whole is so arranged that it gives a feeling of stability and balance. Balance is frequently explained by comparing it with a see-saw.

In a hat, indirect balance may be obtained with a spot of trimming on one side and a turned-up brim on the other. In a dress, a bit of embroidery or ribbon on one side may be balanced by soft drapery on the other. Indirect balance is more difficult than direct balance but the effect is more pleasing because it is less formal and more interesting.

What is Meant by Rhythm?

Lines may be repeated without being interesting or artistic, but when an arrangement of lines is such that it catches the eye and holds it, the effect is interesting. The regular occurrence of lines or figures in a design which arouses a feeling of satisfaction and interest is called rhythm. Everyone understands what is meant by rhythm in music or dancing. One instinctively keeps time when hearing a band play. Rhythm in art brings order without monotony to the design. Lines of a dress which seem to flow into each other are said to be rhythmic. For example, a bit of embroidery on the front of a waist and repeated on the cuffs or girdle produces a rhythmic effect and does not look spotty.

Emphasis

When emphasis is rightly placed, costumes and objects are more apt to be interesting if there is an element of difference or variety present. A design that has variety of design or color, or even both, is usually more interesting and less commonplace and monotonous than one without variety.

The right use of emphasis relieves monotony. Rooms should have a pleasing center of interest to attract the eye as soon as one enters. A center of interest adds charm to a room which might otherwise seem uninteresting. Touches of color are sometimes used on plain dresses to create a pleasing center of interest.

The face is the most attractive part of the body and should be kept the center of interest. The eye of an observer should be directed towards the face of another person by the lines of construction and by the color in the costume, as well as by the trimmings and accessories. A little color placed near the face will often bring out the color of the eyes and enhance the beauty of the skin.

Large areas in clothing are usually a neutral or gray, leaving bright colors to be brought out in ties, scarves, and collars in order to direct attention to one's face. Since the face should be the center of interest, the lines of the neckline and collar are very important. The lines of the collar should emphasize the good points of the face, therefore study your type of face and decide which type of neckline will be most becoming to you. If you have a long, thin face, the neckline should be round, while a V- neckline or a square neckline that is neither too wide nor too narrow is usually becoming to a broad, round face.

Naturalistic and Conventional Patterns.

Decorations are often put on objects for the mere sake of ornamentation. Ornamentation is often found on laces, fabrics, vases, rugs, and other objects and is referred to as pattern design. This pattern or design should conform to the principles above, that is, it should have harmony, proportion, balance, rhythm, and emphasis.

In order for any decoration to be beautiful, it should harmonize with the material on which it is used, with the shape of the article, and with the use to which it is put.

Artists get most of their designs from nature. A design is said to be naturalistic when it is copied exactly as found in nature, and conventional when it follows accepted principles, that is, when it is modified to suit a particular object, space, or material. For example, a rose on a pillow would be naturalistic if one attempted to make it look real, but if the rose were adapted to a general form as a unit for a border repeated many times, it would be called a conventional design. Conventional designs are considered more artistic than naturalistic ones because they can be adapted to the space where they are to be used, and to the texture.

The space of any shape to be decorated controls the dominant lines of the decoration. Then, too, it is inconsistent to put flowers, animals, and birds on table cloths, wall paper, fabrics, and rugs. The design must not be inconsistent with the use for which it was intended, if it is to be artistic.

Good Lines in Dress.

How do we know when a design is good? When is a design harmonious, pleasing, and satisfying? Good design in dress implies that all lines or parts of the dress must be harmonious and seem to belong together. A design is pleasing and satisfying when there is the right relation between lines used for decoration and the dress itself.

What is meant by good lines in dress? The design of the dress should harmonize with the lines of the human body. Even if it is not in accord with the fashion of the day, the proportions of one's figure should settle the style of one's dress. Short, stout people look better in long skirts than in short ones, although short ones may at the time be in vogue. Large plaids, stripes, and other conspicuous designs exaggerate short, fat figures, while vertical lines accentuate their height. One-piece gowns with trimmings that give length are becoming to people who are overweight.

The design of a dress should have harmony and balance the same as that of a drawing. Jerky lines, or lines that lead nowhere, irritate, while a smooth sweep of lines is pleasing. One should be conservative in selecting designs, since some of them are in style for only one season and by the next season look conspicuous and out of style.

The lines of a garment are made by the general shape or cut of the garment as well as by the edges of the collar, cuffs, waistline, and hem of the skirt. For example, a dress may be cut on straight lines as the one-piece dress or in separate skirt and waist, while neck lines may be round, square, or V-shaped.

When trimming, such as lace or embroidery, is used to decorate a dress, the lines made by the trim should harmonize with the lines of the dress.

Finally, remember that artists who have studied the human figure say that the natural lines of the human body are very harmonious. For this reason, clothing that changes the natural lines of the body is not as beautiful as that with simple lines which conform to the normal figure.

How Fabrics Influence Color and Design.

Textures, weaves, and patterns are important factors in applying the principle of color and design to one's clothes. A short, fat girl might choose a dress with long lines and if the dress were made of soft, clinging material, the effect would be pleasing, but if this same dress were made of stiff silk that stood away from the body, the effect would not be satisfactory. Plaids, large patterns, and loud colors may also spoil the effect of good lines. A color in chiffon or georgette is usually softer than the same color in taffeta or serge. Chiffon and georgette will always look lighter because of their transparency; velvet, of like color, will appear lighter or darker as it absorbs or reflects light, while serge, which is heavier and thicker, more nearly shows the true color. Chiffon and georgette soften outlines and make silhouettes indefinite.

Velvet is soft and drapes beautifully, but its thick texture adds bulk which is not good on the stout figure. Serge has a lusterless surface and is rather stiff but lends itself well to straight or curved lines because of its firm, flat texture. There are many, many kinds of material, but these which differ widely are sufficient to call attention to the fact that fabrics influence both color and design and must be taken into consideration if one wishes to be well dressed.

How Fabrics Differ.

What fabrics are you wearing today? What other fabrics have you used? How do the fabrics you wear on rainy days, cold days, hot days differ? What fabrics are especially suitable for house work, for street wear, for a party dress, for coats and wraps? We speak of textures in material as being smooth or rough, stiff or soft, lustrous or lusterless, clinging or fluffy, thick, thin, or medium. Most textile materials combine several of these characteristics, for example, voile and chiffon are soft and clinging, while organdy is thin and stiff. These different qualities are due to the texture, weave, weight, and finish of the cloth. Using the above terms and others, describe the various fabrics in your own wardrobe.

No amount of study about colors, designs, and fabrics will enable us to dress well unless each individual adapts his knowledge of these factors, as well as the prevailing styles, to his own personality. Each person is seen as a whole and the best dressed person is the one whose costume is harmonious in itself and so well suited to his own individuality that details and accessories are practically unnoticed, while only a picture of the whole is pleasantly remembered. In general, when people notice exactly what you have on, your costume is either very harmonious and distinctive or it is inharmonious within itself or with your personality.

It is evident that the buying of a wardrobe is a rather difficult problem which calls for a practical application of the fundamental principles of appropriate dress, color, design, and fabrics. However, no girl or woman can neglect the application of these principles without hurt to her personal appearance.

CHAPTER 10

TEXTILES AND FABRICS

Style in textiles changes as it does in everything else. New materials and new colors appear each season and prices change with their advent. The more one learns about textiles, the more interesting the study becomes. Textiles are accessible and available for study almost everywhere if we but keep our eyes open. Some knowledge of cloth and how it is made is needed that we may know what values to look for when we shop, as well as know what fabrics are suitable for various uses and occasions. Every prospective buyer of textiles should learn how to judge cloth by learning to recognize the different kinds of fibers that are used in making cloth. One should also learn something of how cloth is woven, how it is colored, and how it is finished. A study of standard fabrics and their uses will be of as much value to those who buy all their clothes ready made as to the home dressmaker.

Written information on textiles, no matter how thorough, is at best only a guide. To know quality and values, one must study actual samples of cloth. Study the material in your clothes as well as in the furnishings in your home. Start a textile notebook to which you can add from time to time. Classify your samples according to their use in your wardrobe and in the home. Note briefly any fact that you should remember. Learning how to identify different textile fibers is the first step in textile study.

Characteristics of Textile Fibers.

Cloth is made of the various kinds of fibrous material, which can be spun into yarn or thread such as cotton, silk, wool, and flax. In the raw or unfinished state, we speak of these materials as textile fibers. When these fibers are used in cloth, we speak of the finished products as fabrics, textile fabrics, or textiles.

Cloth is used in making clothing for people of all ages and for furnishing the home with household linens, floor coverings, draperies, upholstery, and many other purposes. The factors which cause differences in cloth are the fiber, the preparation of the yarn, the character of the weave, the color, the design, and the finish.

Fibers having more general use are cotton, linen, wool, silk, and rayon. Rayon was early known as artificial silk or fiber silk but has now passed the experimental stage and has taken its place with the other four staple fibers.

Cotton is the fluffy, white or yellowish fiber that grows on the seed of the cotton plant. Cotton fiber varies in length from one-half inch to two and one-half inches. The best cotton fabric is made from the longer fibers. Cotton cloth made from long fibers has a smoother finish and better wearing qualities. Short length fibers often leave a tiny fuzz on the surface. Cotton is naturally soft in feeling and rather dull in appearance. When cotton cloth is unraveled and the fibers are separated, the fiber has a wavy appearance. Under the microscope, the cotton fiber looks much like twisted ribbon.

Cotton is the most generally used fiber. Cotton is a good conductor of heat and absorbs moisture readily but does not evaporate moisture as rapidly as linen. Therefore cotton does not feel as cool as linen. White cotton cloth washes and boils without injury to the fabric and for this reason makes ideal cloth for garments worn next to the skin. Bacteria do not develop in cotton so readily as in silk and wool. Cotton cloth is desirable for summer garments but does not make good outer garments for cold weather.

Linen is made from a fiber which comes from the flax plant. The bark of the flax plant must be removed to get the fiber. Linen fiber is tan or greenish gray in color, varies from ten to thirty inches in length, and is very irregular. Linen cloth has a rather irregular surface, caused by the unevenness of the linen fiber. The threads in cotton cloth being much more regular than the threads in linen, the surface of cotton fabrics is smoother. Linen is somewhat stiffer than cotton and wrinkles more easily.

Under the microscope, linen fiber is straight and cylindrical and looks like a pointed bamboo rod. Linen thread is stronger than cotton thread but burns like cotton. When linen tears, the ends are pointed and straight. Linen absorbs moisture quickly, dries quickly, and is the coolest fiber known. White linen can be washed and boiled without injury to the fiber. Linen makes an ideal fabric for underwear in summer but because of its scarcity is expensive.

Wool is the wavy, crinkly hair that comes from sheep, and has a springy, wiry feeling. Wool fibers vary in length from one to fifteen inches. The average wool fiber is about four inches long. Long fibers make smooth wool cloth, short fibers leave fuzzy ends raised from the cloth. Wool fiber is composed of scales which overlap like the scales on a fish, but they can be seen only under a microscope. These scales in wool make woolen fabrics difficult to launder, consequently special care must be given woolen garments.

Hot water causes wool fibers to shrink, become harsh, and mat together. Changing from hot to cold water and hard rubbing cause the little scales in woolen fibers to interlock more firmly and shrink. For this reason, we are told to wash woolen garments in warm water, rinse them in water of the same temperature, and dry them in a warm room. Freezing, as well as heating, spoils the texture of woolen garments. Wool is the warmest fiber known because, due to its structure, it holds more air than other fibers, and air, we remember, is a poor conductor of heat. Wool is very absorbent but its moisture evaporates so slowly that it does not feel cold, even when damp. For this reason, wool is especially desirable for outer garments and cold weather clothes. Wool soils easily and bacteria develop in it more quickly than in any of the other fibers.

Wool fibers retain oily, sweaty secretions and dirt, and for this reason woolen garments are not as hygienic when worn next to the skin as those made from fabrics that can be more easily cleaned.

Silk fiber is made by the silkworm. It is the strongest fiber known. Under the microscope a single fiber looks like a smooth, glass rod. The silkworm spins his cocoon in a way similar to that of the common caterpillar. The difference between the two cocoons is that one is silk and the other is a worthless substance. Silk fiber is fine, even, and long. The fibers vary in length from three hundred to fourteen hundred feet. The long fibers make cloth of more beautiful texture than do the short fibers. Waste silk is made from short fibers. Just why some of the fibers are long and others short makes an interesting story. You may want to read about the silkworm and its unusual work.

Silk feels slippery and smooth. It is a poorer conductor of heat than either cotton or linen, but not so poor as wool. Silk absorbs moisture readily but does not dry quickly and feels cold when damp. Because of its smooth surface, it does not soil quickly. Bacteria develop rapidly in silk and it is not so easily cleaned as cotton or linen. Silk does not soil easily or muss quickly, and when of a good quality, wears well. Such silk as pongee or crepe de chine is good for general utility wear.

Rayon is called the man-made fiber because man makes it from wood pulp or cotton waste, which has previously been treated with acid. Rayon has some of the qualities of both silk and cotton. Its fiber is straight and cylindrical. Rayon is a smooth, heavy, cool textile, with a high luster but with less pliancy than silk, that burns like cotton. Rayon wears well when of a good quality and when laundered and cleaned properly. Rayon garments should be laundered or dry cleaned with as much care as silk or wool, although it has better laundering qualities than either. Knitted rayon garments have a tendency to stretch in the process of laundering. Rayon dyes easily and holds color well. Many beautiful effects are now being produced in fabrics made from this fiber.

How Cloth is Made.

Cloth is made from these fibers which we have been discussing by the process of weaving on a loom or by knitting. Cloth varies not only with the kind of fiber used in its manufacture but with the quality of the fiber used, for fibers of the same substance differ not only in variety but in quality. We learned that long fiber makes cloth with a smooth surface while very short fiber produces a cloth more or less rough with tiny, fuzzy ends in evidence. Fibers also differ in fineness, strength, evenness, and color as well as in the amount of twist or tension.

When Fabrics Are Knitted. - Knitted materials are elastic, pliant, and easy to fit. Knitted woolen garments catch dust and lint because of the softly spun yarn, and do not brush off as easily as woven fabrics. Knitted garments do not wrinkle to the extent of other cloth. Rayon knitted garments give excellent satisfaction. Knitted cloth is made from one thread by continually catching one loop and pulling it through another loop. Examine sweaters or stockings closely and you can see how this is done. When one thread breaks, the thread slips through the first loop, then each loop slips through the next and causes a runner. Long ago, when all our stockings were knitted by hand, it took several days to make one pair, but today when stockings are knitted on machines, one person can produce many hundred pairs in one day. You can recognize knitted material by sight and by the feel of the material. You can see the loops or you can stretch the material until the loops are visible. What knitted garments are you wearing today? What others have you in your wardrobe? You will soon discover that there are varieties in the knitted stitch as in weaves.

When Fabrics Are Woven.

When cloth is woven, the threads or fibers are stretched tight on a frame. The lengthwise threads are called warp threads and should be strong. The threads which run crosswise, or at right angles to the warp threads, are called woof threads, or filling threads, and need not be so strong as the warp threads. Cloth woven in this manner furnishes the simplest example of what is known as weaving. There are many kinds of weaves and many varieties of each kind.

The plain weave, the simplest type, is made when warp and filling threads cross alternately as in such fabrics as muslin, longcloth, crash, and handkerchief linen. The yarns (the threads) may differ in color as in checked or plain gingham. Plain weaves are used more than any other.

The twill weave is used in materials where durability and hard wear are desirable. It is stiffer and harder than the plain weave and, with the exception of the plain weave, is used more than any other. Serge and gabardine are examples of the twill weave. In the twill weave the warp passes over one thread of the woof and under two or more, instead of over one and then under the next thread of the woof as is done in plain weaves. In this process, the filling moves forward one thread at a time, thus producing the diagonal ribs that characterize twill weaves.

The satin weave has a smooth lustrous surface on the right side. The threads are woven together in such a way as to leave long threads on the surface of the cloth. The weave in satin somewhat resembles twill. The filling thread passes under one and over six or more warp threads at regular intervals. Satin materials are not so durable as those made from the plain or twill weave because the threads are apt to catch and wear. Sateen and satin materials are made with this weave.

The pile weave is used in carpets, rugs, Turkish towels, velvets, plush, and some coat materials. Pile is made in weaving cloth by projecting yarn from the body of the cloth in the form of little loops which are either cut or left as loops. These loops produce a plush or velvet like appearance. Examine a pile fabric and you will note that the foundation is covered with a soft surface of cut ends, looped or curled yarn. These ends or loops sometimes stand up as in Brussels carpets, or they may be pressed flat as in panne velvet. The foundation cloth is always concealed by the pile.

Pattern weaving is done on a special kind of loom, which is named after the inventor, the Jacquard loom. Pattern weaving is very difficult and expensive since the design must be woven into the material. Table damask, upholstery materials, and drapery materials are common examples of fabrics that are woven on a

Jacquard loom. Other examples of pattern weaving are found in materials for making men's ties and in expensive dress goods.

White and Colored Cloth.

Materials may be divided into four kinds, those that are white, those which are dyed a solid color, those which have a pattern woven into the cloth, and those on which the color is printed on the cloth.

Unbleached materials may be bleached either with chemicals within a few hours, or by the sun, which may take several weeks. When materials are bleached by chemicals, there is danger of their being injured by over-bleaching, which may cause holes to appear in the materials after they have been used only a few times.

Cloth may be dyed either in the yarn or after it is woven. If done after the cloth is woven, it is "piece dyed" and must be all of one color, and if dyed before the cloth is woven it is "yarn dyed" and may be of several different colors. Stripes and checks in ginghams are produced in the latter way.

Prints are made by running cloth between the copper rollers of a printing press on which a pattern is engraved. In this process, which is very rapid, the pattern is printed on the cloth as it passes between the rollers. Percales, calicoes, printed silks, cretonne, and challis are examples of printed materials.

Difference Due to Finish.

We have learned that materials differ in fiber, weave, color, and design. Materials of the same fiber, the same weave, the same color, and the same design might still differ in appearance because of the finish. The finish of cloth refers to all processes or steps through which the material goes after it is woven and dyed or printed. These processes vary with the different fibers. After removing knots, repairing broken threads, etc., the cloth goes through a cleansing process which draws the threads closer together. In woolen cloth, this is called fulling or felting. This cleansing process is practically the same with all fabrics, the object being to clean the material thoroughly and shrink it. During this process wool shrinks more than any other fiber, due to its peculiar scale-like structure. Material which is to have a napped surface is felted and fulled to a high degree in order to conceal all evidence of the weave on the right side.

The napping process consists of pulling the ends of the fiber to the surface. Napping adds to the warmth of both woolen and cotton cloth. Canton flannel is an example of napped cotton cloth; heavy woolen coating and blankets are examples of napped woolen cloth.

The lustering process brings out the natural luster of the fiber or adds luster to the fabric. Lustering is accomplished by steaming and pressing and by the use of chemicals.

Calendering is the process of pressing or ironing to enhance the appearance of cotton, linen, and silk fabrics. This is done by passing the cloth through heavy hot rollers, which results in making it smooth and glossy. The effect disappears as soon as the cloth is laundered.

Sizing is the process of adding stiffening to cloth, which is used to help the appearance of the material. Some materials are purposely sized so as to give a crisp effect, as in percale. Others, such as nainsook, are finished to have a soft effect. Sizing fills up spaces in a material that is loosely woven but usually washes out with the first laundering.

Mercerization is the process of treating cotton fiber to an alkaline bath while the cloth or the yarn is tightly stretched. This process causes the cotton fiber to take a cylindrical form, making it stronger and more lustrous. Mercerized cloth and yarn absorb dye more easily than ordinary cotton cloth. When mercerizing is well done, the material will not lose its silky effect after laundering. Poplins, ginghams, English broadcloth, and chambrays are materials that are often mercerized. It improves the appearance and wearing quality of the material in every way.

Singed cotton cloth is made by passing the woven cloth quickly over a flame to remove the tiny fuzz which, we learned, is characteristic of natural cotton. Singeing gives the cloth a smooth surface. Lisle thread is made of long cotton fibers tightly twisted and finished with singeing and calendering. Lisle yarn (thread) is successfully used in making stockings and light-weight underwear.

Belting or pounding linen until the fibers are flattened brings out its natural luster and increases its beauty. Cheaper grades of linen are sized and calendered in the same way as cotton materials.

Loading or weighting silk is a chemical treatment which adds to its weight and thickness. It is ordinarily thought that the weighting of silk is a finishing process but it is an adulteration. A certain amount of weighting is legitimate and necessary for satisfactory wear. Pure, unweighted silk is very expensive. Overweighting or "loading" is one thing that causes silk garments to wear out too soon.

Crepe effects are produced in different ways. Sometimes the crepe effect is produced in the weaving by holding certain sets of warp threads tight and others loose. Sometimes it is produced by printing stripes of caustic soda on the material. Those parts shrink while the other parts crinkle up, producing the crepe effect. Sometimes it is produced by weaving the cloth out of yarns, with different twists.

Then we find that finishing processes give stiffening, softening, or other qualities to the cloth, depending upon the demands of the season. Materials are sometimes made stronger by the finishing process. Sizing or dressing sometimes protects the yarn from wear or strain. The felting or fulling process makes woolen and cotton garments warmer. Organdy has a finish which is retained after laundering. Some dressings keep cloth from spotting. Rainy day garments are treated with a dressing process to make them waterproof.

Adulteration and Fabric Imitations.

The adulteration of materials usually means that less expensive or less desirable fibers have been added to more valuable products. No hard and fast rules can be laid down as to what fibers should be combined, for materials made of mixed fibers are sometimes very satisfactory, especially from the standpoint of cost and service. Cotton household "linens" are in common use, however one should not pay the price of real linen for cotton or for a mixture of cotton and linen. Some people buy mercerized cotton, believing they are getting pure linen at a cheap price.

Cotton and wool may be mixed, made into cloth, and sold as pure wool. Imitations of wool, silk, and linen have been carried out in less expensive fibers. These imitations are produced by finishing the fiber by a process similar to that used for the finish of the cloth being imitated, or by imitating the weave or the design of the original material. Percales may be printed to imitate ginghams; sateen to imitate expensive silks; cotton and wool mixtures to imitate woolen plaids. "Second hand" wool and poor grades of wool are sometimes sold for the price of the better grades.

Mercerized cotton and rayon are no longer considered adulterations. Rayon is now recognized as one of the staple textile fibers and mercerized cotton is sold as such and is no longer thought of as an imitation of silk.

Fiber mixtures or union materials are often very satisfactory; a little cotton added to wool reduces the price and keeps the material from shrinking so much in laundering. All woolen materials take dye much better than cotton or cotton and wool mixtures. Imitations and fiber mixtures should be sold as such; deception is always wrong. Honesty in the textile world is just as desirable as elsewhere. Laws relating to the correct labeling of textiles are almost as desirable as laws governing the adulteration of foods.

Textile Fabrics and Your Wardrobe.

Fabric is as important as color and design in minimizing your bad points and playing up your good ones. You must make a study of this phase of clothing to know the kind that best suits your individual type. Cloth, like color and design, has a language of its own. The use to which cloth is to be put should receive first consideration, for the use very definitely affects the choice of the texture of the material as well as color and design. Very fine, sheer effects do not usually come in serviceable materials. Dark or subdued colors, conservative design, and firmly woven fabrics suggest service or work, while fine, sheer effects and dainty colors are associated with rare occasions, music, and flowers. Gay colors, rough textures, and loud designs suggest play and out-door activities. Again, certain individuals seem to suggest lace and chiffon, while others suggest the need for heavier, stronger materials.

Style and fashion are two words closely associated with the sale of clothing. Style suggests distinctive dress while fashion refers to the current mode of dress. Fashions are always changing. Individuality is the important factor in dressing correctly and becomingly, for one must adapt the new styles or commonly accepted fashions to one's own personality. A conservative in style of dress is one who modifies prevailing fashions so as not to be too conspicuous. A faddist is one who dresses in an extreme style which exaggerates color, design, or fabric. Good taste in dress usually comes by careful adaptation of prevailing styles to one's own type and individuality.

To keep up-to-date is desirable, but extremes should be avoided, especially when finances are somewhat limited. Choosing conservative styles in the standard fabrics, rather than the "seasonal" innovations, is the keynote to economy in making your textile selections. Standard fabrics are those which are sold under the same name from year to year, such as muslin, gingham, percale, longcloth, taffeta, and serge. How many standard fabrics can you identify? Do you know how to distinguish cotton, linen, wool, silk, and rayon fabrics? Do you know what weaves and fibers are desirable for everyday wear, for underwear, for outer garments, for party dress? Do you know what colors are most becoming to you and most suitable for various occasions? Do you know what designs are best suited to your individual figure and to the various activities in which you are engaged? Do you know what finish is most practical for your school dresses, your party dresses, and your sports costume?

Neatness in Personal Appearance.

In the opinion of others, next to character and ability comes a good personal appearance, which generally is regarded as evidence of self-respect. Self-respect may or may not be indicated by the details of dress in every instance. It is, however, worthwhile to give clothing the right kind of care for a dress may have good lines, beautiful color and design and yet, if there is a button or two lacking, a seam ripped, or a covering of dust or lint, others receive a bad impression of the wearer. Was anyone ever really charming who was ill at ease by being made conscious of something lacking in her dress or her personal appearance? That neatness in dress, which would insure us against the possibility of embarrassment in the presence of others, demands that we keep our clothes clean, well brushed, pressed, and in good repair. Besides contributing to self-confidence and giving the appearance of self-respect, clean clothes last longer and are more hygienic.

Accidents not only can, but often do, happen to clothing; therefore, the art of knowing how to mend, patch, and repair garments is an indispensable accomplishment. Do you know how to clean, mend, and repair your own clothing? What do you need to know in order to assume the entire responsibility of caring for your own wardrobe? Do you hang up your clothing? Do you always put away your hat, shoes, gloves, and other accessories? Perhaps no habit will be of more value to you in later life than that of giving proper attention to the details of clothing care. What are your responsibilities in helping with the family mending? Why should you be concerned about the personal appearance of other members of your family? To what extent do others judge you by your family? You will find the answers to these questions in your own sense of pride.

Brush and Air Your Clothes.

Clothes, if they are to look their best, must be kept clean. New clothes soon look old and dingy if left full of dust and covered with lint. A good whisk broom and several clothes brushes should be found in every home and kept in a place convenient to all members of the household. The need of immaculately clean clothes cannot be overemphasized. Heavy woolen garments, coats, sweaters, and shoes should be kept clean and thoroughly aired. Clothes that must be worn daily should be thoroughly aired at night and at least once a week they should be given a thorough brushing out of doors. Fresh air and sunshine will do much toward keeping clothes fresh and clean. Hang colored garments in the shade, as the bright sunshine causes some colors to fade.

Daily brushing of woolen garments, felt, and velvet hats is necessary to keep them fresh and clean. Silk and other fragile garments should be cleaned with a soft brush. Shaking, out of doors, helps in removing dust and lint from heavy woolen garments. Hang linty garments out of doors on a slightly windy day and brushing will not be necessary.

Hang Up Your Clothes.

Dresses, coats, and suit coats should be kept on hangers. These can be bought and are quite inexpensive. They can also be made of rolled news- papers, tied through the center and suspended by a cord. A smooth covered stick, the width of the shoulders, may be used. More garments may be hung in a small space if one or more rods are added to the usual hooks in the clothes closet. Skirts should be hung from the waist band. Trouser hangers of various types are good for this. Large safety pins fastened to the hanger make good substitutes. Skirts with very bias seams, loosely woven sweaters, knitted garments, and other garments which are apt to stretch, are better kept in a box or drawer.

Protect Your Clothes

It is also well to have some protective covering for your garments, especially if you live where there is much dust or coal smoke. Coverings may be made of old garments, cretonne, heavy unbleached muslin, or argentine cloth. A simple covering can be made of yard-wide material twice the length of the garment, plus one-half yard for extra length. Make this into a plain bag with one-inch hems at the bottom, buttoned together, and a small round hole in the top through which to slip the hook of the hanger. Part of the extra material may be turned up to form a flap at the bottom and fastened with buttons or snaps.

Another style of covering, one that is more convenient and said to be more nearly dustproof, is made with one side of the bag rather than the bottom open, in order to make removal easier. The side vent may be fastened with snaps, buttons, or by the more expensive zipper fastening device.

Dresses in use soil quickly across the shoulders, around the neck, and down the front. Collars, cuffs, and vests which can be easily removed and cleaned will help to keep the dress in better condition. Aprons will also protect the dress. These may be of the cover-all type for use when doing heavy work, or small ones for sewing or working about the house.

Press Your Clothes.

Pressing adds much to the appearance of one's garments. Wrinkled clothes give one an untidy appearance. In fact, if our clothes are not pressed and kept in good condition, we will never be considered well dressed. Woolen garments should be pressed on the wrong side. If pressed on the right side they become shiny. First, place a damp cloth over the garment and press with a heavy hot iron until the cloth is almost dry. This steams the goods, making it easy to press out the wrinkles, on the same principle that sprinkling clothes makes them easier to iron. Be careful not to iron until the cloth is absolutely dry, as this often causes the material to shine. If necessary to press pockets and other parts on the right side, be sure to leave the moist pressing cloth over the goods until pressing is finished. "Shine" is also caused by wearing off the nap and by grease. A tablespoon of ammonia to a quart of cold water is good for sponging shiny material before pressing. Nap may be brushed up with a stiff brush. In pressing materials that are much worn and shiny, if a woolen cloth is placed between the garment and the moist pressing cloth, it will remove the shine and improve the nap. For silk, do not use too hot an iron, as extreme heat injures the material.

Press on the wrong side of the material or garment. Cotton or linen garments can be worn for some time without laundering if they are pressed often. It is sometimes necessary to sponge them with clear water before pressing. Heavy garments should be sent to pressing and cleaning establishments occasionally. Many garments can be pressed at home if the work is done carefully.

Some Old Adages.

"A stitch in time saves nine" is an old adage which is particularly suggestive right here. Habits of neatness are among the first essentials of a well-groomed, attractive personal appearance. Every girl should form the habit of keeping her clothes in good condition and should learn to do the work herself. "Enough is as good as a feast" should be remembered by those of us who buy too many garments. It is not economy to have more clothes than are actually needed. A few garments well cared for are better than many garments poorly kept. Do you have more clothing than you need? It is annoying to have one's closets filled with clothes which are rarely worn and daily going out of style. A minimum number of garments well brushed and kept in repair will enable one always to feel well dressed.

Remember that the daily care of clothing requires the constant and frequent use of irons, brushes, and hangers. Clothes hangers help in keeping garments in shape, brushes keep clothes clean, while the right use of the iron in pressing drives away ugly wrinkles and adds much to the appearance of garments.

Where Do You Keep Your Clothing?

The habit of having "A place for everything and everything in its place" keeps one's clothing in good condition. Adequate space should be provided for keeping things. Closets with shelves, rods, and hooks, chests of drawers, hat boxes, laun- dry bags, dress bags, shoe shelves or bags, and closet door pockets are among the conveniences that make it easy to keep clothes neat and in order. Nothing gives one a greater feeling of satisfaction than to have all her clothing arranged systematically and conveniently. "Budgeting" of the clothing through dresser drawers, closet shelves, and bags is necessary. Do you have a definite place to keep hose, pajamas, and other undergarments? Where do you keep your handkerchiefs, gloves, and other accessories? Where do you put your coat, hat, and other garments when you take them off? Do you have a carefully worked out plan of keeping your wardrobe? Perhaps you can improve your present plan. Garments used every day should be placed in the most convenient places while garments seldom used may be packed in carefully labeled boxes and put in less convenient places.

Care of Dresses.

Wash dresses can be kept especially clean and neat. It is not always necessary to launder the entire dress, if spots are removed carefully when they first appear. The soiled places can be washed with warm water and soap. If the dress is only slightly wrinkled and not soiled, it need only be brushed off with a damp cloth and pressed.

Dresses which cannot be washed, such as silk or wool, should be cared for by airing them frequently, keeping them repaired, and keeping them well brushed and pressed. If an apron of rubberized cloth is worn under the dress in warm weather, it will prevent perspiration from wrinkling and soiling the skirt when sitting.

Care of Hats.

Hats should be brushed and placed in a hat box or bag immediately after wearing. It is sometimes necessary to dampen a cloth and wipe dust from dark straw hats. If the straw has faded, an inexpensive coloring material can be used to make the hat appear fresh and new. A piece of ribbon that has become faded and torn may be replaced at small expense or trouble.

Care of Gloves.

Gloves should be pulled into shape and placed in a box immediately upon removing. If they are of material that can be washed, as soon as a soiled place appears it should be washed out and not be left until it sets into the fabric. Use a neutral soap to make suds; place the gloves in the suds and squeeze the moisture out, without wringing. Rinse thoroughly and place on a bath towel to dry. Doeskin gloves should be rubbed slightly before drying to keep them soft. A little soap left in the rinsing water will also aid in keeping these gloves soft. Always keep your gloves mended.

Kid gloves may be mended with the buttonhole stitch; fabric gloves, with the backstitch or overhand stitch. Worn places in fabric gloves may be darned. For runs in silk gloves, the grafting stitch should be used.

Care of Hose.

Do not let perspiration from the feet remain in the hose, for it destroys the threads. Hose should be laundered after each wearing. It is not much trouble to wash out hose each night in warm soapy water, rinse them, roll them in a towel, and then hang them up to dry. Silk hose do not require ironing. Heat weakens the fiber and lessens durability. Runners should be mended as soon as they appear, as they spread so easily. Colorless nail polish applied to the end of a runner will prevent its running until it can be mended. At small cost, hose can be so well mended at many of the down-town stores that it is impossible to see any trace of the runner. Hose that wear well are reinforced at the heel and toe. Be sure to buy your hose long enough. Toenails should be kept filed evenly or they will punch through at the toes of stockings, particularly if the stockings are too short.

In pulling on a stocking, do not take hold of the top, give it a hard pull, and push your foot down through it. Gather the leg of the stocking and hold it in your fingers so that the foot can be placed at once directly into the foot of the stocking.

Care of Shoes.

Shoes should be aired immediately after removing. If you do not have shoe-trees, place your shoes in a box or in shoe pockets tacked to the closet door or wall. Shoes should be kept clean and well-polished to protect them from moisture and add to their appearance. If they are muddy or soiled, scrape the mud off with soft wood, rather than a sharp knife, clean them, and polish them before putting them away. Leather shoes become stiff if placed too close to the fire after cleaning. Do not let your shoes become run over or badly worn; they may be re-soled and have new heels put on at a reasonable cost. Shoes will last much longer and preserve their shape if repaired before they become badly worn. Having the heels of shoes straightened not only adds to their appearance but helps the health of the one who wears them. Crooked heels cause one to stand in an unnatural position and make walking or running difficult. By polishing your shoes at night, you will save time in the morning when you are rushing to get away to school. If left until the last minute, you might be tempted to wear your shoes without polishing.

White shoes especially should be well cared for if good grooming is the aim. White fabric shoes can be washed but lose shape in drying. One should try to preserve their shape while the shoes are drying, by stuffing them with paper or by using shoe-trees. Unless the shoes are well cleaned before applying the polish, they will be yellow or gray when dry. White shoe powder is conveniently carried in one's purse and while it does not remove the soiled places, it covers them up until the shoes can be cleaned properly. Metal slippers will not tarnish if wrapped in black paper.

Galoshes and Raincoats.

If galoshes are muddy, they should be washed and allowed to dry. Rubber materials should not be placed too near a fire and should be stored in a cool place during warm weather. Torn places can be mended with adhesive tape.

Do Your Clothes Need Mending?

Garments pinned together look very untidy, and an untidy person is never a well-dressed person. Hooks and eyes, snap fasteners, and buttons should always be sewed on as soon as they come off the garment. Stockings should be mended neatly and never worn with holes in them. Garments that need patching should be mended carefully, and if possible, before they are laundered.

To keep clothes in good condition, it is essential to keep them in good repair. Mend the rips and tears; sew on buttons, hooks and eyes, snaps and trimmings; strengthen or re-work button holes; darn worn places or reinforce them by placing a piece of cloth underneath and catching or darning it to the material with ravelings or self-colored thread.

Sewing on Buttons.

Sew the button over a pin so that the stitches will not be drawn too tight. Four-hole buttons may have the stitches form a cross on top of the button or in two parallel lines. What are parallel lines? Fasten the thread securely and neatly on the wrong side.

Sewing on Hooks and Eyes.

Be sure to place hooks and eyes directly opposite each other and far enough from the edge of the garment that they cannot be seen on the outside. You may use the buttonhole stitch in sewing the hooks on as this makes a neat and strong finish. Sew all around the loop of the eye; hold it securely in place. Fasten stitches close to the curve to hold the eye firmly.

Sewing on Snap Fasteners.

Sew the socket piece on the underside of the opening and the ball piece on the upper side. Use a buttonhole stitch, taking several stitches to each hole.

How to Darn.

Darning is the replacing of worn material with a weaving stitch and is one of the very best methods of repairing stockings, sweaters, and all kinds of knit clothing. The thread should match the material in the garment as nearly as possible both in color and kind. Often, threads may be pulled from underneath the hems or seams of garments of heavy material which match perfectly in color and better than new thread.

Darning Stockings.

Trim away the ragged edges around the hole. Strengthen the weakened place by weaving the darning thread in and out to add thickness. Begin the weaving a few stitches to the side of the hole; then when the hole is reached, weave in and out below the hole; carry the thread across to the opposite side of the hole and weave in a few more stitches. Have the thread go in the cloth on the right side once and on the wrong side the next time so that no raw edge will show. Continue until the hole is covered with threads, then weave in and out of the material on this side to strengthen it. You are now ready to fill in threads going in the opposite direction. Weave in and out of the material next to the hole and then weave over and under the thread across the hole; go over one and under one, over and under one, across to the opposite side. Continue in this manner until the hole has been filled in. Be careful not to draw the threads tight enough to pucker them.

Always match the color of the stockings with the thread used. Use two strands of darning cotton for heavy cotton, one strand for thin cotton stockings. Use silk darning thread for silk hose, and yarn for woolen hose. If a worn place is reinforced by darning before the hole appears much time will be saved and repair will be less conspicuous.

Patching.

Patching is a method of repairing that is used when the hole is too large to be darned. If possible, take an old piece of the material as a new one is apt to be of different color and strong enough to tear away the weakened part of the cloth. There are two kinds of patches, a hemmed patch and the overhand patch.

To Make a Hemmed Patch.

Trim the hole neatly in the form of a square or rectangle. Cut diagonally one-fourth inch at each corner, crease a one-fourth inch fold to the wrong side on all sides of the hole. Cut the patch one inch larger than the open space, matching the figure if there is one, and having the warp threads run parallel with the warp threads of the garment. Baste the patch to the underside of the garment with the right side to the wrong side of the garment. Hem down the turned in edges of the hole. On the wrong side of the garment, turn in the edge of the patch and fasten with a catch stitch.

To Make the Overhand Patch.

Prepare the hole the same as for the hemmed patch. Cut the patch one inch larger than the hole in each direction, matching the design if there is a design or figure in the material. Turn a one-fourth inch fold to the wrong side of the four sides of the place to be patched, turn in the edges of the patch so that it will fit exactly into the space to be filled, overhand in place from the wrong side taking care to have the stitches show as little as possible on the right side. Use as fine a needle as will hold the thread. Work carefully or the material will pucker. After overhanding the patch into place, overcast the raw edges on the patch and garment. If new material is to be used and the old garment is faded, place the new piece in the sun until it resembles the color of the garment.

Where Do You Store Your Clothing?

The storage of clothing between seasons and when not in use is equally as important as other phases of the care of clothing. When preparing garments for storage, choose a sunny, windy day. Blankets, furs, and woolen clothing should hang out of doors for several hours. Soiled places attract moths. It is therefore important to remove all grease spots and dirt.

Fold Garments Carefully.

The folding of garments should be orderly and any parts of the garment which are likely to crush, such as sleeves, should have soft, dark tis- sue paper inserted. If you do not know how to fold garments you should ask a tailor or dressmaker for assistance. In folding woolen and silk garments, two parts of the cloth should be prevented from touching each other, by putting paper between the folds. Newspapers are very satisfactory for wrapping dark cloth suits. The packages or boxes should be made secure by pasting pieces of paper over every part where moths can enter. Each box should be labeled. If special care is given to woolen garments, it should not be necessary to put them in cold storage.

Woolen Garments Require Special Attention.

When woolen clothing is stored during the summer it is very essential that it be protected against moths. Moths destroy woolen textiles, fur, feathers, carpets, and upholstery. The damage is done by the larvae or worms which develop from the moth eggs. Prevention is the best method of protection against moths. To keep moths from depositing eggs, hang textiles in the sun and air; beat and brush them to remove eggs that may be present; pack air tight in clean boxes or bags of strong paper. Tobacco, camphor, cedar chips, naphthalene balls, moth balls, or odorless moth powder may be placed in the boxes. Garments which are to be put away should be dry and thoroughly clean. They should also be brushed thoroughly so that lapels and pockets do not harbor moth eggs.

How to Exterminate Moths.

When moths have developed, the housekeeper should give special attention to the closet or place of their origin. First, take all clothing out to the sunlight and brush it thoroughly; wash the closets with strong soap suds; burn sulphur candles; spray walls, shelves, and boxes with oil of cedar, gasoline, or benzine. If gasoline or benzine is used, great care should be taken to prevent fire.

In the northern part of the country moths begin to lay their eggs in April and June, but in warm climates moth- eggs may be found at any time. The little gray moth miller flies about the room trying to find a place to deposit her eggs. Garments which are not clean, well brushed and in use are selected first by the mother moth. The only safe way to care for clothing and furs is to keep the moths away from every garment. This can be done by putting the garments away in tightly closed cedar bags, paper packages, boxes, cedar chests, or heavy tar paper bags. Woolen garments that are not to be put away should have frequent shakings, brushings and beatings, and exposures to sunlight.

Evening Gowns and Party Dresses.

In storing evening gowns, silk dresses or fancy blouses, tissue paper should be used freely in the spaces between the folds. All garments should be carefully pulled into shape before storing. Do not put summer clothing away when starched or soiled. Cotton and linen mildew more quickly than any other textiles and should therefore be kept in a dry place. Heavy clothing should never be left hanging all summer as the shoulders or bias seams are easily pulled out of shape.

Roll Flat Goods.

When putting away flat goods such as linen and ribbons, roll them on bolts or boards in a way similar to the method used in the factories where these materials are made. These bolts may be made with newspapers or wrapping paper rolled over a broomstick. Mailing tubes of various sizes may also be used.

Be Ready When the Weather Changes.

See that hats, wraps, hosiery, and underwear are clean and in good re- pair. Shoes that are not to be worn for the season should be cleaned, put on shoe-trees, and stored carefully.

When is Remodeling Practical?

Remodeling may mean simple alterations or it may mean ripping up the garment and making it over into a new garment. When does it pay to remodel or make over a garment? This is a question that can be answered intelligently only after considering the garment in question. It is usually worthwhile to remodel a garment when the work can be done with little or no expense such as when the material in the garment can be made into something wearable and when the amount of time necessary to rip the old garment, renovate the material, and make over the garment is not out of proportion to its worth. Ordinarily when time must be taken from other important tasks or from much needed rest and recreation, it should not be used in making over old garments.

School girls are mostly interested in "freshening up" their dresses, which consists in thoroughly cleaning or renovating and making such slight alterations as changing or adding cuffs, collars, scarves, belts, or buckles; shortening or lengthening a skirt or sleeves; or altering the position of the waistline in accordance with the prevailing styles.

Another way to alter a dress is to combine it with things one already has, as for example with a different scarf, or by changing the vest. One does not need to spend much money on these new combinations but one does need to devote time and thought in the inspection of fashion sheets and the displays in exclusive shop windows as well as in much brushing, pressing, and sponging at home.

Hats are usually fragile and need constant care and attention. Brushing and cleaning felt hats with cleaning solvents, sponging straw hats with alcohol, adding new linings, and occasionally adding a new flower or ornament will often make old hats finish the season.

Making Something New for Children.

There is real pleasure to be found in cutting down a garment and making it into a much smaller one, and there is satisfaction in the economy of making garments over. When the garments of grown-ups have become worn in places the better parts can often be used successfully in making children's clothes.

Of course making over silk and woolen garments is difficult, in fact, much more difficult than making a new garment from cotton or linen, but since there is little or no expense it is worth trying.

Sometimes old materials can be dyed successfully. Did you ever do any dyeing? Dyes are so carefully prepared, and the directions which come with each kind of dye are so clear and easy to follow, that it is almost impossible to fail with them. Dyes can be bought in different colors for all kinds of textiles, such as linen, silk, wool, and cotton. There are soap dyes, which clean and dye at the same time, and there are dye powders. Most dye companies distribute with their dyes, sheets or leaflets giving such information and directions as are necessary in dyeing both white and colored materials.

In working with dyes, one learns a great deal about color and there is also real satisfaction in creating something beautiful and attractive out of old material.

Curtains, draperies, bedspreads, rag rugs, and other household furnishings can often be successfully dyed, thus changing or harmonizing the color scheme and making the rooms more livable.

How Clothes Are Cleaned.

Clothes are laundered or dry cleaned to keep them fresh, sanitary, and healthful. It cannot be too often reiterated that clean clothes are necessary in order for one to be well dressed and attractive. When soiled clothes are washed in water, we say they are laundered, when soiled garments are cleaned in gasoline or naphtha, we say they are dry cleaned. Garments which cannot be successfully washed in water should be dry cleaned because the dry cleaning process does not affect and alter the garment as does water. Everyone who sends garments to dry cleaning establishments knows that some garments shrink though usually they can be successfully stretched to their original measurements without injury to the fabric. Garments that fit snugly should be measured before sending them to the cleaner and the measurements should be sent with the garment.

The experienced dry cleaner will wash your garments in gasoline or some other solvent and bring them back to you looking much like new ones, with little or no change in size, color, and general appearance. Dry cleaning, properly done, requires skill, and there is danger of fire because gasoline and other solvents are inflammable. Therefore, many people prefer to send their garments to a reliable dry cleaning establishment rather than to try to do the work at home. Visit dry cleaning establishments in order that you may learn to know when dry cleaning is properly done. What garments in your wardrobe should be sent to the dry cleaner? How much would it cost to have all your woolen and silk garments cleaned?

Dry Cleaning at Home.

There is much difference in opinion as to whether or not dry cleaning should ever be done at home. Many people believe that it is much too dangerous because the solvents used are very explosive; others believe that dry cleaning at home is economical and therefore should be encouraged with proper precautions. It is usually cheaper to do dry cleaning at home, but one must be very cautious in the use of explosive cleaning solvents. Gasoline and naphtha are the solvents ordinarily used for dry cleaning. They should be used in the open air away from any possible contact with fire.

Dry cleaning is now being done with technical naphtha which is a cleaning solvent said to have "a low flash touch" which means that it is not so explosive as ordinary gasoline and naphtha.

When garments are badly soiled or very expensive it is much better to have them cleaned at a good dry cleaning establishment even if this necessitates sending them to a distant city.

What Garments Should be Dry Cleaned?

Garments, curtains, and drapes which are made of silk, wool, lace, chiffon, or a combination of these and those which are colored or for any other reason cannot be washed, should be dry cleaned. Sometimes the supplies needed for dry cleaning cost as much as the cost that would be incurred by sending a single garment to a professional dry cleaner. Dry cleaning at home is more economical only when several garments or articles of house furnishings must be cleaned.

Directions for Dry Cleaning.

Before cleaning by any method, all rips and tears should be mended and, if possible, all spots removed. Dry cleaning usually does not remove fruit, grass, perspiration, and blood stains. Spots may be marked with thread before dipping the garment to indicate where more care is needed than with the rest of the garment. Rubbing is done only with the hands and then it is better to do more squeezing than actual rubbing. Do the work out of doors if possible; if not, open the windows and doors and keep away from fire. Have enough fluid to wash the fabrics thoroughly and rinse them twice if possible. A gasoline soap may be used in the first washing. After washing and rinsing shake the garment and dry it in the open air. When thoroughly dry, press it as you would any garment made of similar material.

Removing Spots and Stains.

All spots should be removed as soon as possible after they appear. Fresh spots are easier removed than old ones. It is always better to remove spots before washing or cleaning the entire garment. If one knows the nature of the spot, the work is simplified. Two precautions should be kept in mind in removing any kind of spot; first, not to destroy the surface or finish of the material, and second, not to rub so hard that any of the dye is removed in colored or dark fabrics. It is much easier to remove spots from white materials than from colored ones because there is danger of removing the color from colored fabrics. It is a good plan to experiment on a small piece of goods of like material or on the edge of a seam. This advice applies not only to colored fabrics but to spots of unknown cause and to delicate fabrics. Knowing what kind of material is in the garment is important. Some methods used in removing spots from cotton and linen would cause injury if applied to wool and silk.

White cotton and linen goods can be boiled and rubbed vigorously enough to remove spots but wool and silk are injured by boiling water and by hard rubbing. Careful laundering with a neutral soap, and sunshine will do much in removing ordinary spots but it is a good plan to keep on hand a bottle of non-inflammable spot remover. Follow directions on the bottle.

Classes of Stain Removers.

Stain removers may be divided into absorbents, solvents, and bleaches. Absorbents are used for removing grease spots. French chalk, talcum powder, fuller earth, oatmeal, and starch are absorbents. In using these cover the grease spot with the absorbent, let it stand for several hours, then brush it carefully, repeating the process when necessary. Grease spots may be cleaned by placing the spotted fabric between two sheets of clean, white blotting paper and pressing the paper with a warm iron. Solvents are used to dissolve a stain. Gasoline, alcohol, benzine, turpentine, ether, and chloroform may be used for this purpose when water fails. The spotted fabric should be stretched across a bowl and the liquid should be poured from a height. When other solvents are used, lay the spotted material on a pad of cloth, apply the solvent with a cloth, and rub from the edge toward the center of the spot. Change the pad occasionally. Gasoline, alcohol, benzine, chloroform, ether, and turpentine are all inflammable materials and should never be used in a room where there is a fire or flame of any kind.

Bleaches are used in the last attempt to remove a stain and should be applied very carefully to prevent injury to the fabric. Javelle water, oxalic acid, and potassium per- manganate are more successfully used for this purpose than lemon juice or sour milk but will injure the fabric if not used correctly.

Patience is usually necessary in successfully removing stains. Several short applications are better than one long continuous process. When cleaning with water or any kind of liquid, the chief difficulty seems to be with the ring left after the spot is removed. Try placing the spot over a folded bath towel, moving to a clean, dry place on the towel from time to time. After the spot is removed, begin at the outer edge of the ring and toward the center.

In using these solutions, stretch the spotted fabric over a bowl, dampen with cold water, apply the bleach with a medicine dropper, rinse with clean water, and apply again if necessary.

Javelle water, oxalic acid and potassium permanganate solutions can be bought at a drug store, however, if one cares to mix them at home, the following recipes may be used:

Javelle Water.

Dissolve one pound of chloride of lime in two quarts of cold water. Then dissolve one pound of washing soda in one quart of boiling water. Mix the two solutions, stirring well. After the mixture settles, pour off the clear liquid and bottle. Keep in a dark place. When using Javelle water, stretch the spotted material or garment over a bowl, dampen the spot with cold water and apply the solution by dropping it on the spot with a medicine dropper. Then rinse with clear water. Apply the Javelle solution again if necessary. Rinse again. It is better to repeat the process several times than to soak the fabric in the bleach too long. When the spot has disappeared, rinse well in ammonia water made by adding one tablespoon of ammonia to two quarts of water. Remember that all the Javelle solution must be thoroughly removed or the fabric will be weakened. Never use Javelle water on colored fabrics without first trying the result on the color. Sometimes it is desirable to remove the stain even if a white spot is left on a colored fabric, as this white spot can be retinted with water colors or treated with dye soaps. Do not use on wool or silk.

Oxalic Acid.

Make a solution by dissolving one ounce of the oxalic acid crystals in three quarters of a cup of lukewarm water. Use only half strength in order not to injure the fabric.

Potassium Permanganate.

One teaspoonful of potassium per-manganate crystals to one quart of water. Strain and bottle. In using potassium permanganate it is better to repeat the application several times than to attempt to use a stronger solution, which might destroy the fabric. Do not use on colored fabrics.

Some Common Stains and How to Remove Them.

Stains should be removed before the whole garment is laundered or dry cleaned. This is necessary because cleaning processes set some kinds of stains. Fresh stains are more easily removed than old ones. In removing stains, one should decide, first, the kind of fabric, nature of stain, and the effect of the stain remover upon the color of the fabric, if the garment is colored.

Acid Stain.

Sponge with water containing a little ammonia. Sometimes fumes from the bottle are sufficient. Use with extreme care on colored garments.

Blood Stains.

Blood stains may be removed from cotton and linen by soaking in cold water for several hours. Then wash in the usual way with soap and hot water. Ammonia helps to remove old stains. Hot water if used at first helps set the stain and makes it more difficult to remove. To remove these stains from wool and silk, sponge in cold or lukewarm water. If care is used so as not to injure the color, hydrogen peroxide may be used. Make a paste of raw starch and cold water and apply on thick materials. When starch is discolored, make another application.

Chewing Gum.

Use a solvent such as gasoline or benzine.

Chocolate or cocoa.
Boiling water, borax and cold water, or potassium permanganate if necessary, on white goods.

Coffee and fruit stains.

To remove stains from cotton and linen, spread the article over a bowl and pour boiling water on the spot from a height. Like other stains, these are more easily removed when fresh. Then, too, they must be removed before boiling, for that only sets the stain and makes it immovable. Ammonia removes these stains from white clothes, table linen, etc., but be careful not to use it on colored clothing for it may remove the color along with the stain. In using ammonia, test it on a hem or seam.

To remove these stains from wool and silk fabrics, use warm water, because boiling water would injure the fabric. A little borax added to the warm water will aid in removing the stain.

Cream.

Wash in cold water, then warm water and soap. A solvent may be used.

Fly paper.

Use a solvent.

Grass stains.

Summer brings grass stains. Some of these may be removed by laundering with soap and water. If stains are made on materials that cannot be laundered, remove them by sponging with alcohol.

Remove grass stains from wool and silk by the same methods you use for cotton and linen.

Grease.

To remove grease spots from cotton and linen, use soap and warm water. To remove grease from wool and silk, use some solvent such as chloroform, carbon tetrachlorid, the commercial fluids sold under various trade names, or gasoline, but do remember to keep these fluids from the fire or flames,

French chalk is excellent for removing grease spots and will not injure the most delicate fabrics. When using French chalk, cover the spot on the wrong side with the powdered chalk. Leave it for twenty-four hours, then brush off.

Ink.

The removal of ink stains from cotton and linen is more difficult than the removal of other stains. Ink is made up of different substances hence it is hard to tell what to apply. Wash a fresh ink stain out at once with water. Another method is to soak the stain in milk for at least twenty-four hours, changing the milk as often as it becomes colored from the ink. Of course, the milk will leave a grease spot. Remove this with soap and water. Ink spots on white materials can be removed by applying oxalic acid repeatedly, and Javelle water, which can be obtained at a drug store. Don't forget the warning though that oxalic acid is a poison. Ink eradicators may be used, but they cannot be used on colored goods because they will remove the color.

Milk and water can be used on wool and silk but do not use the cleaning acids on these goods.

Iron Rust.

To remove iron rust from cotton and linen, wet the stain with water and put a few drops of oxalic acid on it. Lemon juice may be used by squeezing the juice on the spot and covering with salt. Expose this to the sunlight and let it bleach. Wash the acid out thoroughly with water, otherwise you will find a hole or worn spot appearing in the garment.

Wool and silk may be treated in the same way as cotton and linen are treated.

Milk.

Wash in cold water, then follow with soap and water or a solvent.

Mildew.

Fresh stains may be worked out in cold water; for old stains apply lemon juice and salt and lay in bright sunshine; also use Javelle water or potassium permanganate and oxalic acid, if necessary, on white goods.

Paint.

To remove paint from cotton and linen, sponge with turpentine, benzine, or gasoline, while the spot is fresh. Apply chloroform, mixed with turpentine, if the stain is an old one, and the stain will yield readily.

Wool and silk can be cleaned by using the methods given for cleaning paint from cotton and linen.

Perspiration.

Wash in warm water and soap, place in sun to dry (white goods). Odor in non-washable material may be removed with a solvent and alcohol or chloroform.

Tobacco.

Apply diluted hydrochloric acid, rinse in diluted ammonia, sponge with soap and water.

Wax.

Scrape off with knife or sharp article. Press between blotters. Alcohol will remove the color from spots made by colored candle wax.

Why Should You Study About Laundry?

What are your responsibilities in seeing that your clothing is kept fresh and clean? Do you send your silk and woolen garments to the dry cleaning establishment? Do you send all your other clothes to the commercial laundry?

What about your hose and silk underwear, your dainty handkerchiefs, your brightly colored wash dresses? Do you know how to launder your own personal clothing? Do you want to learn how to help with the family laundry? Do you know how to prepare the laundry to be sent away to be done? Can you check the laundry when it is returned? Would you know what to do if some of your garments were missing? Would you know whether or not the laundry work was properly done? What is the definition of "wet wash," "rough dry," and "finished work," as applied to laundry work?

Even if most of your laundry is done for you, you should know something about the process of laundering because it may be necessary for you to do an occasional piece for yourself and it may be your responsibility to decide whether the laundering in your home is being done according to approved methods.

Preparing Clothes for the Wash.

When the laundry is sent to the commercial laundry, someone must be responsible for sending it out and checking it upon its return. The laundry will furnish blanks upon which to list all garments and household linens. Make duplicate slips. Keep one yourself and pin the other to the outgoing laundry. This slip should contain instructions as to whether the clothes are to be wet wash, rough dry, or finished. If you do not know what these and other commonly used laundry terms mean, find out from your local laundry.

Inspect each garment as you sort the clothes. Runners or broken stitches in knit underwear and tears which might be made worse in the laundering process should be mended. Spots and stains requiring special care should be removed. Remember that hot water sets some stains such as fruit, grass, and blood.

Silk stockings and underwear, colored garments, hand-made linen, dainty handkerchiefs, and woolen garments may be sent to the commercial laundry if marked "special," but special attention takes time and consequently costs money. For this reason, such garments are usually laundered at home.

Laundering Clothes at Home.

The usual order of procedure in doing laundry work at home is as follows:

1. Sorting the clothes. Dividing them into piles of (1) colored cotton and linen; (2) white cotton and linen; (3) table linen and slightly soiled towels; (4) dirty towels and clothes; (5) handkerchiefs; (6) stockings; (7) silk garments; (8) flannels.

2. Mend torn or worn places. "A stitch in time saves nine." Runners in stockings and broken stitches in silk, rayon, or knit underwear should be mended as soon as they appear. All rips and tears that will be made worse in laundering should be mended before washing. Garments should be inspected after the ironing for missing buttons, torn places, and other needed repairs. Sheets, pillow cases, towels, and other ordinary household linen may be mended on the sewing machine.

3. Remove stains and spots. Garments can be kept new and clean much longer if one knows how to remove spots successfully.

4. Shall we soak our clothes? - Soaking clothes is believed by most people to loosen the dirt, making it easier to wash them. Other people disagree and contend that long soaking, especially in hard water, makes clothes dingy. At least we know that clothes need not be soaked all night or as long as was formerly thought necessary. Soak only very dirty white clothing. Do not soak dirty clothes along with clean clothes. Why? Do not soak colored clothes. Why? Remember that all types of clothing should be wet in cold water before putting into hot water, as heat is known to set stains and spots that might otherwise disappear in ordinary washing.

5. Washing Clothes. - Rain water is soft and is the best kind of water to use in washing. Hard water is of two kinds, temporary and permanent; water which is only temporarily hard can be softened by boiling, while permanently hard water requires the addition of borax, washing soda, household ammonia, or other products of similar kind. Hard water should be softened by boiling, or by using one of the above-mentioned chemicals.

The scum which forms on water in the process of softening should be taken off or the clothes will be covered with dirt. Soaps and washing powders that are prepared especially for use in hard water can be bought. It pays to buy a good, neutral soap for laundry work. Hard soaps are those which have too much alkali and make the hands rough and shriveled.

Hard soap may be used in washing machines on very dirty white clothes. Clothes are usually washed in hot or warm water because the heat causes the threads of the cloth to expand, making it easier to remove the dirt. Soiled clothes are rubbed on a board or washed in a machine as this process helps in removing the dirt. Soap also helps in removing the dirt hence a liberal supply of good suds is considered necessary for the best results.

6. Boiling Clothes. - Boiling the white clothes not only makes them white, clear, and clean, but it also sterilizes them. Before the garment is put into the water for boiling, it should be carefully rinsed. After rinsing, soap the garment well, being careful to soap the spots soiled the most. Then the garment is ready for the boiling process. But remember not to put the clothes into boiling water at first if you want them white and clear. Place them in cold water, sufficient to cover the clothes, and let them boil for about five minutes after the boiling point is reached. Do not pack the clothes in the boiler too closely.

If you boil clothes in hard water, unless you use some kind of softener a scum is likely to form on the top of the water and spoil the looks of the clothes. Many people believe that ordinary clothes need not be boiled, that scalding is all that is necessary, but of course complete sterilization by boiling is necessary if the clothes belong to a sufferer from a contagious disease.

7. Wringing, Rinsing, and Bluing. - Did you know that our success in laundering clothes depends upon rinsing them well and thoroughly? No matter how much you rub them, no matter how much you boil them, if they are not rinsed at least twice and rinsed well, dipped up and down to get the suds out, your laundry will not be clear and clean looking. The first rinsing water should be hot in order to remove the soap and take out the loosened dirt. Cold water will cause a scum to form that will stick to the clothes. Bluing is used to counteract the yellow color of the garments. The yellow color in clothes may be caused by lack of sunlight or by careless rinsing. The amount of bluing to be used in laundry work must be determined by experience — better too little than too much. The last rinsing may be in cold water and bluing added if desired in order to counter- act any yellowness but clothes that are properly washed and dried in the sunshine do not really require bluing. If bluing is added when the rinse water is hot, the first clothes will absorb or take up the bluing and will be too blue or dingy looking.

Right wringing has much to do with the laundry process. In fact, a good wringer is almost essential to good home laundry work. Put clothes in the wringer straight and in folds. Catching a corner in the wringer, thus letting the wringer pull the garment, causes clothes to be torn and stretched out of shape. Fold buttons within the material to prevent so many from being broken or torn off.

8. Starching and Making Starch. - Starch is used to produce an attractive finish on the fabric and to add body to the garment. A starched garment resists moisture and soil for a longer period of time and thus we say that the starched garment wears longer and better. The prevailing style dictates what garments should he starched. What garment are you wearing that has been starched?

In preparing starch for laundry work, add cold water to the starch to separate the grains of starch and form a thin paste. Then add boiling water and boil gently for five or ten minutes until clear. Stir to prevent scorching, then strain the starch through a cloth before using. Use while hot on white fabrics. A small amount of bluing may be added to the starch paste. Wring clothes out well and turn wrong side out before placing in starch. Rub the starch into the fabric thoroughly; then wring out the excess starch.

Uncooked or cold starch is made by combining cold water and starch and is used only on garments to be made very stiff. Do not wring but roll the garment in a cloth and let it stand for about an hour before ironing. The starch is cooked by the hot iron passing over it. It takes experience to do this kind of work successfully.

9. Drying Clothes. - Hanging up the clothes is usually a part of the laundry helper's duties. Mother Goose must have had in mind the spotlessly attired daughter of the household in the role of assistant— clean in person and proud of her purity — when she wrote the jingle about the maid in the garden, hanging out clothes, when along came a blackbird and nipped off her nose. Make sure to have a clean line to hang the clothes on. Wipe it with a fresh, clean cloth. Hang colored clothes in the shade and white clothes in the bright sunshine. The sunshine is a wonderful bleacher. Have you heard how linens are bleached in the sunshine in Ireland?

When you take the clothes from the line, fold them carefully to avoid unnecessary wrinkling, and assemble garments of a kind together. Sheets and towels are not ironed by some busy house- wives. Such details should be decided by each individual family.

10. The Weekly Ironing. - Do you assist with the laundry by ironing the pieces you are able to do well? Do you sprinkle your clothes in plenty of time for the water to saturate the clothes and be evenly distributed, making them easy to iron? Wrinkles cannot be successfully ironed out unless the clothes are sprinkled and the sprinkling well done. Remember to iron the clothing dry as you go, in order to prevent its having a rough appearance. Another important point is to keep the corners square and pull the edges straight as you do in ironing handkerchiefs,

towels, and napkins. In all ironing, keep the shape of the garment in mind. Curtains and pillow covers should be measured before washing, and when ironed or dried, stretched to the original measurements.

No definite rules can be given that will apply to all garments. Iron embroidery and lace on the wrong side over a soft pad. In this way, the pattern will not be flattened by the iron. In ironing tucks and pleats, be sure that each part is dry before beginning a new part. Garments left half dry or half ironed will look rough when finished. Add a second pressing to the hems, tucks, and bands and the appearance of the garments will be much improved. Iron muslins on the right side and prints on the wrong side. Always iron with the thread of the goods.

A heavy iron is better for plain work such as table linen, sheets, and pillow cases, while one of lighter weight is preferable for small articles with ruffles and gathers. The iron should be smooth and clean. Test the iron on a piece of white paper or cloth to be sure that it is clean. No iron is hot enough until it will hiss when touched with the moistened finger.

11. Folding and Putting Away Clothes. - Fold household linen and garments according to approved methods and place them in their usual places.

12. Equipment for Laundry. - What equipment is needed for laundry purposes? Of course a washing board, boiler, tubs and buckets, ironing board, and iron are among the essentials. A good wringer and washing machine are much to be desired, if the laundry work is to be done at home. Nowhere is it more necessary to consider the right height of working equipment than in the laundry. Laundry work is considered the most strenuous work about the house. Perhaps you are interested in making a special study of laundry equipment. Find out what you can about the cost of washing machines. If a washing machine and wringer are needed in your home, perhaps the whole family can join in making or saving money for its purchase. What can you do to earn money? What can you do to save money? Perhaps you can do without something which has been promised you.

Laundering Woolen Garments.

Wool will shrink, felt, and thicken unless very carefully washed. Boiling water causes wool fiber to mat and shrink. When wool is rightly laundered, it remains soft and fluffy. Lukewarm water for both washing and rinsing should be used. Use a mild soap, flakes, or chips to make good suds. Do not rub soap directly on the garment. Dip the woolen garment up and down in the suds, rinse it carefully, squeeze it dry, and then pull it into its correct shape. Do not hang it in the sun- shine or place it close to a fire to dry. Never allow woolen garments to freeze.

Knitted garments should be laid on a bath towel, stretched to correct size and then fastened with pins and allowed to dry. If hung up, they will stretch out of shape. Do not use a hot iron on woolen material. It is a good idea to place folds of cloth over a woolen fabric while pressing it.

To remove stains from woolen garments, use a mild acid such as lemon juice, diluted oxalic or hydrochloric acid. If the stain is very bad, the article should be sent to a commercial cleaner, as one who is not experienced in this kind of work is apt to injure the garment.

Laundering Silk and Rayon.

When laundering silk and rayon stockings, underwear and other garments, use warm water and a mild soap. Dissolve the soap in the water, making good suds. Follow the same procedure in washing silk and rayon as used in washing woolen garments, that is, dip up and down in the suds, squeeze, rather than wring, and rinse in several waters. Crepes and marquisettes should be ironed before they dry to prevent shrinkage. Allow pongee silk to dry thoroughly before ironing it, then iron on the wrong side with a moderately hot iron. Knitted silk underwear and silk jersey should be ironed after they are dry and often must be stretched back into shape. Silk gloves and silk stockings do not need pressing.

When hanging silk garments to dry, arrange so that as little stretching as possible will take place. White silks may turn yellow unless put through bluing water. It is really better to dry silk garments by placing them between towels than by hanging. When almost dry, press on the wrong side with a moderately hot iron. Remember that a hot iron will not only scorch silk but will make it stiff and ugly.

How to Wash Lace.

Lace should be washed in warm suds that are made with a mild soap. Squeeze the lace and douse up and down, but never rub. White lace should be run through a bluing water. Cream or ecru colored lace may be rinsed in water colored with tea or coffee.

When drying lace, pull the article into shape and pin it right side up to a pad. Pin each scallop or point and pull out the points and picots. Keep the lace the correct width and shape by using a tape line or other measure. Lace really looks better when not ironed.

How to Wash Curtains.

Lace or net curtains should be washed in the same way as lace. It is often necessary to use several waters in cleaning curtains. In drying curtains, place them on stretchers to make ironing unnecessary. Curtain stretchers are frames to which the edges of the curtain are attached to draw them back into shape. The stretchers should be adjusted to the size of the curtain before it is washed.

Scrim, marquisette, and other similar curtain material should be washed as other white goods. In ironing curtains, avoid stretching them along the edges. Iron across the curtain, straight with the thread of the material.

How to Wash Rag Rugs.

Cotton rag rugs should be washed In washing machines, with clear warm water first, then in warm suds. The badly soiled places should be brushed with a stiff scrub brush. Rinse through several waters and hang, without wringing, on a line, permitting them to drip dry.

How to Wash Doilies and Other Embroidered Work.

Embroidered doilies should be washed in hot soap suds by dipping them up and down rather than rubbing, thoroughly rinsed, put through a bluing water, and turned face down on a bath towel to dry. They should be pulled into shape and ironed very carefully when only partly dry. Use warm suds to wash doilies embroidered in colors. Doilies with lace should be turned face up on the towel and the lace should be pinned to a pad, the same as when washing lace by itself. Do not iron the lace, though the center may be ironed when about half dry. Folding doilies causes unattractive creases. It is better to roll them around a paper roll to hold their correct shape.

The same careful care as above advised should be given to other embroidered materials and handwork, including fingertip towels, guest towels, and the like.

How to Wash Colored Garments.

Colored fabrics should never be washed in hot water. Hot water may cause the material to fade. Use warm suds made with a neutral soap. Never soak colored goods but wash carefully and rinse quickly and thoroughly. It is better to wash only one garment at a time; hang it in the shade to dry or place it between dry cloths, fold and iron when half dry. Iron on the wrong side with a moderately hot iron. Cretonne used for curtains or pillows should be washed by this method.

Do not sprinkle colored garments, as the color may run. If they are starched, they should be turned wrong side out and starched in warm, not hot, starch, using fresh starch for each color. Rub the starch into the garment thoroughly.

Wardrobe Examination.

Give your wardrobe a thorough examination. List garments needing cleaning, mending or repairing. What garments need airing? Brushing? Pressing? Are you keeping your clothes closet and dresser drawers in order? Well-kept clothes give one a feeling of real satisfaction, add to one's personal appearance, and increase one's self-respect.

Examine your wardrobe carefully and answer the following questions:

1. Are all rips and tears mended?

2. Do any of my garments need hooks, eyes, or buttons?

3. Do any of my garments need patching or darning?

4. Are my hose in good repair?

5. Do any of my clothes need pressing, dusting, or airing?

6. Do any of my wash dresses or undergarments need laundering?

7. Should I take time now to remove spots?

8. Are my shoes polished and ready to wear?

9. Are my collars, ties, and other "accessories" in good repair?

10 Are my rubbers, umbrella, and raincoat ready for use?

Budgets and Care of Clothing.

Clothes, well cared for, effect a saving in money that is sometimes equal to the cost, in considerable part, of a new outfit. Well-kept clothes not only look better but last longer. Clothes that require constant cleaning are expensive. Even though we do our own cleaning, repairing, etc., we should learn to buy clothes that do not require an unusual amount of care. Do you know how much you spend on the care of your clothes? Everyone should have some idea of what is spent each year for general care, repair, laundry, and dry cleaning. Economy in the purchase of clothes is determined by the relation of the original cost to the number of times the garment can be worn. Clothes that are bought at reduced prices or which are on sale, if they require constant cleaning, are more expensive than higher priced garments which do not require so much cleaning and repairing. You should make out a budget for clothing expenses and not exceed the amount budgeted. Upkeep, laundry, cleaning, and repairing are important items in planning a clothing budget. If you are to live within your family's income, you must learn how to plan your wardrobe and buy wisely.

CHAPTER 12

THE WARDROBE CLINIC

Some people with but little money at their disposal can outfit and replenish their wardrobes with a greater measure of success than others can accomplish who have as much, or vastly more, money allocated to the clothing budget. The difference in ability between these two groups is chiefly accounted for by the use of taste in the first instance and the absence of this talent in the latter. It is fortunate for us that taste may be educated, that it may be elevated to higher levels of appreciation for the esthetic. If education and improvement were not possible, we could not become highly discriminating in our choices between good and bad in the arts of music, literature, painting, and costuming the human body. It is not to be supposed that taste has become developed when the stage of passive recognition of such artistic values as proportion, beauty, fitness, symmetry, and the like have been reached. Development must proceed until recognition of the artistic combines with the creative knowledge, skill, and sound judgment which are requisites to the effective use of taste.

Good taste in personal grooming includes the ability to select becoming clothes in color, design, and fabric, and knowledge of how to combine, and when to wear, certain articles of clothing. We say that a boy or girl is well dressed when he has selected clothing that is proportionate in cost with his share of the clothing budget, correctly designed, made of materials suitable to his age, color, and proportion, and appropriate to the occasion when it is to be worn.

Money is not so important a consideration here as knowledge, because it enhances your appearance but little to buy the most expensive garments if you are unable to combine them so as to make a pleasing ensemble. Following are some problems we encounter in choosing an appropriate wardrobe, together with some suggestions for solving them.

1. Clothing for Different Occasions.

A well-chosen costume should be appropriate to the occasion, suited to the individual type and coloring of the wearer, appropriate for the season and the time of day, and in keeping with the wearer's financial and social status. The six most common types of costumes which are worn by the high school boy and girl are (1) school, (2) sports clothes, (3) housewear, (4) street wear, (5) social occasions, and (6) travel.

(1) School clothes should be practical, but this does not mean that they should have no beauty. Printed cottons, ginghams, and rayons all make suitable school clothes for summer, and for winter there are soft silks and light weight wools in attractive colors and designs. SIMPLY MADE wash dresses or wool dresses are appropriate selections for school wear. School clothing should be loose enough to allow room for growth and permit freedom of action which is indispensable for the development of individual grace and strength.

The following list of clothes is considered complete for a boy going to boarding school:

Suits- — -3 sack suits (long trousers) two of tweed for every day, one navy blue for Sunday and dress occasions.

Shoes— 2 brown or black pairs for every day and one pair of black to wear with navy blue suit.

Socks — Thin wool smartest, or else cotton; plain black for blue suit, otherwise subdued colors.

Shirts — Cheviot, collars attached, solid colors, light blue or tan, etc. If climate very cold, flannel with fine striped lines. For Sunday and dress, a few white shirts with detachable starched turn-down collars. Polo shirts and shorts for special occasions such as hikes or scout work of any sort.

Ties— Plain dark blue for blue suit; others of mixed colors not too gaudy.

One or two pairs of old trousers and sweaters of different weights. Windbreaker leather coat, also polo coat and raincoat. For train and in city: overcoat and felt hat. At school: a knit cap or nothing.

(2) Sports Clothes. There is a fascination in sports clothes for both boys and girls. They like the gay, heavy woolens and want to wear them everywhere. Sports clothes may be more individual than other types because of their informal use and background.

In the summer, for informal but not rough wear in the country, at garden parties, house parties, and informal dances, boys may wear white flannel, duck or serge trousers, white buckskin shoes with white woolen or silk socks, and a dark blue coat. White socks should not be worn except with white shoes.

Sweaters and skirts are usually chosen by girls who participate in active sports. Sweaters may be any color but must harmonize with the knickers or skirt and must not be frayed. They should be clean and in good repair. Hats should be plain, not tailored.

Heavy soled, flat heeled or semi-flat heeled walking shoes, wool or silk-and-wool hose are complements of sports clothes.

Riding clothes for girls are strictly tailored. In the city, a riding costume may be purchased from a good sports shop or a tailor consisting of a mannish, tight-fitting coat, a plain mannish hat, worn over hair plainly dressed, riding breeches, and low-heeled boots.

Accessories for sports clothes such as hats, scarves, belts, buckles, and sweaters may be striking and gay but not gaudy.

(3) Housewear. Becomingness of clothes to be worn at home is just as important as elsewhere. Here we are sure of a harmonious back- ground and should be able to choose attractive and becoming garments. Thin woolens and silks are suitable, particularly in winter, and in summer gay cotton prints are both appropriate and attractive.

(4) Street. The street costume should be simple and inconspicuous in design and color, becoming, stylish, and durable. Shoes and hose should be comfortable and well cared for; hats simple but contributing a definite note to the ensemble. A dressy blouse worn with a tailored suit makes it possible to combine shopping with a social engagement.

(5) Social occasions. A girl who goes to dances or formal evening affairs needs an evening dress as well as an afternoon frock, suitable for informal dinners and afternoon parties. With these she should wear dress pumps or slippers or other "dress" shoes which are in vogue and are becoming. To a garden party, a girl should wear a light dress and a simple dress hat, light slippers or pumps, and silk hose. The brighter the colors seen at a garden party, the prettier the effect, but one

should wear only those colors which are becoming. In the country, sports clothes are sometimes worn.

When a girl is a guest at a family dinner, she wears a simple afternoon dress, preferably a light-colored one, silk hose, and slippers.

For a boy whose evenings are full of social activity, or for one who goes to dances and evening parties often enough to justify buying evening clothes, the dinner jacket or Tuxedo is by far the most useful purchase for evening wear. With it, he will need plain black silk hose, plain black patent leather or calfskin pumps, plain black silk or satin tie, plain white waistcoat or plain black silk or satin waistcoat, plain white linen handkerchief, gloves of gray or khaki-colored doeskin, an overcoat and a plain white or black and white muffler when he leaves his own house.

(6) For Traveling. Tailored clothes for girls and business suits for boys are the best general dress to wear on board a passenger ship. A girl will need an afternoon dress for dinner and a boy a dark suit, unless they are traveling deluxe; in which case, a simple evening dress for the girl and a Tuxedo for the boy are correct. During the day, girls may wear sports clothes if they wish, and a soft sports hat that will with- stand the wind. Boys wear tweeds and sports clothes and caps. A bathrobe of plain colors, and good looking but not elaborate slippers are needed on ship-board as much as on sleeping cars.

On the train, a dark suit for boys, a dark dress or suit that does not wrinkle easily for girls, are correct. For going to the dressing room, a dark robe and slippers will be needed.

If a family or party of friends are traveling in an automobile, simple sports clothes may be worn. Girls may wear slacks and sweaters or blouses, depending on the climate.

II. Color in Relation to Type.

Of course we know it is impossible to designate definite types as blond, brunette, or redhead. Very few girls or boys fall exactly in these three classes. Too many other things besides hair, eyes, and complexion go to make up the entire picture.

The three things that influence and perhaps dominate color selection are hair, eyes, and skin, the first two being more or less fixed and fitting better into one's general make-up than any other. Nature has a way of combining colors harmoniously that cannot be approached in perfection by man, and for this reason it is usually a mistake to dye the hair. It makes girls look older and imparts a hard cast to facial features, changes the glow of the complexion, and often does not harmonize with the eyes.

As a rule, eyes of cool colors --green, blue, gray, and very light hazel — - look more attractive with cool ensembles of the same hues, blue, green, violet; while dark or "warm" eyes suggest the warmer colors of red, yellow, brown, and orange.

In dressing to complement the hair, wear shades that accent it by contrast or by repetition, as green to contrast with red hair; black to contrast with golden hair; reds and other vivid colors to contrast with black hair; browns to repeat the tint of brown hair.

Another important factor in choosing color is the tone of the skin. When girls have a healthy, radiant skin, they are able to wear a great many colors. Those whose skin tones are pink and yellow look well in colors that tone down their ruddiness. Girls whose skin tones are orange look well in browns, rust, and gold.

Personality cannot be overlooked in the selection of clothing. Strong, vibrant personalities can wear strong, vivid colors without being overshadowed; but a quiet, reserved personality would be overwhelmed by such colors.

If you study your own personality in its relation to costume design and in relation to your figure and choose every garment accordingly, it will add charm to your figure and make your style of dress distinctive. How does your figure compare with the proportions used by the Greeks? If you will compare your own figure with the Greek standard, you will know which points you want to conceal and which you want to emphasize.

When we look at a girl, our eyes travel a natural line which follows the dominant points of her dress and figure. If you can dress to conceal your bad points and emphasize your good ones, our eyes follow a pleasing outline and we say that you have good lines. For this reason, if you are too tall and thin, your clothes should not have vertical stripes, which emphasize height, but rows running across to minimize your height. In the same way, a plump person would avoid ruffles and lines running around her dress or skirt, which serve only to make her look shorter and fatter, while vertical lines would increase the appearance of her height.

The same principles hold true when applied to the clothing of boys. The vertical stripes in suits tend to add height; the horizontal lines, width. The tall boy should wear figured materials in suits cut to give him lateral lines. He may wear a double-breasted coat, waist line slightly fitted, and trousers wider at bottom, -while the short boy should select clothes with vertical lines such as single breasted coats with narrow lapels, and trousers with bottoms tapered slightly.

A person with a short, fat neck should wear a dress with a V-shaped neckline; one with a long neck should wear a round neckline. A person with a long, slender face should wear collars, hats, and hairdress which minimize length, such as large hats and round, soft collars; while one with a round, square face should select styles in these details which give the appearance of length and slenderness.

In choosing becoming clothes, we have both size and coloring to consider. The tall girl, from five feet seven to six feet tall, instead of stooping to diminish her height which only gives her bad posture and makes her unattractive, should stand naturally and dress so as to reduce the appearance of unusual height and yet emphasize her natural grace. For her are the loose-fitting coats with large collars, cloth or fur, which would make her shorter sisters look dumpy; for her are the large brimmed hats. Her hair may be fluffed out from the face, or, if long, coiled low on the neck. Her dresses should have cuffed sleeves that minimize or conceal her long, thin arms. The wardrobe of the tall girl may appropriately contain sleek satins, graceful organzas, and luxurious velvets. If she is stout as well as tall, then she should avoid the glossier, bulkier fabrics and choose materials which drape gracefully such as chiffons, lace, crepe de chine, and jersey.

The girl whom everyone teases about her diminutive size may laugh at her tormentors if she is guided by a careful study of her figure and knowledge of how to make appropriate clothing selections. Her charm must be expressed and enhanced by daintiness and feminity. Therefore, she should not use horizontal bands or rows, which would increase her appearance of shortness, but instead use vertical lines to give her height. She should avoid wide belts, big collars, and large sleeves. Her sweaters should have straight side lines and but one color; her coats preferably should be of cloth, not fur; her hat should be minus a brim or have only a narrow brim and a high crown. Her hair looks best when it is dressed close to her head, or perhaps when arranged with curls piled high in the back.

The overweight person can appear much smaller by giving careful consideration to details. Her dresses should consist of subdued colors and fabrics, conservative in line and design. Stripes help her to look taller, but they should be narrow and dark. Panels are helpful if they are of the right width. Short jackets and high waistlines are definitely "out" for her. Her skirt must hang straight or flare slightly below the knees. Her evening dress should be of chiffon or georgette which will cling to her as she walks and dances. Her coats, if tastefully chosen, will be plain and simple with straight lines and trim, well fitted sleeves.

Her hat is of great importance since it can either make or mar her appearance. The stout girl should avoid droopy hats with large brims; appropriate hats for her have narrow brims which extend beyond the surface of the face and make it seem less full. The crown should be slanted, or perhaps square.

IV. Building a School Wardrobe.

Type — a blond, blue-eyed, chubby girl. For this girl, with blond coloring and blue eyes, we will build a ward- robe around the basic color of blue, to enhance her eyes:

For classroom wear, a lightweight woolen dress or suit in navy blue would be neat and durable. This costume may be freshened by various collar and cuff sets consisting of white, dull green, Dubonnet, and royal blue. With her round face, the neck-line should, of course, be V-shaped and the collar narrow.

A gay scarf with blue as the predominant color will make an attractive accessory for her black or dark blue overcoat, which should be slightly fitted in at the waist, rather than cut in swagger style, which would make her appear chubbier.

Her summer clothes should have solid colors, or colors with small vertical lines, to detract from her overweight. We will select an evening or afternoon dress of turquoise blue chiffon, designed on long, slenderizing lines, to take care of her social life. Chiffon will cling to her figure and give it the illusion of slenderness. Ruffles, of course, should be avoided, as well as wide belts. Her clothes should be simple in construction; our heroine, therefore, will leave the frills for her slender sister.

A pair of silver evening sandals will harmonize with the evening or afternoon gown. A pair of low-heeled black oxfords for sports and campus wear and a pair of black kid shoes for street and church occasions will give her feet a well-groomed appearance without making them conspicuous.

Her wardrobe may be supplemented occasionally with dark skirts and gayer sweaters of subdued hues.

After the garments needed are listed and their colors decided upon, the tentative cost should be placed after each article. If the total is too high, cut down on the cost of coats and dresses, the best items on which to economize. Accessories must look new and be of good quality, while the dress and coat may be so simple in cut that they look well though made of inexpensive materials.

By planning your entire wardrobe before anything is purchased, you can avoid the mistake of selecting the wrong color or of paying too much for any one item. A purple dress may be very becoming and very beautiful but if it does not harmonize with the rest of your wardrobe, you cannot wear it and appear well dressed.

When you are buying additional dresses, select those that harmonize with the things you have, and avoid choosing a color which would require a special pair of shoes and other accessories to make it a costume. No dress should be bought without having in mind the shoes which will complete the costume. By exercising such precautions as these you will introduce the elements of taste, economy, and business judgment into your shopping.

VI. Undergarments — Should we buy or make them?

There are so many inexpensive, attractive, and well made undergarments on the market today that most people prefer to buy their underwear ready made and use the time thus saved in doing something else they particularly enjoy or find worthwhile.

Undergarments should be dainty, clean, and well fitted so there will not be unattractive bulges in the outer garment. It is also important to our mental poise that they have a clean, dainty feel, and that they have a perfect fit. Soiled underclothes that smell of perspiration or fit uncomfortably affect our outward composure and make us self-conscious.

One of the most unattractive sights, that could be easily avoided, is a slip that shows beneath the dress. The best style of slip is now made with adjustable shoulder straps, which make lengthening or shortening the slip to fit the dress a quick and easy operation.

The most satisfactory materials for undergarments are silk, rayon, and cotton. Undergarments, with your hose, may be washed out in a few minutes just before going to bed. This will keep them clean and fresh for the next wearing and prolong their usefulness.

Girdles are not necessary if the hips or abdomen do not need to be held in.

VII. On Being Ready to Go.

If today you were to receive an invitation at school to attend a small informal gathering tonight, could you accept without hesitation, knowing that you could go home and dress for it immediately? Or would you have to think about the runner in your best pair of hose, the snap that must be sewed on your dress, the spots that must be removed, and the dress itself that needs pressing? It is well always to have one complete costume ready for immediate wear, from the well polished shoes to the well brushed hat. Many people who can afford the best of clothes and have a big variety of costumes never have anything to wear to an impromptu affair because some one part of each costume is soiled or misplaced.

VIII. The Well Groomed Foot

Since few people have feet so dainty as to attract undue attention, the style of shoes as a rule should follow fairly conservative lines in design, color, and material. Shoes should be chosen as everything else, to harmonize with the rest of the wardrobe. Generally speaking, dark colors should be worn in fall and winter; light colors in spring and summer. There are lovely combinations of colors in shoes that may be worn with several different costumes, so long as they match in color or in design some other detail of dress.

In the selection of shoes, the foot should always be measured while standing with your weight on it, as sizes of different brands vary. Shoes should be large enough to insure freedom but not so large as to rub the heel and cause blisters. Corns, bunions, crooked toes, and arch trouble are all caused by ill fitting shoes.

Medium or low heels are more conducive to correct posture, although wearing shoes with high heels occasionally for a few hours will do no harm. Such shoes should, however, not be worn to school, on the street, in sports, or in any activity which entails standing and walking over a long period of time.

Shoes are made from kid leather, patent leather, suede, velvet, satin, crepe, moire, metal cloth, gabardine, and straw. As a rule, leathers are worn for school, street, sports, and church wear and fabrics are worn at evening and party functions.

The choice of becoming shoes, of course, should be decided by the size and shape of the feet. Wide straps and buckles should be worn only by people with small, dainty feet and ankles as they tend to increase the appearance of width.

The correct fit and style of hose are important details in the appearance of a well-groomed foot. Service-weight stockings to harmonize with dresses should be worn at school and on the street, leaving the sheer and less durable hose for dress wear. Hose should be selected about half an inch longer than the feet to give freedom of movement but should fit snugly around the ankles. They should be rinsed out after each wearing.

If your feet tire easily, the following exercises will help to strengthen them:

(1) Practice picking up marbles, pencils, or other round objects with your toes and see if you can walk around the room without dropping them.

(2) Stand, rise high on toes, then lower heels slowly with weight resting on the outside of feet. This exercise will reduce ankles and calves.

(3) Lie on back on floor, arms extended above head, pushing down with toes. Without bending knees, rise slowly and try to touch end of toes with fingers, bending from waist. Chorus girls take this exercise to keep their legs and ankles trim and neat.

(4) Sitting, rotate the foot in a circle, flexing the ankle.

IX. Economical Accessories.

The day of shopping for hose, shoes, gowns, hats and accessories independently is passed. The wise girl will select a complete outfit to make a tasteful, harmonizing whole. By accessories we mean jewelry, flowers, gloves, shoes, hose, handkerchiefs, and bags and purses.

If the clothing allowance is small, it is best to select hats, gloves, and shoes which are dark and at the same time will look well with the rest of the ensemble. If not chosen so carefully as to harmonize, they may mar the effect of the complete ensemble, but if chosen harmoniously, they will seem the one touch needed to complete the effect. The season's wardrobe should be planned in its entirety and all accessories chosen to fit in with the rest of the wardrobe to avoid the expense of buying the correct articles to replace those not found suitable.

Accessories should be worn conservatively. The effect of a gold locket worn with a black dress would be stunning but if you added a flower, a bracelet, a pin, and a few rings, the effect would be gaudy. We need balance in accessories the same as in color and design.

Very little jewelry should be worn by either a girl or a boy. A girl may wear a thin gold chain, a bracelet, or a simple wrist watch, and a simple ring. A boy may wear a little-finger ring and plain gold cuff links.

Bags or purses are an important item in the accessory list. Purses should be of simple design and harmonize in color with the rest of the costume. For economical purposes, they should be of durable material. Suede is smart when in vogue but not durable. Leather purses as a rule are most useful. In the summer, purses of washable fabrics which harmonize with the gay summer prints are attractive. If you can have only one purse for summer use, a white one which can be washed is both inexpensive and attractive and will harmonize with any costume. A gay handkerchief tucked into the flap of the purse will add to its appeal.

Handkerchiefs may be "dressy" or tailored, depending upon their appropriateness to the occasion and the rest of the ensemble, as well as in material and design. The important thing is to have them clean and fresh.

Gloves are of more than minor importance and must be clean and well cared for. Clean, but cheap gloves are much more attractive than expensive ones that are soiled.

Flowers should fit the personality as well as the ensemble. Gardenias for the girl who is fond of sports and who wears tweeds; orchids for the sophisticated woman in satin or chiffon; a rosebud for the wearer of a tailored street dress or suit.

Perfume should be used sparingly. If you cannot afford expensive perfume, do not use any. The smell of perfume should be subtle and only faintly discernible.

X. The Clothing Budget.

How much have you expended on your clothes for the past twelve months? The annual cost of clothing for those living on moderate incomes should average about fifteen percent of all their expenses. Have you ever thought about the cost of the clothing you wear and how much money your family is required to provide in order that you may be dressed throughout the year? Are you giving in return service equal to the cost of your clothing?

Many people spend more than is necessary by buying unwisely in such ways as selecting materials that fade or are not suited to the occasions for which they are needed, or are not durable. If clothing of good quality is properly cared for, clothing expenses will be materially reduced.

Buying fads, novelty materials, and exaggerated styles is exercising poor judgment since such things can be worn for only a short time.

List the clothing you have on hand and your clothing needs for the next year. Build your wardrobe around a definite color scheme becoming to your type.

In making a budget, clothing may be divided into three groups: (1) outer or protective clothing; (2) under-garments; (3) accessories. Under (1) list coats, dresses, skirts, waists, suits, hats, shoes, hose, and sports clothes; under (2) list slips, brassieres, pajamas, garters, step-ins, shorts; under (3) list gloves, handkerchiefs, and purses. After each item, put the number you think you will need, and the cost.

XI. Boys' Clothes.

Boys' clothes present fewer problems in that boys do not "cater" to the new in clothes as girls do. The best sort of grooming for boys has an aspect of casual negligence about it. The typical boy's clothes fit rather loosely; his collar is not too high or too tight, his tie not too stiff or thick, and his shoes and hose are comfortable.

One of the most important items in dress for boys is that of good shoes. The leather and workmanship should be of good quality. Then too, it is important that good care should be given them by polishing them often and putting them on shoe trees at night.

Tweeds are good for day time wear; serge is good for street or school occasions. A color scheme of blue and gray or brown and tan is a good one around which to build the boy's wardrobe. Men's clothes are more neutral in color than those of women and hence it is easier to select harmonizing supplements. Tan shoes, brown socks, and a dark tie might be worn with either a grayish brown suit or one of olive brown.

The best all-round investment in the way of a suit for any boy is a dark suit. A dark suit is suitable for school, calls, church, and very informal dances and dinners. With a soft felt hat, gray suede gloves, and black shoes, a boy will appear well dressed if:

His suit is cleaned and pressed
His handkerchief white and immaculately clean
His shoes black and well polished
His collar immaculate
His socks and tie conservative and harmonizing with each other and with the suit.

XII. Shall We Dress in Fashion or in Style?

Fashion in dress is the accepted or popular method of wearing our clothes. It is determined by many passing things — such as (1) our mode of living with its accent on health which keeps in fashion the shorts and slacks that girls now wear in sports because they allow freedom of action; (2) a national event of importance, such as the development of aviation which popularized airplane prints in dresses; (3) the taste of some one of importance as illustrated by the popularity of "Eleanor Blue" the favorite color of Mrs. Franklin D. Roosevelt, wife of the President; and (4) a sensational event such as the wedding of the Duke of Windsor and Mrs. Simpson, which has given rise not only to changes in designs and colors of dresses, but in hairdress as well.

When important and interesting world events transpire, there often follows a "change in fashion." But since great events are constantly happening and we never follow one fashion long at a time, "Dame Fashion" gets blamed for our own fickleness and inconstancy.

Style, however, fundamentally applies to the appropriateness of designs, colors, and fabrics in relation to the personality of the individual. Hence one can always dress in style without blindly yielding to the dictates of fashion. When we have style in our clothes, they become us in color, design, and fabric. On the contrary, we may be dressed in fashion and yet look incongruous. Regardless of how fashionable plaids may be, the short, fat girl who wears them is sacrificing her appearance to fashion. Better for her the more subdued colors and lines that minimize the disproportions of her figure.

It is never necessary to expend a lot of money to dress correctly. Study the fashion trends and pick the permanent from the passing fancy. Above all, avoid fads.

CHAPTER 13

THE HOME BEAUTY CLINIC

A radiant, attractive personality is inseparable from both physical and mental health; we can no more neglect one than the other. This truism applies as well to the girl with perfectly chiseled features and well moulded form as to her plainer and less fortunate sister. The former can claim no more than the semblance of beauty if her mental growth is neglected; and the latter places herself at further disadvantage if she neglects the care of her health and personal appearance.

Those of us who were not fortunate enough to be endowed by birth with "good looks" must not think that we can develop alert and interesting minds at the expense of health and physical self-care. Every girl must give constant attention to the care of her voice, skin, hands, eyes, figure, and dress. The obligation to be well groomed, if it applies with more force to one girl than another, falls more heavily upon the girl with few claims to physical beauty.

Since one's face is the point of interest that first attracts other people's attention, everyone should want a fine, clear skin as the outward and visible sign of a good constitution, sound nerves, and abundant vitality. Although the skin is adaptable and resilient, habitual carelessness will in time give it a sluggish look. If one has a normal, healthy skin, it may be cleansed by washing thoroughly with mild soap and rinsing with cold water until all the soap is gone. If soap is not thoroughly rinsed off, it injures the skin.

The use of facial creams and lotions is not altogether a matter of personal vanity and extravagance. Soap and water alone have a difficult time keeping our skins clean or beautifully young. We have to combat not only climatic conditions but steam heat, grime, dust, and smoke. Cream is used for cleansing, lubricating, softening, and massaging to prevent wrinkles or crow's feet, and to give protection and normalize a skin which has been neglected. Today everyone must look her very best. It is not necessary to spend hours at the beauty parlor; the same results can be obtained at home with a few moments of intelligent care.

"Beauty culture is as old as the human race. When the tomb of King "Tut" was opened in modern times, it was found to contain perfume and unguent vases. In the days of Cleopatra ladies sought to make themselves more beautiful by the generous use of paint. Henna was liberally applied to the fingernails, the palms of the hands, and the soles of the feet. The eyes of Egyptian beauties were regarded as their most alluring feature. It is said that they painted the skin under the eyes green, and the lids, lashes, and brows black. Even today beauty preparations of the East are much like those of the ancient times when Queen Chesha cooked donkey's hoofs with the fat of black snakes and applied the resultant concoction to her skin. In America women of refinement seek to emulate natural youth; women in Egypt and India strive to improve upon Nature.

"The Romans were noted for the luxury of their baths. They had rouge and lipstick much as we know it today, and women in the heyday of Rome bleached and dyed their hair. Incidentally, bobbed hair is not a modern fad. It was popular during the reign of Louis XIV of France; the 'Dutch Bob' was the accepted style when James I was king of England."

Skin Types.

The human skin is usually divided into three types— normal, dry, and oily. However, one's skin may vary during the different seasons of the year and indifferent climates. A normal skin sometimes appears oily in summer and dry in winter. A few people have dry and oily patches at the same time. Proper care, which includes cleanliness, a well-balanced diet, and the sensible use of cosmetics, will do much to keep the skin lovely, soft, and smooth with a clear, healthy color. The normal skin is ample evidence of good health, physical and mental, controlled emotions, a sunny disposition and sensible habits of living. A balanced diet and cleanliness are necessary to keep the normal skin in good condition. Good soap and warm water, with thorough rinsing, are used for cleanliness, and cleansing cream, if one can afford it, to remove all dirt and make-up. A good cold cream may then be smoothed on and wiped off just before retiring.

The Dry Skin.

Dry skin is thin, chaps easily, and feels and looks drawn. A dry skin often looks very shiny, but this dry shiny skin should not be confused with that of an oily skin. Dry skins line and wrinkle early in life unless care and constant attention are given. Soap and water should not be used on the dry skin; use clear, cold water in rinsing and cleanse the skin with a good cleansing cream, wipe off with tissue, put on skin freshener, and then apply tissue cream. In reality a nightly facial should be given to keep a dry skin in good condition, youthful, and unlined.

The Oily Skin.

Oily skin is usually of a coarser texture than either the dry or normal skin. It is shiny and when rubbed gently makes the tissue used look wet. Powder does not stay on the oily skin very well and it sometimes makes the skin look gray. Oily skin often has black- heads and pimples because it is hard to keep clean. Therefore it should be cleansed frequently — every night, and every time the face is made up if possible. First, wash with a good alkaline soap, then use cleansing cream, wipe this off in a few minutes, and then apply pads of cotton dipped in an astringent. Powder base cream is usually not needed with an oily skin.

A Combination Skin.

Some skins have both dry and oily patches and consequently treatment for both types should be used. Dry cheeks, oily nose and forehead are examples. Use cleansing cream and astringent but use more astringent in oily patches. Use cream on dry places -every day, such as the cheeks, but seldom on the nose and forehead. For make-up, use a cream base on the cheeks and an astringent on the nose and forehead.

Facials.

In the nervous and fatiguing life of today, facials will do much toward keeping women buoyant, well poised and happy. A good facial with proper massage will take years off the face and do much toward giving an expression of greater self-confidence, and, in fact, brighten up the mental point of view as a whole.

The first step in a facial should be to secure relaxation of the entire body in order to rest the nerves. The face and neck should then be thoroughly cleansed, the pores of the skin opened to remove poisons, the circulation of the blood stimulated through massage, the skin softened and lubricated to help prevent lines and wrinkles and to eradicate any which may be present. The pores should then be closed by rubbing the face gently with ice, after which the make-up should be applied.

A facial should benefit the whole body; rest, relaxation and complete quiet are therefore urged. In a serene atmosphere, nerves relax and strain disappears, leaving the face years younger. When giving a facial to yourself or another, thoroughly cleanse the hands and lubricate the skin with a little cleansing cream;

knead deep into the muscles at the back of the neck and down the spine to un-kink the tired nerve centers; then upward, kneading the muscles at the side of the neck to make the blood flow more quickly through the great arteries which nourish the brain.

The Cleansing.

Pin a towel around the neck of the dress to protect it and an- other towel around the hair to keep it out of the way.

Apply a generous amount of cleansing cream to the face and neck and gently smooth it on; then wipe off as much of the cream and surface soil as possible, working gently with upward movements. Apply more cream, wring out a bath or linen towel in hot water and fold it around the face, with room for breathing space, and leave it on until it cools. The warm towel opens the pores and softens the blackheads. Wipe off the excess cream with cleansing tissue.

Massage.

Apply tissue cream with long upward strokes over the face and neck generally. Follow the line of the jaw and cheek bones with firm yet gentle strokes. This procedure will help to firm the muscles and prevent sagging. Then slap gently with the finger tips, up the line of the jaw, and along the jaw to the temple and around the forehead. "Creep" the fingers upward, stroke very, very gently round the eyes, outward and upward and inward and beneath. Do not stretch or pull anywhere. Pads of absorbent cotton wrung out with skin freshener, or witch hazel, and placed over the eyes are refreshing. Massage the throat directly under the chin, using long, firm molding movements, work from the chin to the ears and from the middle of the back of the neck forward to the ears. Most of the cream will be absorbed, but wipe off the excess, gently, with tissue.

Stimulation.

To remove the cream, apply skin freshener if the skin is dry, an astringent if the skin is inclined to be oily or blemished. Pat it on generously, covering the entire surface. This should leave the skin glowing and soft with a fine clear appearance. One should feel rested after a facial.

Frequency of Facials.

How often should facials be given? The frequency with which one should be given a facial depends upon the condition of the skin. The young girl with a fresh complexion needs facials only occasionally, only to keep her skin dainty, lovely and beautiful. The person with a dry skin should give the skin careful care every night and every few days a real facial. The person beginning to show signs of age, wrinkles, and crow's feet needs a daily facial. Persons with oily skins need facials only for extra stimulation; once every two or three weeks is sufficient.

Acne.

Acne is a skin disease caused by the inflammation of the oil glands which become plugged by blackheads. Stoppage of these glands causes pimples which sometimes become infected and may cause boils and sometimes even permanent scars. Acne usually affects the face, shoulders, and back. It occurs most frequently among boys and girls in their teens. It is curable when proper treatment is given but with improper or no treatment, difficulties arise. Sometimes adults suffer all their lives with acne because of neglect and an improper health regimen. Acne is really a disease of the oil glands lying directly over the blood stream. Internal treatment is usually most necessary. Highly seasoned foods such as chop suey, chow mein, chile con carne, and soda water should be indulged in but rarely or not at all. Thorough bathing is necessary together with plenty of sleep, exercise, and plain food. Fruits and vegetables are required to build up the body and help it throw off this condition, which is really a disease. Proper elimination and plenty of water are necessary. A daily bath in rich suds that are thoroughly rinsed off is a necessity. Be sure that the hands are thoroughly scrubbed before starting treatment. Picking at blackheads and pimples causes serious trouble. The pus in the pimples is highly infectious and may cause similar sores anywhere it comes in contact with the skin.

Blackheads.

After washing the hands and face thoroughly in warm water, sterilize the blackhead remover in boiling water or pour a reliable antiseptic on it and press gently on the blackhead. If the blackhead will not come out leave it for the next treatment. If the blackhead comes out, touch the spot with an antiseptic astringent.

Whiteheads.

Whiteheads, like blackheads, are symptoms of an infected skin, that has become so because the pores are inactive and oil has collected in the glands and formed a hard white mass underneath the skin. Blackheads are formed in the outlet to the gland by oil near the surface which collects dirt and makes the "blackhead"; but whiteheads are formed underneath the skin. Use a sterilized needle to make an opening and gently press the hardened material out; then apply an astringent.

Pimples.

Pimples which are not headed should be left alone. Those which are headed may be opened with a sterilized needle and the pus gently expelled. Touch the spot with absorbent cotton which has been saturated with astringent. Now apply cleansing cream, working lightly over the affected parts, and then wipe off the cream with cleansing tissue. Finish up by wiping the face with cotton saturated with astringent. A light application of cream to the sore place will help it to heal quickly and prevent permanent scars.

Very little make-up should be used when suffering from any kind of skin disease. Lipstick and mascara of course will do no harm but never use a powder puff twice, particularly with acne. It is best to use absorbent cotton, never putting the cotton back into the box for more powder. The germs which get into the powder puff may get back into the skin and cause trouble since acne is infectious. No one else should use the wash cloth, towels, or anything else used by one who has acne.

Enlarged Pores.

Enlarged pores usually accompany an oily skin. The treatment is therefore the same as for oily skin. Use a good soap frequently with plenty of warm water and rinse thoroughly, afterward applying cleansing cream and an astringent to make sure the skin is absolutely clean and the underlying tissues stimulated. Every other night apply pore cream before retiring. Never make up without removing the old make-up and thoroughly cleansing the skin. Keep powder puffs clean.

Freckles.

The best way to treat freckles is to prevent them. A good powder base and a darker shade of face powder than one would ordinarily use gives much protection from sun and wind. Bleach cream may be used at night; use a bleach cream that does not peel the skin but gradually lightens the skin. Freckles are those single small flat spots which vary from light-salmon to darkest brown. Some brown spots are caused by internal disturbances and should be under the doctor's treatment. Those who freckle should use a bleach cream at night the year round and good powder base. For covering freckles use liquid powder as a base and apply regular make-up over the liquid powder.

How to Select and Apply Make-up.

Make-up of a good quality does not injure the skin. We should, however, use immaculate puffs and apply make-up only to a clean skin. Powder does not disguise a bad complexion, so your skin should be smooth and healthy. Powder and rouge should be blended well into the skin and all make-up should be applied in front of a well-lighted mirror since you are likely not only to use too much but to apply it unevenly.

Choose powder and rouge to harmonize with your general coloring. Brunettes, with their basic coloring of orange, usually choose from cream, ochre, and suntan shades, while the blond, with her delicate violet-pink coloring, usually finds natural, flesh, and peach more harmonious. Violet-pink rouge harmonizes better with the blond's coloring and orange with the brunette's. In summer, powder a shade or two darker than that for winter use may be used. Lipstick should be chosen which does not clash with the color of your dress.

How to Apply Rouge.

Rouge is generally applied in the shape of a triangle and carefully blended into the skin because no harsh line should show where the rouge is applied. When one has a too round face, rouge should be placed on the side of the face and gradually extended up to the temple and down to the lobe of the ear. One with a long narrow face should start the rouge near the nose on the cheek bone, gradually carrying it up to the temple and down to the lobe of the ear, blending most carefully. The person with a well-shaped face neither too round nor too long starts the rouge on the cheek bone just below the pupil of the eye, then gradually takes the rouge up to the temple and down to the lobe of the ear. In each case, the general shape is that of a triangle. One is long, one is wide, and with the regular featured person the triangle is equilateral. Going up and down narrows the face, going across widens it.

How to Powder.

After the rouge is applied, powder should be added. It should be fluffed on the face gently, not slapped on carelessly. An immaculately clean powder puff is necessary for the wellbeing of the skin; absorbent cotton and swansdown make excellent powder puffs. Relax the face when powdering; screwing the face up makes the powder go on unevenly. Wrinkled parts do not receive the powder evenly, especially when the face is not relaxed. Fluff the puff lightly on the face with a downward stroke, then turn the puff over or get a clean one and go over the face lightly again. Brush off excess powder. When powder is correctly applied it softens the features and really protects the skin.

Liquid powder is really a powder suspended in a slightly astringent liquid. Apply it by shaking the container thoroughly and pouring out a little on a sponge; then smooth the liquid on the skin, after moistening the fingers. Add regular make-up. Liquid powder is a make-up base and should not rub off. It is used on the arms, neck, and back in the evening make up.

How to Apply Lipstick.

Lipstick is said to give the final touch. It really protects the lips and keeps them from aging and cracking. Some mouths need a little coloring; some lips are too pale, too thin, or too thick. Some mouths are too large, others too small. Lipstick rightly used will improve such things. For the too thin mouth, lipstick is rouged over both upper and lower lips, all over. The too thick mouth is rouged only partly and powdered up to the rouge line. Cupid's bow is accented when the mouth is too large and powder is used over the corners. The too small mouth is rouged to the full extent. Lips are moistened before applying the lipstick. The lipstick is then rubbed over the part on which the accent is desired and the little finger is used to work it in. Biting with the lips on a fold of cleansing tissue takes off the excess cream and prevents an artificial look. Powder brushed lightly on the lips helps to prevent the artificial appearance disliked by so many people.

Selection of Make-up

If a girl or woman has no natural coloring, she should gently pinch her cheek or hand and compare the color with the plaques of rouge on the color catalog, removing make-up first, of course. The rouge which is nearest one's own natural color is the correct color. When in doubt, select the light shade.

Cream rouge is the easiest to apply; it is blended with a powder base of cream, a liquid. Cream rouge is perhaps more natural in appearance and lasts until it is removed.

Eye Make-up.

If given half a chance, eyes will take care of themselves. Do not abuse them by reading in a poor light or by straining them. If in reading the eyes tire easily or if the prints run together on the page and if there is a tendency to squint and to have frequent headaches, the eyes should be examined by a good oculist. Do not buy glasses without first being examined by a dependable oculist.

When mascara is used, it should be used in the right way and only standard products should be used. For giving eyes a bigger, brighter appearance, mascara is applied to the eyelashes, darkening the whole length of the eyelash.

Eyelashes are really lighter at the tips and for that reason do not seem as long as they really are, hence a little darkening really makes them seem longer. The application of mascara is really simple. Use the long brush which comes in the box, moisten the brush and rub over the cake of mascara, then touch the tips of the eyelashes with the brush. Do not apply it thickly and do not make the lashes look beaded. If by accident some gets on the cheek or eyelids, rub it off with a wet cloth at once ; and remember it must be removed while wet as good mascara is smudge-proof. Blonds usually look better with brown mascara, other types with black mascara.

Eye shadow should be used sparingly and only at night. Blue eyes may be given depth by blue eye shadow, dark eyes by light brown, blue, or green. Do not use eye shadow that is darker than the eyes. To make small eyes appear larger, draw a line around the eye with an eyebrow pencil, extending it beyond the outside of the eye. With the little finger, rub the line lightly so that it will not be definite.

If the eyes are prominent, apply comparatively heavy shading on the lower part of the lid. If the eyes are too near together, place the shadow away from the nose. If the shadow is placed near the bridge of the nose, the eyes appear to be closer together.

Teeth.

Have the teeth examined at least every six months by a good dentist. Keep them well brushed and clean. Clean teeth are beautiful and much less likely to be accompanied with diseased gums than those which are neglected.

Hands.

The hands receive harder use and less attention than almost any other part of the body, and since they are constantly in view, care should not only be given to them but to the nails as well. Hands should be kept out of very hot water and should not be washed with strong soap.

They should be dried thoroughly after each washing, and if the skin is dry, a hand lotion should be used. Gloves should be worn for rough work and during exposure to the wind and cold.

Keep the nails clean and relatively short. Dirt may be removed from beneath them with an orange stick tipped with cotton. The cuticle should be pushed gently back each morning to prevent its clinging to the nail. White vaseline rubbed into the nails and cuticle each night before going to bed will keep them smooth and prevent their cracking and breaking.

Stains may be removed with cuticle remover, lemon or tomato juice. Either powder polish or liquid polish may be used, the former by brushing briskly with a buffer. Liquid polish is applied with a brush and wiped off quickly from the half moon and end of nail.

Brightly colored nail polish is considered in poor taste and much too bizarre for everyday wear.

Hair.

Good health is the foundation of beautiful glossy hair. Daily care is also essential. The color of the hair is unimportant if it is clean, glossy, and well brushed. Dirty and oily hair cannot be beautiful. Mothers should care for their children's hair from infancy, brushing it daily, and keeping it scrupulously clean. Illness affects the condition of the hair and good care should be given to it after an illness of any kind. Hair grows normally at the rate of about one inch every six weeks. New hair is important. Regular scalp treatments, massages, and oil treatments will do much to make new hair continue growing normally and beautifully. Combs and brushes should be moderately stiff and washed frequently.

The "hundred strokes every night" rule is still a good one. Combs with short edges which catch and break hair should not be used.

Types of Hair.

There are three types of hair, in conformity with the skin, dry, normal, and oily; and each type takes special care:

Dry Hair.

Dry hair is usually stiff and colorless, often "wild" or fluffy and rather unmanageable. To test for dry hair, rub cleansing tissue along a part; if the hair is dry the paper will not show any discoloring. Oil treatments are a wonderful help for dry hair. Pour a little oil in a saucer, set it in hot water, and heat it. Dip a bit of cotton in the warm oil and rub it along the part and all over the scalp in both directions so that every bit of the scalp is covered. If the ends of the hair are dry, rub a little oil on the hair itself. Then wring out a bath towel in hot water and wrap it around the head to open the pores of the scalp. When cool, take the towel off and massage by planting the fingers firmly on the scalp and rotating the hand and scalp too. The healthy scalp is easily moved. If the scalp seems tight, it should be loosened by massaging. Remember it is the scalp one treats, not the hair. Oil should be left on overnight if possible. Specially prepared hair tonic for dry hair massaged into the hair daily will be of much benefit. Brilliantine brushed into the hair will add gloss and help to make the hair more easily managed.

Oily Hair.

Oily hair often accompanies illness, nervousness, extreme fatigue, and digestive disorder. The cause of oily hair is important and should be remedied if possible. Oily hair should be shampooed as often as it needs it. Oil treatment just before the shampoo will be helpful but do not leave oil on overnight. Specially prepared hair tonic may be used nightly according to directions. Wash hair brush and combs and keep them scrupulously clean.

Normal Hair.

Normal hair will remain lovely, barring ill health, as long as kept clean. When the brush appears soiled, it is time for a shampoo. Use hairdress or brilliantine to make hair more glossy. An occasional hot oil treatment and massage are beneficial to normal hair.

Permanents

Cheap permanents are apt to be frizzy and unattractive, as a result of the cheap and harsh chemicals that are used and the poor workmanship of improperly trained operators. Straight hair emphasizes youthfulness; waves at best have the disadvantage of making us appear older than we are.

Coiffure.

The hairline, texture of hair, shape of head, and facial features should determine the style of coiffure for each individual face. The hair is a background for the face. If the features are clear cut and the hairline beautiful, straight hair is usually more becoming, as it indicates youthfulness. But if you are unhappy without a permanent, then use curls and waves only to emphasize the beauty of lines in the face or head or to disguise bad features.

If the features are small, keep hair off the face. If features are not good, a soft wave on the hairline will minimize them. A simple wave on each cheekbone makes the broad face look more oval. Hair should always be dressed to emphasize the personality and lend color to it. Its biggest value is in showing off the head and face to the best possible advantage.

If you have a short face, keep the hair off your forehead; if your face is broad, bring the hair forward on your cheeks, keeping it flat over your ears.

Unit 4

THE HOUSE

CHAPTER 14

THE HOUSE WE LIVE IN

There are a number of important needs to consider in planning your home. Next to food and clothing providing suitable shelter is the most vital social and economic problem that confronts the individual family and the nation as a whole. The problem has some aspects that concern only the individual family; others that are fast becoming matters of concern to society at large. If the economic means are at hand with which the individual family may enlarge the house and improve its surroundings in order to create a happier home environment, the problem is one which concerns the attention of none but the members of that family. If, however, many, many families are compelled to live under conditions of housing and shelter that are inferior to actual physical, social, and spiritual needs, the solution of the problem ceases to be a matter of individual responsibility and falls upon society.

The children of parents who are too poor to rent homes or apartments that sufficiently provide shelter, are hampered and handicapped in their development during the very period in which they need most the comforts and conveniences that adequate shelter provides. Society is paying, in large part, for the education and training for citizenship of all such children. Therefore, society has the right to demand that the owners of property for rent by poor tenants shall render services commensurable with the prices they charge for houses and apartments.

Characteristics of a Good House.

The concept of house and that of home are not vastly different although much has been written in both prose and poetry to set forth the difference between house and home. In these tributes, by common consent the home is pictured as a sort of spiritual edifice built out of no more tangible substance than the emotions and attitudes of the family. Home is given a definition by these panegyrists from which the dependence upon physical shelter is entirely removed. Yet how well do we know that the house itself, its location, and its physical surroundings, must be satisfying in order that our emotional and social natures may find the means of normal expression. The protection, security, and privacy that are symbolized in the word home really emanate from the capacity of the house to furnish space, shelter, and convenience adequate to these needs. Therefore, if the house is comfortable, convenient, beautiful, and attractively environed, the emotional and spiritual attitudes that give home life its beauty have a congenial atmosphere in which to develop.

In the location and arrangement of the house, provision for the health of the family should receive first consideration. Requirements in this respect call for ample ventilation, adequate heat and light, plenty of sunshine, good drainage, clean streets, sufficient room space for members of the family, and a sanitary and otherwise desirable neighborhood. The requisite sanitary conditions and facilities include running water and sewage disposal, sunshine in every room some time during the day, screening against flies and other harmful insects, good drinking water, clean streets and backyards.

Not only should the house give protection from extremes of weather in all seasons, but it should be so located and constructed as to exclude noises from the street and from one part of the house to another. The privacy and opportunity for solitude, that are the due of every member of the family, the house should provide. And while it is ideal but not always practical for every member of the family to have his own bedroom, satisfactory provision can be made for privacy in many respects. In the sod or log house, the wigwam, or even the trailer, it is not expecting too much for every member of the family to have a place for his personal possessions — some space he can call his own.

More often than otherwise economic and social factors must be taken into consideration when the size of the house is in the process of determination. Many large families, finding it an economic necessity to limit space, have solved the problem of size with the use of three bedrooms, one for the parents, one for girls, and the other for boys.

Rooming together under these conditions has some distinct social advantages; valuable lessons in cooperation and mutual understanding are learned. It was Emerson who said, in his essay on Compensation, "For everything you have missed, you have gained something else; and for everything you gain, you lose something." Large families find enough joy and happiness in each other to compensate for the sacrifices they find it necessary to make.

A neighborhood free from moral hazards, which has the protecting influence of churches, good schools, playgrounds, and parks is much to be desired. Many cities pass housing laws which give protection to very poor people and the very ignorant but leave much to the good judgment of the average citizen.

Houses should conform to the laws of beauty and order. Good judgment in the selection of a site and plans for building a house and taste in the selection of its furnishings are only attained by much study and careful investigation. Because the house is the center of family life, time devoted towards making it as nearly ideal as possible is time well used.

It is well for a family to select some site for the location of the house and imagine themselves living in that locality long enough to learn whether or not home life there would be enjoyable. In this imaginary picture, place each member of the family at his daily task, as for instance, the younger children going to school, studying at home, and playing in the yard or nearby park, older children entertaining friends at home, going to church, and participating in the social life of the community. If satisfied with the ad- vantages the picture discloses, build there and make your home. If you are not satisfied, other locations should be studied.

For Future Home Owners

Whether we rent a home or buy one, there are certain advantages and disadvantages to be taken into consideration.

Home ownership affords a greater sense of permanency; it develops a feeling of pride and civic responsibility; it promises security in the period of old age. It has been said on good authority that ninety per cent of the divorces are procured by people who do not own their own homes. On the basis of this divorce record, the inference is easily established that home ownership provides a better home life for children; better social standing; better credit rating; more permanent marriages.

It is the usual procedure, and often a necessary one to finance the building of homes through installment loans. Paying these installments often develops the habit of thrift and of saving, and after the home is paid for, the family still continues to save the amount formerly applied on installments.

There are, as in everything else, disadvantages in owning a home. There is the possibility of financial loss through decrease in property values; there are increased responsibilities; should it be necessary to change locations, there is difficulty in renting to satisfactory tenants; and there is the possibility of losing money on a forced sale.

No one can begin too early to observe and compare advantages and disadvantages between owning and renting a home, as it is a decision which ultimately confronts almost everyone. It is well after deciding either to buy or rent to observe and compare the various types and features of houses so that a suitable choice may be made.

These factors should have a determining influence in making calculations for the expenditure of money in the purchase of homes:

1. Size of income. It is seldom that the amount spent in building a home should exceed twice the amount of one's annual income.

2. Size of family. It is obvious that a large family has more need for spacious shelter than a small one. The requisite number of bedrooms and bathrooms particularly depends upon the size of the family. Some families like to have an additional bedroom as a guest room for friends or relatives who visit them often. Additional space is sometimes needed for household employees.

3. Standards of living of the family. Is your family much accustomed to the art and practice of entertaining? If so, you require a larger living room than a family that seldom or never entertains. Also, if your family is musically inclined, you may require a music room. Many families have recreation rooms. Both the cultural background of the family and its personnel should be guiding influences in the choice of a home. It is also important to select a site where other families are of approximately the same financial and social status.

The most important problems in buying a home are:

1. Amount of Money the Family Can Afford to Invest. The most difficult condition or element in the problem of selecting a home is finding one that will be satisfactory without absorbing so much of the family's income as to lower their general living standards. The following considerations should influence the decision as to the amount to spend:

a. What is the family income? Is it stable or is it likely to decrease or increase? If the head of the family is a wage earner, or works on a salary, is there danger of his losing his job? The person who has sufficient savings to pay in full has, of course, no problem in financing the purchase of his home, but most people can make only a partial payment and must borrow the remainder and repay it from their earnings.

b. How much money does the family now spend annually for rent? If as much as one-sixth of the income is being spent for rent, one-fourth should be a safe percentage to spend in buying and maintaining a house, since this amount will include both rent and savings. Allowance must of course be made for repairs, taxes, insurance, water tax, improvements or additions, interest payments, and installments on the principal of the loan.

c. How much are the family's annual savings? Most families who buy a home must pay for it out of their savings. As a rule, they should have on hand, in cash, at least one-fifth of the value of the house and lot. The larger the cash payment, the lower the amount of interest. After the initial payment, the family should devote a certain amount of current savings toward paying off the loan at regular intervals. Since greater economy and saving are necessary, the wisest thing to do is to start a budget and cut down as many expenses as possible. Savings should be placed where they are safeguarded and yet yield a fair rate of interest.

d. Will anyone except the head of the family be able to contribute financially to the family income? Often during the period in which the home is being paid for, another member of the family is able to secure a job and help with the payments. High school boys and girls frequently secure work during the summer and help with their earnings in paying for their homes. It gives them a feeling of pride and a sense of ownership if they have contributed a small part towards purchasing the home they live in.

e. How much could the family afford to expend each year in making payments and for upkeep of the house? The majority of people, while paying for a home, are using between eighteen and thirty-five per cent of their annual income for these expenses which include payments and interest on the loan, taxes, insurance, water, fuel, gas and electricity, etc. The annual expenses involved in purchasing and maintaining a home obviously vary from one community to another. Thus a family with few children or residing in a community where living costs are low, can afford to pay out a larger proportion of their income toward buying a home.

2. Methods of Financing. The three methods of financing home ownership most often used are (1) paying all cash, (2) paying part cash and raising the remainder on a first or second mortgage, and (3) buying on a contract plan, which calls for making a small down payment and paying the remainder in monthly installments. Borrowing money to buy a home is no disgrace but on the contrary is a normal business practice and in many ways desirable.

Obtaining a loan is a simple matter when as much as from forty to fifty per cent of the cost has been made as the initial payment. The problem becomes harder as the proportion to be borrowed grows larger.

It is well for a person inexperienced in real estate matters to borrow from a responsible loan institution whose officials can give advice concerning the validity of the title, prices of property, back taxes and special assessments, insurance, and the tendency and range of property values within the next few years.

Borrowings may cost as much as ten or even fifteen percent a year. Loans may be made through building and loan companies, life insurance companies, savings banks, trust companies, mortgage companies, and national banks.

The building and loan associations were created for the promotion of thrift and home ownership. They provide a method of saving and lend their funds for the purchase and construction of homes. The most common plan used in this connection is by the members subscribing to "shares" and making regularly stated payments on them until the sum of the payments added to the dividends, obtained through the lending operations, is equal to the face value of the shares. Their loans are made for periods as long as twelve years; the interest is occasionally higher than that asked by savings banks and trust companies, but usually they pay a higher rate of returns to their depositors than is obtainable elsewhere. Lending policies and methods differ among the associations.

Life insurance companies make loans through local agents, banks, trust companies, and mortgage companies. Their loans run for periods as long as fifteen years; they seldom lend their funds for construction purposes, hence when a family builds its home, the money for construction must be supplied from some other source. The advantage of a loan from an insurance company is that the period over which the loan is made is so long that the borrower can usually avoid the necessity, trouble, and expense involved in renewing his loan.

Savings banks loans are usually made for short periods of one, three, and five years and are payable in full at the end of the term. However, an increasing number are making long term loans which are repayable in installments similar to those of building and loan associations and life insurance companies.

Trust companies have funds available for real estate loans. Their lending policies and methods are similar to those of savings banks.

Mortgage companies are not generally so closely confined in their activities by legal restrictions as other lending agencies and the use they make of their funds is left more to their own wishes. The loans of mortgage companies are made for short terms and long terms and on the amortized or straight basis. Many of them devote a large portion of their funds to construction loans.

National banks are so constricted by both federal and state laws that they have not been lending on real estate to any considerable extent. They do have large savings re- sources however and are a potential source of funds for home owners. They are permitted to use as much as one- half their savings deposits in realty loans for periods up to five years.

3. Maintenance Costs and Other Expenses. Besides the actual money used in building or buying a home, other expenditures include those for repair and upkeep, taxes, insurance, water, and miscellaneous items and improvements.

Expenditures for maintenance vary according to the quality of workmanship and the family's inclination and ability to make repairs promptly. This requirement cannot be determined by any fixed rule.

A house that is well maintained and kept in good repair by the latest improvements will not decline appreciably in value over a long period of years. Some of the maintenance costs that are most common are for repainting and repapering the interior walls every few years, repairing the interior, planting and caring for the grounds, repairing leaking roofs, replacing door and window screens, installing new water, sewer, and gas mains and electric light lines, adding such conveniences as a sleeping-porch, storm doors, or an extra bathroom. Maintenance cost also includes fire insurance, the cost of which depends upon the location of the house, the material of which it is built, and other factors.

4. Future Value of Property. In purchasing a house, it is well to find out the tax rate and the assessed valuation, so that an estimate may be made of the amount of taxes to be paid each year. A responsible loan institution will advise you as to whether the property you are planning to buy is likely to decrease in value within a few years. Naturally the future value of the property is an important factor in determining both the amount of money you will have to pay for your home, and the location of your home.

5. Methods of Lowering Home Building Costs. The high costs of building houses and the difficulty encountered in financing these costs are responsible to a large

degree for the low percentage of home owners in the United States. Our greatest housing problem is that of lowering home building costs without lowering at the same time our standards of living. Some methods which already have been tried as devices to reduce costs are mass production, use of factory-made parts whenever possible, less expensive improvements, cheaper land, elimination of waste in construction materials, standardization of building materials, better use of materials, substitutes for costly materials, cheaper financing, uniformity of building codes, omission of expensive built-in equipment.

Contributions of Government. During the past few years the Federal Government has encouraged home ownership by lending money to individuals wishing to build homes, at a very low rate of interest. The Federal Housing Administration guarantees loans made by banks, mortgage companies and similar institutions to the extent of 90% of the value of the property. These loans cover taxes, insurance, and interest as well as the principal and are re-paid monthly over a period of years, usually 20 years.

As a rule, a family that owns its own home takes more pride in it, gives it better care, and receives more pleasure from it. The owner cannot be evicted for failure to pay rent and can use money that would go to pay rent for other living expenses. He can make whatever changes or alterations he wishes without the consent of a landlord. He can truthfully say "My home is my castle." Democracy itself is made more secure by home ownership.

Will You Rent?

Delightful as owning your own home may be, there are also compensations in the rented house or apartment. For one thing, there is less responsibility in the care of house and property. Renting is preferable to buying or building, also, when one's position makes frequent moving a necessity or when taxes, the cost of maintenance, upkeep, and financing are too high. The main disadvantages in renting are that the family is less likely to plan for the future; the standards and ideals of living conditions are often lowered through inability to secure from the owner the desired repairs and changes; tenants may be requested to move at inconvenient times because the owner has decided to sell the house, or another tenant has offered him a higher rental.

Nevertheless, the house we live in, whether rented or owned, is undeniably associated with our physical needs — food, clothing, and shelter, and for that reason housing conditions will continue for years to come as one of the most vital problems of the nation. The importance of this problem cannot be minimized in either its social or its economic aspects. Shelter in a comfortable home or in a room, even for varying lengths of time, actually gives the feeling of security, the sense of privacy and of belonging, so necessary to the mental poise and peace of the individual and the masses of our population.

When the family has decided that it is wiser to rent than to buy a house, there are still other factors which must be decided, the most important of which is the type of home to rent. The type which usually meets best the requirements of the family is the "one-family house," however types may range from the hotel room or suite, and the efficiency apartment, to the huge house with many rooms and the requisite staff of servants.

After deciding the type of home to rent, the family should decide how much rent it can afford to pay. Not more than twenty per cent of the family income should be spent for rent without heat, or twenty-five per cent when heat is included, otherwise other essentials such as food, clothing, and recreation must be neglected. It is sometimes necessary to live in less desirable quarters in order to provide other important items in the budget. It is sometimes possible to reduce rental costs by taking a lease on the house or apartment for a definite period of time. Many property owners will not rent to a tenant unless he takes a six months or year's lease. This arrangement serves to protect the renter from having to move during the period of time covered by the lease, or from having to pay more rent should property values and rentals increase. Houses may be rented either furnished or unfurnished, the same as apartments, the rent of course being somewhat higher for furnished ones.

One of the disadvantages often encountered in renting apartments is the lack of garden or yard space, and the distance from a park or other recreation center. If possible, an apartment or house should be selected which is near enough to a park that children may go there for play and adults for amusement or meditation.

An advantage often found in an apartment not found in a house, is the convenience of free garbage and yard service. Often also, in an otherwise unfurnished apartment, there is an electric refrigerator on the same meter with the other apartments in the house which rids the budget of the necessity to take care of the unstable item of electricity.

Although there is not so much responsibility for the care of property in rented houses or apartments, a great many tenants take exceptional pride in their rented homes and do their best to keep them in good repair. Because a family rents, it is not to be inferred that they do not care for beautiful and attractive surroundings. On the contrary, they may appreciate and admire beauty in the homes of others as well as in their own. Often we find a lovely collection of beautiful vases and bottles adorning the rooms of a rented house or apartment; family heirlooms are cherished as much here, as in other homes, although perhaps not so often, due to the danger of loss by breakage and frequent moving. The following poem is characteristic of the best type of renter:

RENTED HOUSE

"You rent this home?" I asked, amazed,
The place looked so contented.
"This home is mine," she proudly said,
"It's just the house that's rented."

— *Gladys Warwick*

Choosing the Home Site.

In selecting the location for our home, whether we are to rent or to buy, the following factors must be considered:

Health conditions
Character of neighborhood
Nearness to church, school, friends, business
Transportation facilities
Scenery and surroundings
Protection of property
Size of lot
Cost

Sunshine and fresh air are essentials that should not be ignored in the search for a healthful site, because sunlight prevents the growth of bacteria and fresh air carries away the impurities which collect. For this reason then, it is wise to select a site that rises above its surroundings and is not too much shaded by trees or other buildings. A supply of fresh water, and the conveniences of gas and electricity are important from the viewpoint of health. A lovely view is another valuable asset. Some people prefer an attractive lot that is already set out in trees and shrubs;

others get a great deal of enjoyment out of taking an unimproved lot, fixing it up, selecting and planting the kinds of flowers and shrubs that would harmonize with the other surroundings, and caring for them from the first.

For families with children, a yard is especially desirable. It is doubly important, if there are children, that the character of the neighborhood should be of the type in which children would have wholesome associations as they grow into young manhood and young womanhood.

If the prospective home site is not within walking distance of churches, schools, and stores, there should be a nearby bus or street car line. In determining the cost of the location, on either a rental or a purchase basis, it is necessary to consider transportation costs. When locations are not within walking distance of work and school, it entails car fare and occasional meals away from home. On the other hand, perhaps there is less danger of contracting disease, which would reduce the probable expenditure for doctors' bills; and perhaps there is room for a garden, which would be an economic asset as well as the means of providing recreation and exercise.

Before buying the lot, an appraisal should be made by a disinterested third person. Usually a building and loan company will give a fair appraisal. The judgment of dependable real estate dealers is always worthwhile.

If you want to base your home-building project "on solid grounds," literally as well as figuratively, you should "look beneath the surface" of the real estate deal — figuratively as well as literally!

A home is more than just a house. By the same token, a proper home site is more than just so much dirt. It may or may not have the qualities that make it desirable as a permanent location for a dwelling, and profitable as an investment in real property.

So here is a list of thirty items by which to judge whether the lot you are thinking of buying is mere real estate or a good home site.

1. Buy the knowledge of a dependable real estate expert; that is, patronize a dealer of high standing in the community.

2. Buy an appraisal. Consult a second disinterested real estate man or a professional appraiser and pay him his relatively small fee for making an analysis of the value of the property before you purchase it.

3. Buy an absolutely clear title. You may require the seller to establish his title to the property before you buy it, or you may employ a lawyer or a title guarantee company to search the title for you. This is vitally important and is worth the expense.

4. Buy exact boundaries. Don't take the seller's word as to property lines but see that they are accurately established at the time when the title is purchased.

5. Buy sunlight, not smoke and dust. If you are going to the trouble of acquiring your own permanent home, you might just as well have it in a location that is sure to be healthful for your children.

6. Buy exposure to the winds that prevail in summer. When looking over the lot, keep in mind the house you intend to place on it and try to see whether or not it will be comfortable.

7. Buy enough land. The minimum should be from 40 to 60 feet of frontage. Old-style 25 and 28 and 30-feet lots in crowded districts are poor investments. The wider your lot, the greater your chances for a price increase.

8. Buy solid earth. In filled-in tracts, or "made" land, there always is danger of poor drainage or a chanoe that the house will settle. Either settling or bad drainage will damage the structure.

9. Buy high land. This is necessary if drainage is to be satisfactory. A low-lying lot may mean a water proofing problem.

10. Buy level land. Filling a lot to bring it up to the desired level is almost as costly as excavating.

11. Buy land of good shape. A lot of irregular outline may prove difficult to sell.

12. Buy good soil. Remember that excavating in rock may prove more expensive than you wish to undertake, that quicksand or other defects of the soil may result in damage to your house, but that under-surface sand or gravel may be an advantage if it is of such quality that it can be used for the mortar, plaster, or stucco.

13. Buy land fully developed or already under development. It is safer, though more expensive, than acreage which may be developed in the distant future.

14. Buy water and gas mains, graded and paved streets, sewers, walks and curbs already installed, or else add the estimated cost of taxes for these improvements to the price of your lot. Property with all these utilities in and fully paid for should not cost you more than 30 per cent of the total investment you plan to make, though 20 per cent would be a much safer figure. Land without these improvements should not cost more than 10 per cent of the total.

15. Buy moderate taxation. If you have any choice as to the state, county, or city in which you intend to build your home, acquaint yourself fully with the taxing policy of the authorities and estimate what the taxes will add to the cost of maintaining your dwelling.

16. Buy good transportation to your work, church, schools, and shopping centers. Measure the distance, not in miles, but in time it takes to get there. The ideal home lot is three or four blocks from transportation lines and stations.

17. Buy good collateral on a building loan; that is, choose a lot on which a bank or building and loan association will advance you at least 50 or 60 per cent of its value. If they won't lend you more than 40 per cent you may question whether or not you are paying too much.

18. Buy fire and police protection. See that your neighborhood is well served by these city departments.

19. Buy partnership in the community. "Restricted residential districts" may serve as protection against persons with whom your family won't care to associate, provided the restrictions are enforced and are not merely temporary.

20. Buy the right to build according to your own standard of living. The building restrictions may call for a more expensive house than you can afford to build and maintain.

21. Buy a well-balanced investment. That is, don't put much more or much less than one-fifth or one-fourth of your total funds into the lot. The construction should cost you three or four times the purchase price of the land.

22. Buy a sound investment, so far as you and your appraiser can judge future values. Population and transportation are the two chief elements in increasing home-site values. Be sure your property is in the line of residential, not industrial or commercial growth of the city.

23. Buy freedom from easements; investigate thoroughly to find out whether or not anyone has any right to lay pipes or erect poles or make a right-of-way on your lot.

24. Buy a good location within the block. Remember that a corner lot may be double-assessed for streets and sidewalks and that it will require longer fences. See that your lot is such that your neighbor's kitchen or garage won't be a nuisance.

25. Buy a real share of parks, playgrounds, and schools. An ideal location is about half a mile from these.

26. Buy freedom from traffic dangers and noises. A through street may prove a menace to your children and to the daily comfort and nightly slumber of the whole family.

27. Buy a chance at future favorable development. Examine the chances of public utilities, parks or boulevards being brought closer to your property in the future — and then be sure that such developments would be to the advantage and not to the detriment of the property.

28. Buy "a sure thing." If at all possible, it would be well for you to rent and live in a neighborhood for a year before undertaking to buy and build there.

29. Buy beauty. Too many trees are better than too few; natural objects of beauty will save you the cost of development and will help you dispose of the property advantageously when the time comes.

30. Buy a home, not a speculation. You would accept many things in buying just to make money which you wouldn't consider if you were buying for permanence. Set your ideal high — you probably will have to modify it, but it's safer to modify a high ideal than a low one.

Of course, a home lot possessing all these thirty advantages may be more than an ideal — it may be a physical as well as a financial impossibility in your town. But these are the things you should have in mind before you buy. Don't let anyone "talk you out of them."

CHAPTER 15

HOME ARCHITECTURE AND LANDSCAPING

Architecture is classified as a fine art along with music, painting, and sculpture. In these fields of endeavor the finest creations have invariably been the products of composers, painters, sculptors, and architects who possessed both genius and talent and above all the capacity for mastering the underlying theories and techniques of their arts. How fortunate are we who love beautiful things that some individuals are endowed by birth with creative talents and aspiring souls — souls that will not be satisfied until the ideals of the brain take physical shape, form, and substance in those works of art we most dearly prize.

The rewards of the true artist have ever been public recognition and appreciation of his creations rather than the money they brought at sale. Yet artists must live and we must have the products of their art to beautify a world that is constantly being made more drab and smoke filled as the result of industrial expansion into one new area after another. Thus as we grow in recognition and appreciation of the artist's work, we supply incentive and inspiration for him to carry on and to that extent at least do we become the patrons of his art.

Unfortunately, there is the spurious in art, the offensive, that which violates the principles of taste. For this reason, the layman should have access to information by which to judge and make tasteful selections in the purchase of the works of art. In recognition of the universal need for information by the coming generation, this chapter is devoted to a discussion of architecture and landscaping from the viewpoint of the future home maker who at some time will have to exercise the knowledge at her command in plans for her own home life.

"Architecture," said the poet Goethe, "is frozen music." The poet's metaphor signifies that architecture has all the elements of beauty that are heard in good music such as rhythm, emphasis, measure, proportion, repetition, variation, balance, and harmony. It is frozen only because its beauty is fixed and conveyed to us through the sense of sight rather than through the vibrant and warmer sense of hearing.

As a rule, the fine arts make their best contributions to human society in the production of objects that in purpose and function are wholly cultural. Unlike the other arts, architecture, the glorious exception to this rule, has a function of practical usefulness, separate and apart from esthetic considerations — that of providing shelter for man in the various forms his activities demand. The need for shelter, as acute as that for food, could have been met without calling upon art to render assistance, by the use with slight variations in purpose and design of the crude forms of shelter that primitive man devised for his protection. But as man grew in intelligence and feeling, his un- adorned home abode and surroundings provoked a state of mental unrest and a craving for things that would satisfy his mind. His first efforts to meet the demands of his mind in this respect mark the dawn of art in architecture.

From the birth of his desire for beauty in his surroundings, man has ever manifested that desire by his efforts to apply art to the structures he has created for shelter purposes. Traces of these efforts are found along the entire pathway of history, beginning with the crude color decorations of cavern abodes, and ending in the triumphs of accomplishment that are signalized by the achievements of the modern architect. It is not to be inferred that architecture is classified as a fine art merely because its products are made beautiful by the use of color and the expression of correct form and proportion. It has other claims than these — the purpose and function must be truthfully expressed. For example; where strength, stability, and resistance are demanded of certain structural parts these qualities must not only exist in actuality but suggest themselves in the appearance of such parts. The exterior must also suggest the meaning and uses of the structure such as solemnity and dignity of form in churches; simplicity, strength, and character in bank buildings, etc.

Architecture makes use of such laws as proportion, harmony, balance, emphasis, and rhythm. These laws call upon mathematics for help in the expression of form. Scale enters the picture too, as an enabling factor in estimating size and form. The layman who is a prospective builder or purchaser needs information that will enable him to act intelligently in making the transaction. It is not expected that he should try to fathom the intricacies of scientific and artistic knowledge with which the architect must equip himself. Such study is unnecessary because the layman needs only to acquaint and familiarize himself with the standards by which the products of architecture are judged to be in conformity with the principles of taste — -laws of beauty and order, purpose, use, and use of description of some of the most important of these standards seems necessary at this point.

Proportion, literally meaning share, is used in architecture as a term to express the correct relationship of one part to another or that of a part to the whole. A church tower too high or too heavy for the rest of the building, windows, or doors would immediately attract more than its share of attention and thereby create a dissatisfying effect. The same tower, if built in the right relationship of height and width to the whole, would give a pleasing effect. You can multiply examples of windows, doors, roofs, and lawns that annoy you by being out of proportion as well as examples that please you by being correct in all the details of proportion if you but use your eyes as you go about.

In architecture, balance has several uses also. It may have the meaning of weight equally distributed, equality of size between objects, equality of open spaces one with another, or the restful effect upon the mind when things are seen in a satisfying relationship such as window with window, windows with doors, or the distribution of shrubbery.

Rhythm, which you recognize in music and dancing as the flow and regularity of movement, has a similar meaning and application in architecture. As a term it is used to mark the regular recurrence of like features in the design, or the regular alternations of features and elements. It is a fundamental principle of beauty in all decorative work for the exteriors and interiors of buildings.

Harmony, as used in architecture and the other arts, adheres to the general meaning of agreement. It was derived from a Greek word which in that language means joint. The critic of architectural products would give to the word substantially the following meaning: "Such an agreement between the different parts of a design (or finished building) as to produce unity of effect or a pleasing whole." Conflicts with the principles of harmony may be recognized in such ugly aspects as lack of balance, the distorted pro- portions of a single feature, disagreement between parts, broken rhythm, the appearance of instability, and failure to suggest the purpose or function.

Emphasis is expressed by giving prominence to a particular feature that by tradition or special use enjoys the right of prominence, as for example the steeple of a church or the dome on a capitol building. Magnified emphasis defeats the possibility of a pleasing effect in the structure as a whole while the effect of giving no emphasis to features that should be more prominent than others is monotonous in the extreme.

Color enters the design of the exterior as a feature that may not be dismissed lightly. It should be chosen so as to make the building fit naturally into its surroundings. Ivory, buff, gray blue, and gray green colors are admirably suited to this purpose. Generally, houses are painted in one color in order to present to the eye a unified picture. Where contrast in color is desired, white with green window shutters is a popular selection.

The study of architecture provides a worthwhile vocation for the talented few and a delightful avocation or hobby for those who must content themselves with an appreciation of the beauty expressed in buildings. Appreciation of beautiful homes, churches, and civic buildings, joy and delight in the artistic homes of others, and a developing appreciation for good taste in lines, proportion, and color may be shared by home owners and renters alike.

Expression in Architecture.

Why is a building beautiful and in good taste? Not necessarily because it closely resembles some architectural style of the past. All factors should be taken into consideration. In other words, we should see the completed picture in which design, function, beauty, and use are all included. While good, artistic expression is often found in buildings which exist for beauty only, that is not proof of goodness in an architectural sense of meaning. Most beautiful buildings serve a useful purpose such as giving shelter to people or to valuable things. Certain types of buildings have naturally come to express definite functions. Do you easily recognize a church, a school, a library, a state capitol, or a municipal auditorium? A building should seem to belong to its location or site and it should be suited to its purpose. Its design should somehow express simplicity, fitness, harmony and unity, or what is sometimes referred to as "architectural good manner." A building which is supposed to express strength and security, such as a state capitol, should show strength in lines and proportion as well as in building materials. All adornment or decoration should be in harmony with the whole building. Buildings of any given period of time should be representative of the beauty, climate, and social conditions of that time.

Buildings may show character and individuality as do people, but individuality in buildings should be governed by the basic purpose of design and color and that illusive something called good taste.

Simplicity and suitability to purpose sound the key- note to beauty in architecture as in everything else. Architectural beauty is not achieved by accident but by careful planning and much study on the part of those interested in making a more beautiful world in which to live. We cannot expect to get beauty in a building unless the building fulfills its purpose, belongs to its type, and in part and whole gives a complete, unified picture.

Styles in Architecture.

Changes in architecture are as apparent in each epoch of history as are changes in social customs and the clothes we wear. The extremely large homes and large rooms of the South, for example, were primarily the concomitants of a social life in which there were servants to care for the house as well as to lift the heavy burdens of entertaining. Today, home life is changing practically everywhere and all types of women are giving more and more time to civic and philanthropic activities outside the home. Hence the smaller house with its simpler type of housekeeping is in demand in most localities.

Various styles of architecture which have been used in America have been adapted to meet the special needs of locality and climate. Changes have been brought about by discovery of new construction materials, new ideas, and new habits.

Styles in architecture and their adaptation to present day use are of interest to everyone. When building a new house, remodeling an old one, or when renting an apartment or house, it is a source of much satisfaction to have definite knowledge of the fundamental principles of art that are applied to buildings and their surroundings. Such knowledge is also a source of satisfaction when you are driving around for pleasure. Beautiful public buildings and artistic, well kept parks should bring happiness to everyone in the community as well as to visiting friends or strangers.

The good American home should first of all be designed to meet the individual family's needs and special requirements. Though the health, safety, comfort, and happiness of the family should be the first consideration, good appearance need not be sacrificed for these essentials if the builder knows the fundamentals of good architecture, or if an architect is employed.

As has been previously mentioned, the climate, the location, the size of the family, the economic status, and the individual likes and dislikes should influence the choice of architectural style. While each architectural style has a definite character, there are very few pure architectural styles to be found. The most common domestic styles in America are colonials, adaptations of English, French, Spanish, and Italian.

Colonial Houses.

The colonial house is typical of the early American home but the styles of colonial houses differed in type even in early colonial days, hence we have Northern, Southern, and Dutch Colonial. Formal balance of windows and doorways, simple gabled roofs, wooden shutters, small window panes, hooded doorways in a house depicting simplicity through every feature, briefly describes the Northern Colonial. Southern Colonial houses show the same simplicity and formal balance in windows and doorways but they are larger and much more pretentious with tall columns and enormous porticoes. Comfortable and elaborate in type, they fit beautifully into the picture on large plantations, depict a life of leisure for their owners, and suggest a staff of capable servants. Colonial style is the inspiration for the greater part of American homes, perhaps because one of its attractive features is that it can be built from so many types of material —wood, brick, cement, stucco, etc. Colonial architecture may and often does reflect the influence of English, Spanish, French, and Dutch ancestry without detracting from its Americanism.

Dutch Colonial.

The Dutch Colonial style of house had fixed itself as a domestic type of architecture before England had supplanted Holland in ownership of the area now comprising the state of New York. This type of house was distinguished by whitewashed limestone walls, tall chimneys at the ends, and steep gables. In time, features of the Dutch Colonial type crept into the buildings of adjacent sections in New Jersey and eastern Pennsylvania. It was logical that the type would undergo modification due to surrounding influences and certain adaptations to need that the Dutch settlers were able to make as they grew in wealth. The roof slope was lessened, and the over-hang of the eaves was increased. The height was extended to two stories, and piazzas or verandas were eventually added.

Modern reproductions (descendants) of this type are very popular with builders at this time. These are characterized by a stoop at the main entrance that may or may not be flanked by seats on both sides. The windows have an upper and a lower casement, each consisting of six small square panes. If shutters are used, they open outward from the center and fasten at both sides against the wall. Two tall narrow windows balancing in height with the top of the door may be placed at the main entrance. The materials used in the construction of the modern Dutch Colonial type of house consist of the following: brick, stone, clapboards, stucco, shingles, or concrete blocks for walls; asbestos shingles, slate, composition shingles, tile, wood shingles, or metal for the roof; hardwood for floors.

The English.

A home structure of half stone and half wood that has a very steep roof, prominent chimney effects, and windows grouped together, is typical of the English style of home building now prevalent in the United States. It was but natural for our earliest settlers to erect houses as nearly like those to which they had been accustomed as the limitations set by distance from home and the scarcity of materials would allow. Thus English architectural influences, dominant at the very first as a very natural course of events, have persisted until this very day. These influences are manifest both in colonial revivals and uses of the modern type of English house. The English type now so much used in new city subdivisions is more popular than any other.

The Spanish.

The first houses of Florida, Texas, New Mexico, Arizona, and California although crude in the beginning followed the style of building that at that time was characteristic of Spain. At first, of course, they were constructed of the crude materials at hand, but eventually sun dried (adobe) bricks or stone supplanted these materials. The patio, or courtyard, occupied the center space, and was enclosed on three sides by the walls of the building. In the center of the patio was a fountain or well which was surrounded on all sides by a profusion of growing things, flowers, trees- — orange, palm, lemon, shrubs, and ferns. Inviting walks of gravel or brick led from the patio entrance to the fountain and thence in a well-executed pattern to the doors of the building that opened out on a long porch which extended the full length of the walls on three sides of the court. Whitewashed walls and red tiled roofs were characteristic of the exterior. Inside, the walls were whitewashed and the floors and porches were paved with tiles or brick, square in design. It is easy to see that climatic influences were taken into consideration. There being no great necessity for heat, the ceilings were open and fireplaces were not always in evidence. In parts of New Mexico and Arizona, houses of the Spanish type borrowed something in the way of atmosphere that can perhaps be attributed jointly to the influence of climate and the impress of Indian life.

The French.

The best examples of the French Colonial type of architecture are to be found in New Orleans and other parts of Louisiana. But even there, revivals are not numerous in present building activities. It is to be regretted that such is the case for in failure to retain the French tradition as it is expressed in architecture and other forms of domestic culture, we are losing a source of enrichment that could come from no nation or people other than the French.

Unlike the patio in Spanish designs or the spacious front lawn of the modern mansion, but rivaling them in beauty, the courtyard of the French Colonial house was excluded from view by the walls of the building or by a tall board fence if there were a court entrance from the street. It was a retreat for family recreation and only to be shared with guests and friends. The front of the house, also suggesting privacy, was plain and unbroken except for doors and window casements extending to the floor and arched or flat at the top. Since, in New Orleans, houses extended out to the sidewalk with no yard in front, the lower casements were provided with shutters of heavy material. The upper part of the plastered, pink-tinted, yellow, or green facades were crossed at the junction of the first and second stories by wrought iron balconies latticed with iron and supported by trellises or posts of iron.

It is a source of wonder that architecture in Detroit, St. Louis, Mobile, Vincennes and other centers of former French activity exhibit so little in historic reminder of our gains from contact with a national and family culture that the world has never seen surpassed.

The Modern House.

The modern house in America gives expression to the desire for convenience, comfort, and leisure. Simple decorations, many windows, strong and durable construction using much steel and glass, sun decks and sun porches, and glass walls are all beginning to appear. Some houses are made entirely of steel. A new architectural style, better suited to American life and ideals than the older styles, seems to be in the making.

Let us study the traditions of the past and the conventions of other countries and profit by their strength and beauty but let us hold fast to the ideal of eventually perfecting a house that is truly American, clean and sanitary, comfort- able and convenient, beautiful and charming, with structural ornament and decoration — a completed picture that seems to belong to the American people with enough variation to suit the hillsides, the rolling prairies, the flat plains, the small lot in town, or the more pretentious home in the country.

A study of the different types of architecture is interesting and worthwhile, and every effort should be made to analyze the strong and weak points of the styles of the past and of other countries and adapt them to present day use and materials. Such a study would be valuable, not only to those who plan to build or remodel an old house, but for all of us who want to enjoy the fine points of architectural beauty. Our aim should be to choose designs that are beautiful and at the same time suited to our environment and our individual needs.

Are we developing a type of architecture of our own? Is our demand for convenience and comfort in our homes causing a new type of architecture to be developed? It is almost the unanimous opinion of architects and other authorities that periods have been carried too far. We should not let traditions of the past or the lovely things of other countries influence our choices to the extent that we choose a house which does not fit into the native setting.

Briefly, a building should fit its location, serve its purpose, express its aim, be free from sham or pretense, be suited to the type and place and social condition of its environment, and have all decoration or ornament in keeping with the structural design. In short, the best architecture will always reflect the life and activities of its time.

Architecture always has a conscious or unconscious effect upon us. Ruskin says that "Architecture should contribute to our mental health, power, and pleasure."

Principles of Landscaping.

By landscaping, we mean the scientific arrangement about a building of walks and drives, lawns and gardens, flowers, shrubbery, and trees so as to create pleasing effects. In landscaping, the design of the land surrounding the house is made in accordance with principles that are as finely drawn, as definite, and as important as the design of the house itself and as true to art. The appearance of a lovely house can be spoiled by inharmonious landscaping just as a lovely ensemble can be spoiled by incorrect dress accessories.

Proper landscaping entails knowledge, forethought, and careful, detailed planning. Planning is a prerequisite in landscape architecture and it should be done even before the house is built, if possible, so that the house may fit ideally into the location. Even if the house is already built, much can be done to give it a more congenial atmosphere by carefully laying out plans for changing the surroundings and putting them into execution. It is well to have the completed plan on paper before beginning work.

Some Things to Keep in Mind in Making Your Plan.

A house should, first of all, seem indigenous, if that were possible, that is, to have grown out of its surroundings, and nothing contributes so much to this appearance as well chosen, appropriate plantings about the foundation. A house rising directly from the ground seems isolated and unfriendly, even though a perfect lawn surrounds it.

The foundation for a good lawn is rich, deep, well-drained soil; about eight inches of good top soil is desirable. Fertilizer should be incorporated before the lawn is seeded.

High places in the yard should in general have special attention and low places should be built up. New soil should be added to places where the soil is poor or was made poor by filling up depressions with poor soil. Money used in the purchase of good fertilizer and additional soil is money well invested when the groundwork for a beautiful lawn is being prepared.

Locate trees so as to frame the house, usually at the corners, leaving the middle of the front open; or place them at the back to provide a setting for the house. The size of the trees at maturity should be taken into consideration when planting. By intelligent planning, even shade trees can be introduced to add beauty to the completed picture. Trees are used both to provide shade and to give beauty. If the back yard is large enough to be used for recreation, trees that yield shade make an especially attractive feature by serving both purposes. A croquet ground well shaded by trees, or a tennis court where there are large shade trees under which to rest between sets, are welcomed by everyone.

Shrubbery makes for an air of permanence and gives the feeling of unity and harmony between the house and the lawn, while the absence of all shrubbery makes the house look deserted and temporary. Shrubbery is for the purpose of framing the house and emphasizing its good points in structure. Choose shrubs which will fit your house when full grown. This requires exact knowledge and planning that is based upon such knowledge before planting the shrubs. Placing shrubs is much like placing furniture in your rooms, tall and short, large and small are needed to relieve monotony. Repetition of the same size violates the principles of harmony.

Shrubs are usually planted close against the foundation of the house, at corners and in angles of the house, and in angles of the steps at porches. The corner of the house, a porch, or a long bare wall without windows are ideal places for shrubbery.

Corners and entrances are key places to add emphasis and interest. Clumps of shrubbery along boundaries, irregular in size, and varying in width and height can often be used effectively. Shrubs may also be used to break long, straight sides. Vines and shrubbery should be placed so that they will hide work areas, garbage cans, clothes lines, and any other unattractive features. Screening off service areas and the seclusion of garden spots can be accomplished by choosing shrubbery of irregular sizes. Since shrubs help to insure privacy, the small lot requires tall, narrow shrubs, such as a trimmed hedge, in order to take as little space as possible, while the large ground may have shorter, spreading shrubbery. A landscape gardener or an architect will be able to give valuable suggestions concerning the kind of shrubbery to use in order to have variety in size and color and also concerning the care of shrubbery. The cost of employing a landscape architect would bring good returns even to the builder of a small home by assuring a tasteful appearance to house and grounds. Your own state college of agriculture sends out free bulletins telling which trees and shrubs grow best in your state, with suggestions for planting them.

Gardens, flowers, grass, and shrubs not only add beauty to a home but, when rightly placed and cared for, they add to its monetary value. Gardens, too, are restful and beautiful and provide an ideal place for rest, meditation, and solitude. For this reason, they should never be crowded or cluttered up. A secluded garden spot in one's own back yard, even though small and unpretentious, is priceless.

Communion with nature has its own peculiar way of bringing serenity, comfort, and happiness to old and young alike. The philosophy that working with growing things brings new enthusiasm and new vision applies with as much force to the care of the potted plant on the window sill, the window box, the small box garden in the back yard of the tiny apartment house, or the cozy nook in the corner of the children's play yard, as to the more pretentious gardens of palatial homes.

Walks should be few and most carefully laid out in order to give as much unbroken space as possible. If the house is set close to the street, the walks should lead straight to the house, and not curve. When planting flowers bordering a path or walk, keep in mind that the main purpose of the path is to serve the pedestrian, and that while we want our walks as artistic as possible, we must not let the flowers interfere with their usefulness. Walks should be dry and conveniently arranged.

The smaller the place, the more planning is necessary. Simplicity must be the keynote of the small yard; in this respect it is comparable to the small house which must utilize every bit of space. It is the effect of spaciousness that we want and must strive for in the smaller place. Straight lines express or amplify space more than curved ones. The lattice or wire fence with vines growing over it is more appropriate here than thick shrubbery. All possible lawn area should be seen in the rear. The small yard has an advantage not shared by the large one. For example, arrangement may be unsymmetrical with one feature balanced by a different one on the other side rather than repeated. This gives a more subtle and interesting effect although it is rather difficult to obtain.

The love of flowers is innate in most of us. Many people who say they do not care for flowers may have been prejudiced from seeing the wrong arrangement much of the time. Flowers should be grown in the back yard, rather than in front. The front yard should be clear and unbroken, thus giving a harmonious foreground for the house and flower garden in the rear. This is particularly true of the small lawn, where every bit of space must be made to count.

The vegetable gardens in small areas should be arranged for planting so that the tall growing plants will not shade the small ones. When enough space is available for the exercise of choice between locations, vegetables should not be planted near large trees. Trees utilize the minerals and water from the surrounding soil and exclude it from the sunshine. The lack of fertility and sunshine in such an area would necessarily cheat vegetables of their growth. Vegetable gardening is most successful in soil that is free from rocks beneath the surface and has plenty of sunshine and moisture.

An Outdoor Living Room.

Have you ever thought of your yard as being an outdoor living room? You would not think of going to a furniture store and picking up a yellow chair, a red chair, or an orange chair, with no thought of how it would harmonize with your rug and other furnishings, yet we sometimes go to a florist and pick at random a number of packages of seeds with no thought whatever of whether flowers grown from them will harmonize in size and color with the rest of nature's furnishings in our gardens. Color in flowers is subject to the same rules as color in dress or in interior decoration.

Plan carefully just what design you wish to make of your outside living room. If possible, have it so situated that it may be viewed from the inside living room, so that you and your guests may step from one living room into the other without the inconvenience of going around the house or through the kitchen.

A lot which is properly landscaped fits into its natural environment and makes a completed ensemble of house and lot. Each house with its yard of course presents its own individual problem, but by having a tentative yard plan on paper with which to work and make comparative notes, and by observing yards in which similar details have been satisfactorily solved, one should be able to evolve a satisfactory plan for making the yard an attractive, inviting living room.

CHAPTER 16

THE HOUSE WITHIN

Planning, Equipping, Furnishing

Homes reflect the individuality of a nation more than any other type of building. Collectively, they give an excellent picture of the ideals of a people. Beauty can be expressed in houses without sacrifice of the useful features that contribute to happier and more wholesome family living. Thus, as we learn to live more sensibly, we build more sensibly. Many people who do not build homes buy, alter, or redecorate them, hence the need on the part of all people for knowledge and information of the types of service that meet specific needs.

We have learned that different types of architecture were developed to correspond with different modes of living and that the mode of living should dictate the floor plans and the interiors of our homes. The well-planned exterior adds beauty which may be enjoyed by everyone, even those who pass our homes; but the keynote to a livable house within is a well-planned floor that provides for comfort, convenience, and safety.

It may be years before you build a home but you will build a better home if you begin now to take note of the beauty that architecture has to offer you in the appearance of public buildings and homes of others.

The House Plan.

After the lot is selected, its shape and size impose certain limitations upon the plan of the house. For example, a long narrow lot would require a long, narrow house, while a lot nearly square suggests that a square house would be more suitable. Symmetrical balancing can be achieved in the square house where the entrance is in the center, with windows and porches arranged in formal balance. If the entrance is on the side, balance is more difficult and must be achieved by windows, porches, chimneys, etc. On the large suburban lot or on the farm, personal preference should be the influencing factor in planning the shape.

On a hillside, high, vertical lines would fit better than the horizontal lines which would be suitable on a level plain.

In a town or city, there are zoning rules to take into consideration. Here the plan must be in keeping with the rest of the neighborhood or the immediate vicinity.

Since there is such a close relationship between the floor plan and the exterior, it might be advisable, on account of the peculiar location, to select the exterior first and then make floor plans accordingly, but usually the floor plan is made and the exterior is made to conform.

One who has made a few floor plans and has seen the consequences of poor planning knows that mistakes in building are not only expensive from the standpoint of the money it costs to make corrections, but also from the standpoint of safety, convenience, and comfort if the mistakes go uncorrected. "A little knowledge is a dangerous thing" in house planning but thought given to floor plans will at least give some basis of judgment as to the correct selection, even though an architect does the planning. Serious mistakes in building can best be averted by consulting an architect; yet the builder should have sufficient knowledge for making suggestions.

Altogether, we must take into consideration before making a house plan the location or site, the family's likes and dislikes, the number in the family — whether children or adults, and the amount of money that can be invested. On the basis of this information we then should try to build a house of good design that in all respects conforms to "architectural good manners."

The topography of the site should influence the design of the exterior and should also influence the floor plan. For example, a sloping lot demands one type of floor plan while the pitched roof of a mountain home and the adobe of the western plains suggest other needs. Activities of the family also influence design. If the family likes to read, there may be need for a library, but if the members are seldom at home, a library is impractical. The reasons why the doctor's family should have a different kind of house than that of his neighbor are easy to imagine. The large family would select by preference and because of necessity a large living room and a large kitchen which could be used for informal family meals and gatherings, and the members might have to use a combination library and dining room for their more formal meals in order to have enough sleeping space. A playroom in the house where there are children is a boon to the adults in the house as well as to the younger members, as it insures more privacy to both groups. Too, if there are servants in the house- hold, a different type of house would be needed from that for the smaller family without servants. It is thus seen that the size of the family and the type of life the family leads help to determine the kind of house that should be selected or built. The amount of money available is of paramount importance but by no means should the lack of money result in the construction of a house with a commonplace, ugly exterior or an awkward, inconvenient interior.

Floor Plans

Floor plans give no perspective of depth but show size and relation to each other of rooms, doors, windows, etc. The study of floor plans provides a simple, direct method of securing definite information about building. The knowledge of floor plans thus gained will be helpful to the student who rents a room, to the family renting a house or apartment, or to those who plan to build. Everyone should therefore learn to read floor plans or blueprints, as it will help him to see how his furniture would fit into the available space.

A blue print is a print of an original drawing, usually made by an architect. Architects have symbols of their own which they use in designating various parts of a building, such as doors and windows. The architect's drawings are so accurate that they locate exactly where doors, windows, chimneys, plumbing, electric lights, etc. are to be placed. Some knowledge of these symbols is necessary in order to study intelligently the architect's plan or blue print. To read it, you must imagine depth, the third dimension.

Imagine yourself going through every room in the house, looking out the windows. Cut stiff paper and cardboard to scale and arrange furniture. Build with paper and pencil and with words before actual construction begins. Begin observing and measuring the houses you live in.

Everyone interested in floor plans should make use of a yard stick. Measuring floor space, windows, doors, and furniture, the height of sinks, the width of closets and shelves in the house we now live in and the homes of our friends will reveal many essential points to us. After all, our only intention in studying floor plans is to learn to translate or interpret them in terms of our own needs and interests, and the comfort, safety, and convenience of the family within. Nowhere are accurate measurements more necessary. Space poorly planned wastes money as well as energy and means discomfort in everyday living.

The architect who plans the exterior of our homes puts beauty in design and color and suitability to site first; but when floor plans are under consideration, health, safety, convenience, and comfort take precedence.

Fixed standards which have grown out of the experiences of architects and builders should not be ignored. These fixed standards are in reality the generally accepted standards used in furniture sizes, and heights of tables, chairs, beds, musical instruments, etc. Standard heights are also used in the construction of working tables, sinks, and lavatories. It is advisable to use these standards, which the architect will offer, unless it is desirable to adapt the house to an individual family. For example, a very short woman would need a lower sink than the standard height, while the very tall woman would want it raised a few inches.

Architects are trained in the principles that underlie efficient designs, beauty of lines, good workmanship, and sound construction. An architect will be able to analyze and reconcile your own plan with good taste, adequate living conditions, and suitability of the lot; and he may help you immeasurably in the elimination of waste. Do you know why most dining rooms are square or nearly so? Why most people prefer a long living room? Should the living room always be in the front and bedrooms and kitchen in the rear, or do our ways of living today make new demands, even in floor plans? Today we have the auto drive at the back, guests entering from a side door, and living rooms that look out on a beautiful lawn or flower garden in the rear. A new grouping of rooms may be in the making.

Before we actually build, we should have the contractor submit prices on definite plans and specifications. After these are agreed upon, most home builders desire changes, minor ones usually, but they are very expensive to make. These last minute changes are usually the cause of building costs exceeding the budget. It is the architect's business to study the arrangement, size, and number of rooms and estimate the probable cost per cubic foot. If the number of rooms desired cannot be built for the amount of money available, then satisfactory substitutions can be arranged. For example, a roll-away bed, or a studio couch could be provided for guests if a guest room is prohibited.

Cost.

The cost of building depends upon local markets and the quality of material, and these vary from season to season and in different localities. The cost of the site is, of course, determined by its size and location. Things to consider in choosing the site are nearness to business, schools, churches, parks, etc. All these details and more should be taken into consideration before actually buying. When ready to build, the amount of money available plus the amount of indebtedness one dares to shoulder should be the determining factors.

Type of Material.

The kind of material which is to be used in the finished house is of vital importance. It is true here as elsewhere that we usually "get what we pay for" but those who have had experience know that some knowledge on our part is necessary to make this saying come true. Good building materials should be used. We do not want a cheap house that is not durable, even though we must sacrifice some of the other things we would like or make the rooms smaller in order to have a house of good building materials. One way to economize is on the woodwork. We might like walnut woodwork, but cheaper material, yet very attractive, might have to be used.

Room Arrangement.

The floor plan is much like a dress pattern. Each room must be considered separately and in connection with the whole plan. The room arrangement can be divided into three parts: the living rooms, such as the sitting room, library, reception room, dining room, entrance hall; sleeping or rest rooms, including bedrooms, bathrooms, sleeping porch, dressing rooms; and work rooms, including kitchen, laundry, and store rooms.

The sleeping rooms should be located in the quieter, more secluded part of the house; the living rooms should usually be grouped together in the most accessible space for they are used by guests and visitors as well as the family; the work rooms should be grouped together in the rear. The living rooms should open into each other, so that when opened in entertaining a large group, the effect of having one large living room is produced.

The Living Room.

If the living room is in the form of a rectangle, it will provide for a convenient and pleasing furniture arrangement. It should, of course, be convenient to the dining room as well as to outdoor living areas, and should be so located as to afford the best possible view from the building site. The size of the family, its needs, activities and desires, are important. From the health angle, it should be planned for air motion, ventilation, and sunshine. Do not forget the articles of furniture that will go into this room; leave enough wall space between windows and doors to provide adequately for their use.

For purposes of entertaining and making the house seem more friendly, it is desirable to have large doorways between the dining room and living room and library or reception room. Doorways should of course conform to one style in size and shape to keep a harmonious and unified appearance.

The Dining Room.

The dining room, first of all, must be easily accessible from the kitchen so that food can be served immediately after preparation. The dining room is generally square in shape, although if the family is large or if much entertaining is done, a rectangular room is preferable and more in harmony with the long, rectangular dining table which is required by necessity. Three or more feet of space should be left between the table and the wall to permit ease in serving. In small houses, built-in cup- boards and pass closets to the kitchen are desirable. A pleasant view, plenty of light, and sunshine are other factors to consider.

The Bedroom.

Good ventilation should be an outstand- ing feature of the bedroom. This room should provide privacy, with an entrance from the hall, easy access to the bathroom, adequate closet space, and also enough wall space clear of windows to prevent dressers, chests, or other high pieces of furniture from interfering with ventilation and breeze from the outside. The bed should be so located that it may be reached easily from either side. Bedrooms and living rooms should not connect in ways that force members of the family to go through the living rooms to reach their bedrooms.

The Kitchen.

In planning the kitchen, think of it as a domestic workshop, and plan it accordingly. Study its relation to the rest of the house, seeing that there is easy access to the dining room, to the front and back doors, to the cellar and second floor, to the stairway, and to the telephone. Good lighting and ventilation are particularly important in the kitchen, both from the standpoint of health and convenience.

In the small house, it is advisable to have the entrance to the kitchen in as direct a route as possible.

Stairways and Halls.

Space may be saved in the small house by placing the basement stairway directly under the main stairway. In the very large house, where a back stairway is needed, the basement stairway may be placed under the back stairway.

Halls should not take up more room than absolutely necessary as a hall is merely an entrance into the house or a passage from room to room. The entrance hall should be convenient to the living room. If there is a stairway, whenever possible it should lead upstairs from the entrance hall and there should also be an entrance to the stairway from the kitchen.

In order to insure the health and safety and as much comfort and convenience as possible for all members of the family, most careful consideration should be given to the arrangement of rooms. The relation of rooms to each other, together with the necessary attention to the principles of design and color are to be considered. Fine workmanship and good grades of structural materials, decorations of beauty and simplicity, well-proportioned rooms, pleasing views, privacy, and provision for the needs and desires of the individual family members should be the aim in making the floor plans for a happy, healthful home.

Equipping Heating Systems.

How shall the house be heated? What is the best heating system? What is the most economical heating system? These questions and others might be asked concerning the heating of houses, but no one, not even an expert, can supply the answers for any given house without making a careful survey of such factors as size, location, and construction of the house, climatic conditions, size of rooms, health of members of the family, etc. A poorly constructed house which fails to keep out the wind cannot be warmed by any type of heating system, and to achieve even fair success in heating such a house each room must have at least one direct heating unit, such as a stove or radiator.

The four most commonly used systems of heating are hot air, hot water, steam, and the modern "air conditioning" each with its own advantages and disadvantages. The hot air furnace is least expensive, giving quick heat and providing ventilation when the cold air box is connected with the outside air. The furnace, however, does not heat adequately those rooms farthest away that must be reached by long pipes. The space occupied by the pipes is another unsatisfactory feature.

Factors to consider in choosing a hot water system are economy of fuel, cost, and capacity for heating. A heating plant should have sufficient capacity to more than heat the house as it is more economical to run a large plant slowly than a small plant forcefully.

An efficient heater must be kept clean to give good service. A collection of soot naturally lessens the quantity of heat given out. Covering the hot water and steam pipes as well as the heater with asbestos covering will help to conserve fuel.

Hot water heating for homes is very satisfactory since after the radiator has been heated to the desired temperature the water continues to circulate after the fire has gone out. However, since so much water must be heated the temperature of the room cannot be modified quickly, which makes it inconvenient during extreme changes of weather. Also, if the water is heated over the boiling point the "expansion tank" located at the highest point may boil over and cause damage.

In the pressure hot water heating system, the water can be heated over the boiling point, thus giving more rapid circulation, and making it possible to use smaller pipes and radiators.

For large houses and apartment buildings, a steam heating system is considered the most effective system of heating that may be used.

"Air conditioning" is becoming increasingly popular as a means of ventilation both for coolness in summer and warmth in winter. This system dehumidifies, filters, and circulates the air. The direction of the air is controlled by outlet grilles. The ducts or risers are concealed in the walls and only the inconspicuous grilles show in the rooms. The upper grilles circulate the warm air and the used air passes through the lower grilles for reconditioning. Air conditioning eliminates the unsightly radiator and is otherwise an attractive heating system. Its main disadvantage is the initial cost of installation, but it reduces laundry and cleaning bills caused by exposure of curtains, rugs, bed covers, and upholstery to dust and smoke, saves time by eliminating furnace tending, and protects furniture, floors, and walls against cracking and peeling.

Cooling Systems.

The most popular method of cooling homes, and the least expensive, is by means of an electric fan, which aids the circulation of air. In particularly warm climates, however, the air itself is so warm that this system is rapidly giving way to the "air conditioning" system of cooling, particularly in business houses, hotels, and the larger homes. Recently, smaller homes in the hot climates have adapted this system to fit their own needs on a less expensive scale by the use of a window box, an electric fan, excelsior, and dripping water that is supplied from a hose connected outside the house. As the water drips over the excelsior, the fan blows the cooled air in through the window.

The disadvantage of this device is the high degree of humidity it produces, but this is more than compensated for by cooling breezes which are in delightful contrast to the dry, stifling heat outside.

Lighting.

There is no hard and fast rule by which to be governed in lighting the various rooms of a house, but there are fundamental principles which should be observed. For instance, the light should not be excessively brilliant or glaring; lights should be artistic and useful in character; light should be toned to fit the decorative schemes; and lights should not cast shadows.

Of the three methods of artificial lighting — gas, oil, and electricity- — the most effective and the one which nearest approximates natural light is the modern "indirect" lighting system provided by electricity. Besides the inconvenience of caring for oil lamps and gas lights, their light is neither constant nor adequate. Since seeing what we should to be safe in this bustling world involves the best use of our eyes, nerves, muscles, and minds, the process should not be made more complicated by poor lighting. Therefore, the modern homemaker insists upon good home lighting because it is scientifically sound and healthful.

Lighting, when well done, enhances the beauty of rugs, furnishings, and pictures. Therefore, lamp bulbs should not be exposed so as to cause glare. In the indirect lighting systems, the diffusing bowl used under the lamp shade softens the shadows.

Plumbing.

What is plumbing? Plumbing is the system of pipes, fixtures, and other apparatus used for bringing in the water supply and removing waste. The plumbing fixtures in a building include the pipes for distributing the water, fixtures for using water, drainage pipes for removing water, and pipes for removing sewage. Needless to say, the water supply and drainage system are mutually dependent. The values of good plumbing consist of an adequate supply of water to keep ourselves and our houses clean, and provision for carrying waste water away from the house.

Cost of Plumbing.

The cost of plumbing varies any- where from six to ten per cent of the total building cost, the smallest system consisting of the fixtures for one bathroom, one kitchen sink, and two laundry tubs. Rooms which require the most plumbing are the bathroom, kitchen, and the basement for which the fixtures include a laundry and hot water tank.

In cities, plumbing is a simple problem but in the country it is a difficult one. A simple plumbing system for a rural house consists of devices by which spring or well water is carried to the house and the waste water carried out.

The three essentials of a good plumbing system are an adequate supply of water under pressure, proper fixtures, and an adequate system for disposal of waste. Factors which influence the supply of water are the daily needs of the family, the water available for different seasons, and the power for pumping. Sources of water include springs, wells, cisterns, and city water works.' Usually water in cities is treated with chemicals in order to make it safe, since absolutely pure water is found only in the laboratory. Sometimes water that is safest is not so palatable as that in the spring or open well, which may be quite unsafe.

Daily Needs of the Family.

It is estimated that for each person on the farm, from ten to twenty gallons of water per day is used. Cities furnish a much larger quantity than this, but much is used for community service, such as cleaning streets, watering lawns, etc.

Proper Fixtures.

The installation of good plumbing, including fixtures, is an economical measure. Fixtures should be well constructed and of good material. Sanitary plumbing fixtures, adequate water, and a good sewer system help to assure health protection in homes. Brass is desirable in pipes used for the distribution of the water supply in the home, since it does not break down or rust or become stopped up with lime deposits. At least the pipes about the heater and hot water tanks should be of brass if one cannot afford to use brass altogether. Iron and steel are used on the underground pipes.

The waste system should be impervious to gas, acids, etc., and sufficient in capacity to carry off all wastes but small enough to be well flushed.

Bathroom fixtures come in different colors and sizes to harmonize with the rest of the rooms and to satisfy individual preference. Sinks of every desired size and color, as well as different materials, are available. Some of the things to look for in the sink are good back and drain boards, made with as few joints as possible and curved corners instead of sharp angles. The floor around the stool in the bathroom should be of nonabsorbent material. Care should be taken in locating each plumbing fixture so that its use and care may be made convenient. Water splashes on both the bath tub and water closet when the lavatory is placed too close to either and causes an unattractive appearance.

The cheapest kind of stopper is made of rubber and has a chain attached to it. It is just as satisfactory as the more modern waste stopper. Stops should be placed on the water faucets to prevent their getting out of order. Faucets may be cheap or elaborate, of light metal or solid brass. Well made faucets require few repairs and those which are required are easily made. Finishes may be nickel or chromium, the latter being preferable since it neither rusts nor stains and is therefore worth the extra cost.

If at all possible, arrangements for the plumbing should be planned in advance so that the main piping can be put in when the building is being constructed. Fixtures may be added later without great expense and without marring walls and floors.

Plan for Other Equipment.

After the plumbing, lighting, and heating systems have been planned, a plan for other equipment for the home should be made. This usually includes the tools that the housewife or her assistants need for the preparation of food, for cleaning house, and for doing laundry work. Some of these are essential, while others are desirable for making housework more pleasant. The plan for these is just as important as the floor plan or as the plan for one's wardrobe. It must be made for the individual family in accordance with the size of the house, the vocations and avocations of family members, and the special desires of family members as to comfort, convenience, beauty, and cost.

The plan for equipping must accord with the size of the entire house, size and exposure of the rooms, position of doors, windows, etc. Furnishings and equipment are actually one form of investment. The more limited income requires more careful planning because the furniture must be bought over a period of time. It is better to get a few essentials, adding durable, suitable and beautiful articles which are desirable, gradually as one can afford them. Why not use the installment method of adding rather than the installment method of buying? Until the desirable bedroom suite can be bought for cash, why should not the young homemaker make a dressing table from orange crates and use an inexpensive bed, perhaps purchased from the second-hand store?

Choice of Equipment.

A list of essentials and of desirable pieces of equipment is given to serve as a checking list for those who are contemplating the purchase of additional new equipment and for those who are having the joy of buying equipment for the first time. Possibly no two people would desire exactly the same kind of kitchen tools. Therefore, no list of equipment can fill the needs of every family. Too much hinges upon personal interests, likes, and dislikes. The family that is fond of outdoor life would select a new fishing reel in preference to the bestselling novel selected by the family that likes to read. Another factor which should govern the choice of equipment is the health of the family members. The strong, energetic woman might find joy in the physical activity of difficult household tasks while a frail woman would need the advantage of every possible labor-saving device.

How should we decide which type or brand of equipment to buy? Should the comparison be made on the basis of the original cost, the cost of operating, the amount of time and energy used in operation? Yes, all these, but you may ask how are such facts to be discovered. And rightly so, for no one today would dare guess at the answers to these questions or to take the salesman's word for his products. Most advertising, newspaper and magazine as well as radio, is directed to women who mainly do the buying for the home. With them rests the responsibility of choosing for their families, and since they can- not entirely depend upon the word of advertisers and salesmen, it is to their interest to educate themselves as consumers and buyers.

One of the things to take into consideration in buying is the reputation of the manufacturer. Some manufacturers have put out good products over a long period of years and have become so well established and so well known for the good taste and character of their furnishings that the inexperienced person might well take advantage of their advice. The home economics department of your state college or university will probably be able to give you the names of reputable manufacturers. Usually a reputable manufacturer will guarantee his products. Unless he does, it is generally unwise to buy them, particularly if you are inexperienced.

Equipment sold by stores of reputable standing in the community and made by reputable manufacturers can be depended upon for durable and satisfactory service. But perhaps it is unfair to say that because a company is new or just beginning, its merchandise is not so good as some of the older concerns. New impetus may be given to the education of consumers through the competitive service of new concerns. Always keep in mind that whenever we buy, we are encouraging manufacturers to produce. For that reason, we should demand good quality and thereby discourage the manufacturer of products of poor quality.

Another consideration in the choice of equipment is the care it takes to keep it in a satisfactory condition. For example, one family bought an electric dish washer and found that it took more time to take care of the electric machine than to do the dishwashing, since the family was small and there were not sufficient dishes to justify a machine although, for a larger family or a boarding school or hotel, the electric dish washer would be a real labor saver. This may be true of some smaller utensils such as machines for making cakes, skimming milk, etc.

Cost of Equipment.

Because in the choice of equipment consideration should be given to the elements of cost, a careful study of different types should be made. This should include the original cost, the cost of operation, and the cost of repairs. Cheap equipment is high at any price. Equipment should be durable. Pans that are used only occasionally such as certain types of cookie pans or cake pans, will last for years even though of light weight, but preserving kettles, and tea kettles need to be of more durable material.

Renewal and upkeep of equipment would naturally be one of the items of the budget. Sometimes this item is forgotten and when replacements or repairs are necessary, the cost is taken out of some other item of the budget. Replacement needs should be carefully thought-out; a plan of replacement for bed linens, kitchen utensils, dishes, etc. should be made in order that there be no unexpected drain upon the financial budget.

Electric Equipment.

What is the first piece of electrical equipment that is purchased in the average home? The electric iron! The electric iron is certainly a friend to the household and a real labor-saving device. Toasters and washing machines usually come next followed by vacuum cleaners, percolators, curling irons, chafing dishes or grills, sandwich toasters, dish washers, mixers, and electric stoves.

It is important that everyone know more about electricity and its uses. Most electrical supplies are accompanied by a book of directions on how to use them and how to care for them. However, many people destroy or misplace the directions or fail to interpret them correctly. Local electrical supply companies usually furnish information and service on the use and care of electrical supplies.

Kitchen and Laundry Equipment.

The efficient kitchen needs (1) a separate working surface for each kind of work to be done, such as a table for the preparation of food and a table for serving it; (2) arrangement of large equipment to save steps; (3) the placing of equipment at convenient heights to eliminate unnecessary stooping and stretching; (4) the grouping of small equipment around the working surface where it is first used; and (5) a compact working area.

One of the largest pieces of equipment in the kitchen is the cupboard. This should extend all the way to the ceiling or it will be difficult to care for, since an exposed top will serve as a dust catcher. Tables in the kitchen should be of the right height to insure comfort for the worker; with sufficient space for knee room when sitting. The kitchen stove may be fueled with gas, electricity, oil, or coal, the main consideration being the type of fuel available, with personal preference and cost as influencing factors. The stove should harmonize in design with other furnishings and equipment, be easily cared for, and have little or no ornamentation.

An ice box is necessary for the storage and preservation of food. The refrigerator may be operated by electricity or gas, or it may be ice cooled. It should be so arranged that it is easily cared for.

Smaller kitchen equipment and cooking utensils should include wares of each desirable type. In selecting utensils, the things to consider are durability, design, size of family, amount of entertaining, and uses of articles. Handles of articles should be securely attached and able to withstand weight. The article itself should be free from cracks or crevices which harbor dirt and germs.

For laundry work, we need a washboard, at least one tub, and some kind of iron and ironing board. Desirable things to have are an additional tub or two for rinsing and a wringer or some kind of washing machine. An electric washing machine and an electric mangle for ironing are desirable, but they are luxuries. Washtubs should be of smooth, nonabsorbent material, easily cleaned and cared for; the wash benches should be adjusted to the height of the worker to prevent fatigue. Washboards may be glass, zinc, or galvanized iron. The latter two are more durable, but the former is more easily cared for. The laundry should be supplied with soap and soap flakes. A small board for ironing small garments and lingerie, such as underwear and handkerchiefs, is a convenience.

Furnishing and Equipping the House.

Demands of the living room include at least one sofa, two chairs, and a floor covering. Desirable additions are occasional chairs, end tables, book cases, lamps, pictures, and ornaments. A piano would be a luxury.

The dining room needs include the dining table, chairs, table linens, and silver. A buffet is not essential but is desirable for use in providing storage space for table linens and silver, and for other aids in serving.

The minimum bedroom equipment includes as essentials the bed, a chest of drawers, and a floor covering. Desirable additions might include a bed lamp, a table and water bottle, a rocker, and a dressing table.

Porch and garden furniture, desirable rather than essential, might include a glider, a hammock, sun chairs, and a table with chairs or stools for use in serving refreshments and outdoor meals.

What considerations, then, should determine the quantity and the kind of furniture and equipment that are needed? Furniture and equipment may be classified as essential, desirable, and luxurious. What constitutes a luxury as opposed to what is desirable is a question that arouses conflicting opinions in the minds of different people. The bare necessities would likely be agreed upon but after all much depends upon what the individual family is accustomed to in its standards of living. Things that are desirable make work easier and more enjoyable. Things that cost more but render no better service than those which can be obtained less expensively may be regarded as luxuries. In a kitchen, for instance, some of the essentials would be the cook stove, and the necessary cooking utensils and dishes. A refrigerator would be desirable, but an electric mixer would be considered a luxury because it is less needed and adds to the cost of equipment.

When buying, list the essential things you need in order to provide satisfactory living conditions in each room. Ordinarily we would not recommend installment buying, but sometimes it is an economically sound procedure. For example, a washing machine, or a vacuum cleaner, should be bought on the installment plan because of the energy and time it saves. It is also justifiable for the family that is inclined toward music to buy a radio or perhaps a piano on the installment plan if interest is sufficient to induce each family member to contribute something toward the payments.

The basis for determining the value of furnishings and equipment would be the usefulness of each piece to the family and what it contributes in the way of beauty and convenience.

Furniture and Equipment List

This list is only suggestive. What would you add to your own list? What would you omit?

Kitchen:

Biscuit cutter
Butcher knife
Cake box
Cake racks (wire)
Cake turner
Can opener
Casserole
Chopping bowl
Kitchen
Coffee pot
Cookie cutters

Cupboard
Dishcloths
Dish drainer
Dishpan
Dish towels
Double boiler
Dutch oven
Egg beater
Egg poacher
Electric mixer
Electric toaster
Flour sifter
Funnel
Fruit juice extractor
Garbage can
Ice box of some kind
Knives, forks, and spoons
Match box
Measuring cup
Mixing bowls
Muffin and cake pans
Paper towels
Paper baking cups
Paring knives
Percolator
Potato masher
Pot holders
Pressure cooker
Refrigerator dishes
Rolling pin
Saucepans, various sizes
Scales
Scissors
Skillet
Spice, cereal, and coffee jars
Step ladder
Strainer
Stove
Spatula
Tea kettle

Tea strainer
Towel rack
Tray
Vegetable brush
Waffle iron
Waste paper basket
Waxed paper

Laundry:

Bowls
Clothes basket
Clothes horse
Clothes lines
Clothes pins
Electric washing machine and mangle
Floor mop
Floor mats
Funnel
Ironing board
Scissors
Sprinkler
Tubs
Washboard
Wash bench
Whisk broom
Wooden spoon
Wringer

Living Room:

Sofa and chair to match
Coffee table
2 occasional chairs, one with 2 End tables
Ottoman
2 Candlesticks
Rug
2 Vases

Radio
Pictures
Desk
Book cases

Dining Room:

Table
Silver
Chairs
Floor covering
Buffet
Tea cart
Glass ware
Service table
China
Pictures

Bed Room:

Bed
Dresser
Mattress
Bed lamp
Mattress pad
Floor lamp
Chest of drawers
Table
Closet equipped with hangers, shelves, rods

Linen Closet:

For Dining Room:
4 table cloths
3 luncheon cloths
12 napkins
Table pad

3 tray covers
12 tea napkins

For Bedroom:

4 sheets for each bed
4 pillow cases for each bed
2 light weight blankets for each bed
2 mattress protectors for each bed
2 bedspreads for each bed
2 heavy blankets for each bed

For Bathroom:

12 bath towels
12 wash cloths
3 bath mats
12 guest towels
24 hand towels

For Kitchen and Laundry:

Dish cloths
Tea towels
Pot holders
Dust cloths

Personality in our Homes.

Does a house reflect the personality, charm, and individual character of the family within? Does it have a way of inviting people in or does it coldly suggest that no one is at home? Do we want our homes to be hospitable and friendly as well as beautiful, comfortable, and convenient? Consciously or unconsciously, our choices in houses, their surroundings, furnishings, and equipment express our personalities, our individual tastes, and our characters.

Our homes are not attractive by magic or by accident; to make them so takes careful planning, some knowledge of art and obedience to its basic principles of beauty and good taste. Why not devote our time and thought in an effort to make our homes beautiful and artistic? Efforts directed towards the beautifying of our homes increase our capacity for self-expression, develop in us a keener appreciation of the beauty which is to be found all about us, and teach us how to look for it. Through study and effort, people who can neither draw nor paint and do not consider themselves artistic in any sense, often become most appreciative of the fine works and possessions of others. They also become appreciative of the beauty to be found everywhere. such as in a beautiful sunset, harmonious lines and proportions in a well-constructed building, a bit of lovely pottery, a choice piece of tapestry, and the grandeur of distant mountains.

We all live in houses and they must be furnished in some way. The difference between right and wrong in furnishings is by no means accounted for by the difference in costs but rather by the good taste expressed in the correct choice and the absence of taste in the wrong choice. Taste, which is here but the application of the fundamental rules of design and color harmony, helps us to make better use of the things which we now have and also helps us in the selection of new things.

Things selected in good taste bring their own rewards, for daily association with lovely furnishings instills an ever-increasing appreciation of beauty and good design. Thus do houses take on new character and charm in the proportion that growth in appreciation of beautiful furnishings creates the desire in the minds of their occupants to add attractive pieces and remove those that detract from a harmonious whole. Thus do we all write the nature of our preferences and dislikes and even our personalities on the walls and floors of our abodes.

Types of Homes.

Homes may reflect the influence of other nations or of other years, or they may be truly expressive of our own activities. A study of their domestic architecture will reveal much of the thought and modes of living of any race of people who built houses and called them homes. What is meant by period furniture and period architecture? Period furniture and period architecture refer to styles which were popular during a certain historical period, usually in a certain country. Each architectural style has definite characteristics. Needless to say, houses adapted from these styles should be furnished in keeping with their period.

Learning the story of domestic architecture and of period furniture would for some of you be an interesting and romantic adventure that would make an ideal hobby and be a constant source of pleasure in the opportunity it gives to form an appreciation of beauty. A list of books relating to these subjects may be secured from your city, county, or state librarian or from the home economics department of your state college of agriculture or your state university.

Good domestic architecture is that which is based on the needs and requirements of family life and adheres to the laws of beauty and order. Good furniture is furniture of good structural design with decoration in keeping with its structure, adequate in size and shape for comfortable use, beautiful, harmonious, restful, and in good taste always.

The house in relation to its background is comparable with a gem in relation to its harmonious setting. The pretentious diamond requires a different setting from that of the simple amethyst, but the setting for each must be appropriate and harmonious in general effect. In either case, if the gem is genuine and correctly set, its charm will be found in the fidelity with which background and gem unite in obedience to the laws of order and design. Likewise, the small frame house and the large stone mansion each has its place to fulfill and each has its own individual charm in a harmonious background.

The type of furniture and furnishings to be chosen for any given house would depend, of course, upon the type of architecture and the general color scheme. For anyone to rent a house with no historic style and then to furnish it in period furniture would seem incongruous. Keep a picture in mind of the completed unit as you wish it to look and select each article with the completed picture in mind. The whole house also must be taken into consideration in choosing furnishings, for each room in the house should be furnished in a definite relationship to every other room and to the house as a whole. All rooms in a house furnished in the same colors and with the same type of furniture would be monotonous. On the other hand, conflicting color notes and too much variety in furnishings would present a picture of confusion and disorder.

It is by the right selection of furnishings and their arrangement that we create an atmosphere of peace and restfulness. We can violate the principles of design in the selection of furniture and thus spoil our homes, and it is equally easy to spoil our homes by violating the principles of design in the selection of minor furnishings, such as pictures, vases, or the clock on the mantle. Often it is in the minor things by which we most definitely express our personalities. Would it spoil the individuality of your room to have the furnishings selected by some person other than yourself, even though he is an expert in interior decoration? Rarely could any artist select furnishings that would express the personality of another, but the artist can be of invaluable assistance to all of us and we should avail ourselves of his service.

What is Decoration?

Things are in good taste only when they fit the purpose for which they were intended. Not everything decorated is in good taste. The basic principles of line and design control decoration, and beauty in decoration is possible only when it conforms to these principles. When decorative material is added merely for show or when applied to any object without reference to its structure, it degenerates into mere ornamentation.

Whenever anything requires decoration it must be incomplete in itself. When things are beautiful and complete in themselves, decoration becomes mere ornamentation and spoils the whole effect. To decorate, there must be a place which needs decoration and this decoration should conform to the structural or natural lines of the thing decorated. Simplicity in background is the foundation of decorative possibilities. A great artist has said that "Art is creation, not imitation." Natural flowers, beautiful in themselves, painted on rugs or kitchen floors and other usable articles are not in good taste, for the more natural they are, the more inappropriate they seem when found out of their natural environment, or in an unrelated atmosphere. Apples, pears, and peaches look well on trees and on tables, but they should not be painted on useful articles whose conventional lines give them an inharmonious background. If their design is conventionalized to harmonize with the lines of the article, the effect is harmonious and therefore pleasing.

Real art is creation. It is expressing one's self and should be the result of a need for something that is practical in purpose. For example, a chair should first be usable and comfortable, then beautiful and artistic; a living room, comfortable and convenient, then beautiful. Standards of beauty are almost as fixed as standards of usefulness, for when the principles of harmony are understood and applied, beauty will be the result. Milton says that "for want of consideration of things in their right order, all the
world is in confusion."

Study and discussion of the laws of beauty will help us to develop standards of good taste as art is merely "refined common sense." A cultivated taste springs from appreciation of the beautiful, and appreciation is but the outgrowth of knowledge. The modest home or the tiny room in a crowded apartment district can be charming and peaceful if one understands and applies the principles of design and color harmony in the selection and arrangement of the furniture and furnishings.

To freshen our memories and enable us better to apply the principles of art in the selection of furniture and furnishings, let us review briefly harmony, balance, proportion, rhythm, and emphasis.

Harmony.

Harmony means unity, right relationships of color and line, conformity in shape and arrangement. Just as people live in harmony with one another, so the things placed together in the house must give unity and harmony — a pleasing, unified picture of fitness.

Balance.

Balance means equal distribution of weights in color and size, a feeling of rest and equilibrium. "You will go most safely by the middle way" is a proverb that applies here — not top heavy, not lopsided.

Proportion.

Proportion means beautiful spacing, pleasing widths and lengths, relationship of lines and spaces to each other. The Greeks had a fine sense of proportion and they used the ratio of 3-5, 4-7, 5-8. The space relationships of the normal human body are the most beautiful to be found anywhere. The Greek's motto was "Nothing in excess."

Rhythm.

Rhythm means easy flowing lines — rhythm in furniture and furnishings expresses movement, life itself ; it is the dancing art principle. It indicates smoothness of movement and seems to tie one line to another.

Emphasis.

Emphasis is a demand for attention as the center of interest. Emphasis, if not overdone, relieves monotony and prevents commonplace and ordinary effects. The center of interest which is not pleasing may be calling attention because it represents a violation of art principles.

Movements in a room should be restful, the eye traveling from one line to another in a smooth, easy flowing way.

Some of us have more talent for creating beauty than others, but all of us can enjoy and appreciate the loveliness of nature and the beautiful things which others create. We can be artists by our choices of the things with which we live, our homes, our clothing, our gardens, and our friendships. Emerson says, "Though we travel the world over to find the beautiful we must carry it with us or we find it not." The ability to appreciate the beautiful makes our lives richer, fuller, and happier.

Color is one of the chief factors, if not the most important one, in decoration. Color adds cheerfulness and life to the house. The study of color is most interesting. If you were to take a box of paints and select the red, the blue, and the yellow — the three colors known as primary colors — you could, by combining these in various ways, produce every known color. By mixing the three you will have gray. By mixing any two primary colors, you will have what is known as the complementary color of the third, as blue and yellow produce green, and green is the complement of red; yellow and red produce orange, the complement of blue ; red and blue produce violet, the complement of yellow. Green, orange, and violet are called secondary colors.

Color Harmonies.

Color harmonies might be divided into two general groups, namely the related color harmonies and the contrasted color harmonies. In the related, we have the self -tone harmony (sometimes called dominant or monochromatic) which in reality consists of different tones of the same color, as when several shades of browns and tans are used together. Another related harmony is the adjacent or analogous, which is a combination of two or more consecutive colors on the spectrum, as blue and green.

In the contrasted color harmony group, we have first the complementary combination, as red and green, blue and orange, yellow and violet, and the triad color combination, when three colors located at equal spaces on the color chart are used. Examples are red, yellow and blue; orange, green, and violet.

If we mix equal parts of any color and its complement, for example red and green, the result will be gray. If the proportions are unequal, the predominating color is grayed or neutralized. By this, we mean softened in tone.

Colors may be brought into harmony either by graying or by "keying." Those which are keyed have some one color in common. Pure red and yellow do not harmonize but by graying them, mixing green with red and violet with yellow, we have dull red and tan, which make a good color combination. Or by keying them, mixing blue with each, we have violet and green, another good combination.

Black, white, and gray are neutral colors and may be added to any color harmony without definitely changing it.

Soft colors such as grays, greens, and warm tans are best for backgrounds and large surfaces because these give a feeling of restfulness. Bright colors such as scarlet, rose, orange, and bright blue are used in small areas such as in flowers, pottery, and pictures. Bright colors are irritating and too stimulating for some personalities when used in large proportions.

Evolution of Color in the Kitchen.

Kitchens were once dark and dingy, because colors that would not show dirt or dust were desired. Then we went to the other extreme and had pure white kitchens, which, while they were an improvement over the dark kitchen, were still dull and monotonous. The kitchen has now come out of the white stage and has become one of the gayest and most livable rooms in the house. Gay colored curtains and utensils and flowers are to be found there. Bright copper cooking utensils hang in plain sight and harmonize with the rest of the kitchen furnishings. Simplicity, order, cleanliness, harmony, and appropriateness should be criterions in selecting all kitchen furnishings, in order to create a cheerful, restful, and beautiful atmosphere.

Color Enjoyment.

Do you really enjoy color? Do you realize that color is the most dominant note in every room? And more, do you realize that as a rule every individual unconsciously gives a definite color note to the world? Do you know people who definitely express warmth and cheerfulness? Others who suggest distance and reserve? How interesting it is to analyze the color note of others, of rooms and homes, of ourselves.

Seasons, too, are expressed with color— autumn with its orange and red and purples; winter with it purples and blues; spring with its blues and greens; and summer with its greens, yellows, and orange.

Decorating the Rooms of the House.

Perhaps you have gone into some newly papered or newly furnished room and wondered at the change in atmosphere. The difference was probably brought about by a change in the color scheme. The colors from yellow through orange and red to violet are called warm colors and usually produce a very cheerful effect. Those from yellow through green and blue to violet are cool. For a room with much sunshine, you may choose a cool appearing wall paper, but for a room with little sunshine use a warmer color such as buff (a grayed yellow).

If the color predominating in your room is light and pale, the room seems larger, but if dark, intense colors predominate, the size is seemingly reduced. If you have a dark room you should study samples and select a paper that will make your room look brighter and more cheerful. If you select a light color your room will look lighter; but, if you choose a dark color, such as brown, dark green or gray, then your room will look even darker than it really is. In a dark room, brilliant red or brilliant yellow cannot be used because both are too bright. A soft shade of pink and a pale cream yellow make good colors for a dark room, because they are light as well as warm in effect.

Decorating the various rooms of the house will seem much simpler if we will let Nature be our guide. In nature, the softer colors — blues, violets, and grayed greens are seen in the distance, or background, while the more intense reds and yellows appear closer to us. Nature uses blue for the distant sky, for the spacious ocean; we use blue as a background in a ceiling or rug, but not in our walls which we want warmed and softened. The warm colors are irritating when used in quantities and the cool colors, on the contrary, are restful. Nature uses the greens and blues for the restfulness of space, of skies, of grass, of water; and in smaller proportion she uses the warm colors found in vivid sunsets, in flowers, and even in trees for a small portion of the year.

Through the years we have come to associate definite colors with definite emotions; green with restfulness; red with warmth and cheer; black with somberness; yellow with gayety. With this in mind, we use red in our reception room to welcome visitors; our living and sleeping rooms are furnished with restful colors; our kitchens are cheerful and gay.

"Oh, scarlet hurts, like some strange lust;
Mauve stills your heart like sleepy things;
Blue dreams forever; yellow laughs;
But green — green sings.
Oh, silver is a shining peace;
And purple throbs, like Bacchic kings;
Opal has quick, fairy mysteries;
But green — green sings."

Backgrounds.

No matter how well selected your furniture and furnishings, or how artistic the floor covering, if the wall is not decorated in such a way that it keeps its place as a background, then it spoils the effect of the whole.

Since the primary purpose of walls is to shut off the rest of the house, and since walls are flat solid things, you should aim to continue this idea in decorating them. A plain colored wall may be a very bad background even though it has no pattern. This is due to the fact that strong, bright colors refuse to remain in the background but seem to advance and make the wall seem nearer to you.

There are different finishes for walls, and at varying costs. Perhaps the most common finish is wallpaper. If you will experiment with samples of wallpaper you will discover what a difference in appearance different shades of wallpaper make. Take a lot of green samples; study them and see what effect they have on the appearance of the walls. Then try the same experiment with samples of pink wallpaper. Some of these will make the walls seem nearer, and hence not so flat. You will also find that paper that has large trailing vines, big figures of animals, parrots, large flowers, large designs, does not preserve this idea of flatness, but causes the walls to "stare" at one. Artistic wallpaper will cause the wall to look just as flat and solid as it really is. Pictorial wallpaper, by which we mean wallpaper that has roses, houses, or other objects in the design, does not produce a solid looking appearance and hence is in bad taste. When the wallpaper is figured, the important thing is to be sure that the decoration is conventionalized and subdued and stays in its place as a back- ground rather than as a foreground. Soft neutral shades, such as warm gray, putty, sand, and buff are pleasing background colors.

Collect samples of wallpaper, or better still get a book of samples from a wallpaper house or a department store and compare them. You will notice that some of the papers are smooth, others rough, and that some have a mingled composite color in which other colors seem to blend. The quality of roughness or smoothness in paper influences the intensity of color, just as the quality of texture in cloth influences its appearance. Textures in wallpaper differ as do paints. While wallpapers are not so shiny as enamel paint, they sometimes reflect too much light. Some wall- papers have a mingled color effect, due to texture, that is pleasing.

Woodwork.

The wallpaper and the finish of woodwork appear to affect the size of the room. Light color makes a room seem larger and cool colors give the feeling of spaciousness.

The color of the woodwork is very important as it in- fluences the color scheme of every room in the house. Unless the woodwork is really beautiful in itself in every room, it should be subordinated rather than emphasized. Ordinarily strong contrast between walls and wood-work should be avoided.

Highly polished or glazed woodwork has destroyed the beauty in far too many homes. It is better to paint the woodwork, even though hard wood, than to permit it to destroy harmony in the whole house.

When entering a room, do you notice the doors and windows? No doubt you do, either consciously or unconsciously, for the wood-work in these plays just as important a part in the appearance of the room as the furniture or finish of the walls. Since the color of the woodwork is not changed frequently, special attention should be given in the selection of a color suitable for the woodwork. Most people paint the wood- work around the doors and windows.

The woodwork is really a part of the wall and should be so considered in its decoration. It is usually advisable to have the color of the woodwork and walls similar, with the walls a shade or two darker. In the matter of color painted woodwork makes a simpler problem than wood, even in its natural finish. For example, when the woodwork is dark and the location of the room, due to its exposure, calls for a light wall and ceiling, it would be better to paint the woodwork a light color to harmonize with the lighter wall. Natural wood when stained should not be too dark, but should be of middle value. Walnut and mahogany stains should be used only when the wood-work is of excellent quality and can well be emphasized.

In some colonial houses, the entire background is made of wood and is very effective. The woodwork should not shine, as this causes it to reflect light. It should be part of the background and therefore unobtrusive. After varnishing, woodwork may be rubbed with pumice stone to remove the gloss, or it may be waxed instead of varnished. Painted woodwork can be highly polished or it can be somewhat dull, and therefore more pleasing to many people.

The finish of the wall and the texture of material used are also important items to be considered. Rough texture is being used in some plastered houses and is very effective, particularly in Spanish and Italian types. Ordinarily, paint on a smooth plaster is not pleasing; however, the paint can be treated in such a way as to give a mottled, broken effect, as when it is stippled. This treatment is somewhat expensive and for that reason most people prefer to select wallpaper that gives a similar effect.

Since walls are the background of the room, any paint which produces a glare or reflects the light unpleasantly is not a good finish. Sometimes plastered walls are left with a rough finish to prevent their having a shiny appearance when painted. Calcimine is a kind of water paint that is often used. However, this spots with water and cannot be easily cleaned. Dull finish paint made with oil is some-times used. This can be cleaned.

In the kitchen and bathroom, we need highly polished walls and woodwork because of the extra amount of cleaning necessary. When walls are too high, decorators can make them appear lower by dropping the moldings and letting the ceiling paper cover the upper part of the wall.

Ceilings.

A ceiling should be lighter in value than the walls. When ceilings are too dark or too highly colored, or papered with patterned paper, they seem top heavy and give us an un- comfortable feeling.

When finishing the walls, cost must be taken into consideration.

Calcimine put on at home often looks very streaked and botchy. Do you think it economical to do the work when you cannot do it in a workman-like manner? This work, as well as any other, can be mastered of course, and once learned, it would be economical for the novice to do it himself.

In papering, the cost is computed by rolls. Wallpaper comes in rolls twenty inches wide and eight yards long. Another size is thirty inches wide and five yards long. To figure the cost of papering the room, first measure the room, getting the length, width and height. From this, compute the number of strips to be used on each of the four side walls, and in addition, the number for the ceiling. Doors and windows in the room will reduce the amount of wall-paper necessary but something must be allowed for matching the pattern. After computing the number of rolls of paper required, multiply this number by the price per roll.

Floor Coverings.

Floor coverings include carpets, rugs, and linoleums. No matter what kind of floor covering is chosen, remember that floor coverings are a background for the furniture. Rugs with prominent designs, such as animals, large flowers, etc. are tiring and out of place as they become a foreground rather than a background.

In choosing floor coverings, it is well to consider the following questions: Is the covering under consideration durable? Is it easily cleaned? Is it substantial enough to lie on the floor? Are the colors and pattern good? Does it harmonize with the furniture?

The main purpose of the floor covering is protection. It should make the floor warmer and more comfortable, protect it from hard wear, deaden sound, and cover rough and unsightly places. It also should function as a part of the decoration of the room.

Kinds of Rugs.

Ingrain, Brussels, Wilton, and Axminster are the most common makes of rugs and carpets. In addition to these there are oriental rugs, fiber and grass rugs and mattings, and many variations of the old-fashioned rag rug. Did you know that all the floor coverings at Mount Vernon are rag carpets and that the looms on which their counterparts were woven may still be seen at the home of General George Washington?

Ingrain carpets and rugs are particularly good for use in bedrooms. They are easy to clean, inexpensive, and not heavy. Ingrain carpets and rugs wear better and look better if they are well padded with a layer of good carpet lining. Several thicknesses of newspapers tacked to the floor will answer the same purpose. Where an unfinished floor is left bare, plain ingrains make a good background for small rugs, or a cover for the space around the edges of a large rug.

Brussels Rugs.

Brussels rugs are so called because they were first made in Brussels, Belgium. You can tell a Brussels rug by the small loops covering the surface. If you run a wire hairpin under a row of these loops, you will notice that the loops were made when the rug was woven. These loops are made by passing the yarn over wires. This weave, where some of the yarns are left raised from the surface in the form of loops, is called the pile weave. A mg made from the pile weave is more agreeable to walk upon than a rug made with a plain, flat weave. The quality of Brussels rugs depends to some extent on the thickness of the looped pile. Good Brussels rugs should have not less than nine loops per inch.

There are two kinds of Brussels rugs. The genuine Brussels is made by weaving different colored yarns into the fabric so as to form a pattern. By examining the back where the colors show through faintly you can distinguish this rug. A cheaper Brussels rug is called Tapestry Brussels, which is lighter in weight than the genuine Brussels. In the Tapestry Brussels, the colors are either printed on the yarn before it is woven, or the rug is woven and the colors printed on the fabric. The back of the tapestry rug shows no color at all, only the plain grayish tan of the foundation cloth.

Wilton Rugs.

The name Wilton rug is derived from the name of the place where it was first manufactured — Wilton, England. This rug is made in exactly the same way as a Brussels rug with the yarn woven over wires to form loops. In the Brussels rug, you can put a hairpin under all the loops, but if you try to do the same with the Wilton, you will notice that the loops have been cut, as with a sharp knife. In making these rugs, wires having a knife-like edge are used and as the wires are pulled out they cut the loops. The ends of the loops stand up as in fur and are called pile. The Wilton rug, having this pile, is more difficult to clean than the Brussels, and the Brussels is much softer as a floor covering. The quality of the Wilton rug, just as in the Brussels rug, depends partly upon the closeness of the pile. If the pile in a sample is thin and poor, then that rug would be a poor one to select.

The Wiltons, like the Brussels, may be made up in cheaper rugs by printing the colors on. When the Wilton is made in this way, we call it a Wilton velvet or a velvet rug. When the colors are printed on instead of being woven, naturally the rug is not so durable. When the printed rug becomes worn a little, the color wears off the top and the rug begins to look old and gray. The velvet rug can usually be detected by the pile which is short and thin.

Axminster Rugs.

Axminster, England, was the home of this rug two centuries ago. The Axminster has a longer pile and a more uneven texture than the Wilton rug. Instead of the pile being made over wires as is the case in Wiltons, it is made by pulling in each tuft of yarn separately as the weaving progresses. Formerly these tufts were knotted in by hand, but now they are put in by machinery. If you bend an Axminster rug back sharply, you will be able to see these tufts. The greater the number of tufts that are put in, the thicker and better the rug will be. The Axminster rugs have long, soft pile, but the cheaper grades are not very durable because the nap wears off and comes out easily when cleaned.

Oriental Rugs.

Rugs from the Orient, Persia, Turkey, and China, are sold in this country as oriental rugs. The pile is all knotted in by hand with an especially firm knot so as to show the foundation weave. These rugs are considered the most durable and beautiful that have ever been made and there is so much to learn about them that some people have made a life study of them. It is interesting to study the different patterns, how the yarns are dyed, and about the lives of the weavers.

Rag Rugs.

In the time of our grandmothers and great grandmothers, the most common floor covering in America was the rag rug. These were made with strong cotton or linen threads for warp and strips of cloth for filling threads. Many people used to take the strips of cloth and braid them, after which they sewed the braided rags into oval or circular shaped rugs. People have found these rag rugs so attractive and charming that they are manufactured in quantity and may be obtained in almost any furniture or department store. Rag rugs are usually used in bedrooms, in the bathroom, and in the space between rugs of one room and another.

Other Types of Rugs.

Rugs made of jute, grass, linen and hemp are of a coarse, harsh texture. These are suitable for porches and summer cottages because they are cool and do not hold the dust.

Linoleum makes a particularly suitable floor covering for the kitchen as it is nonabsorbent, does not hold grease, and is easy to keep clean.

Care of Rugs, Carpets, and Mattings.

First of all, before laying floor coverings of any kind, see that the defects in the floor are remedied. If this cannot be done, cover up the defects by padding with material for this purpose. Several layers of carefully arranged newspapers will do. Newspapers make an especially good padding under mattings or grass and fiber rugs, because the dirt which sifts through can be removed simply by folding and destroying the papers.

When a large removable rug is used with ingrain or other carpet tacked down around the edges of the floor, the padding in the middle of the room may be covered with strips of heavy manila paper. The manila paper must be carefully laid, with the strips overlapping each other. The carpet will hold it in place. This will prevent dirt from getting into the padding and provide a smooth surface which can be easily brushed when the rug is taken up.

A carpet should be carefully fitted to the space over which it is to be tacked. If it is so large that it wrinkles, it will be uncomfortable under foot and may be torn when moving heavy furniture. If it is stretched too tight, the threads may break. Turning under one edge of a carpet or rug when it is too large should be avoided if possible. Turning under forms a ridge which not only looks clumsy, but also wears and soils more quickly than the rest. Rust proof tacks should be used to fasten rugs and carpets to the floor.

Matting lies more flatly and wears better if laid with the edges close together and tacked near the edge with brads or small tacks. The cut edges of matting should be bound or turned under at once to prevent fraying.

Choosing your Rug.

Since small rugs on the bedroom floor make cleaning that room easier, many people prefer small rugs to a single large one. When choosing a rug, make allowance for a large part of the bare floor to show around the edges of the rug. Choose a rug so heavy that the edges will not curl. Do not purchase a cheap, gaudy rug for you will soon tire of it. No matter what kind is chosen, remember that floor coverings are a background for the furniture.

Choosing Furniture.

It is a good thing for us to make a study of the different periods of furniture so that we may adapt the proper ones to our homes. Reed and wicker are in good taste depending upon the type of house you live in and whether you live in a house or apartment. Furniture that is well made, with good lines and color harmony should he selected. Choice may be influenced by personal taste, cost, suitability to purpose, and durability.

Furniture lasts a long time and is often handed down from one generation to the next. Some people have heirlooms of generations before them. If you start out to purchase a winter coat, you study the style, durability, cost, etc. Just so when buying furniture, you should study these same points, but since furniture is more enduring than any clothes we may buy, we should use our best judgment in its selection. One should buy the best he can afford in furniture. A visit to a furniture factory will be instructive and will give you many new ideas concerning the construction of furniture and its durability.

Many housewives buy a fine piece or two of furniture every year. This procedure enables them to make a collection of good furniture, whereas, if they bought several pieces the same year and did not feel able to buy durable furniture, in the end they would be left with a large amount of old, shabby furniture that would be short lived and unsatisfactory. We must take into consideration the pieces we already have and buy those that will fit into the scheme we have chosen, or gradually change the scheme if we are dissatisfied with it or tired of it. Some pieces of furniture will fit into almost any selection; fiber chairs and colonial chairs may be used as informal pieces to fit any scheme.

Other points to take into consideration are good lines and proportion, kind of wood, color, and finish.

Good Lines.

Good strong lines with curves, simply formed and with decoration conforming to the structure of the article itself, form the basis for harmony in home furnishings. The size and shape of a chair should be determined first by its usefulness or purpose. All decoration should seem to grow out of the lines of the chair and should seem to be a part of it. Furniture which should first of all be useful and comfortable, should depend largely upon its structural design for its beauty rather than on any type of decoration. As most of our furniture is boxlike in shape, naturally all the structural lines are straight. However, if curved lines are added, the rectangular lines must not be interfered with by the curves. Curved furniture is attractive but when the curves are decided and exaggerated, they give furniture the appearance of being weak and wobbly and of being unable to sustain weight and serve the purpose for which it was intended.

Good Proportion.

Good proportion exists when the different parts of a piece of furniture are spaced so as to balance. When all the spaces are exactly alike a monotonous effect results. Go into a large furniture store and study the various pieces of furniture. Notice those with unusually good proportion.

Kinds of Wood.

There are many woods used in the manufacture of the furniture on the market today and we should give them all study. Walnut, mahogany, oak, red gum and maple are the ones most commonly used.

Walnut.

Walnut is a hard wood and is difficult to distinguish from mahogany, as they both take a smooth, lustrous finish. Being such a desirable wood for furniture, it is imitated, just as mahogany is imitated by the use of cheaper woods. The substitute for walnut is gum wood. Circassian walnut is in reality not a walnut but is a kind of ash, with a prominent grain. Because the swirling lines are so conspicuous in Circassian walnut, it is not held in as high favor as some other woods.

Mahogany.

Mahogany is finished with different shades of red and brown stain. It shows little grain in the finished wood. Since it takes a very smooth and lustrous finish, it is particularly desirable. Sometimes birch is used as a substitute to imitate mahogany. Much furniture that is advertised as mahogany is merely an imitation, made of birch with a mahogany finish. The manual training teacher can show you how to tell mahogany from other woods. What pieces of furniture have you seen made of mahogany?

Oak.

As oak is a very durable wood, very strong and hard, it is used largely for the massive and larger pieces of furniture. Golden oak is so called from the light brownish color or finish. Some people do not like this bright color but prefer the soft dark brown color given to oak, which is very beautiful and agreeable. Sometimes it is finished in a greenish gray tone; this too is very beautiful. Oak is often imitated. The imitation oak is hard to distinguish.

Veneering.

The finish of furniture has much to do with the general appearance. Two chairs of oak made exactly the same in every respect except the finish will have different effects. One with a bright yellowish color, varnished so that it is shiny, will produce a poor effect, while the same chair stained a soft, rich brown, and then rubbed until it has a lustrous glossy polish, will be beautiful and attractive. In order to produce cheap furniture which at the same time looks well, the manufacturers use a process called veneering. This consists of gluing a thin layer of wood on to the surface of a cheaper piece of wood. The drawback with veneered furniture is that it often becomes unglued and the thin layer pulls off or the corners catch. However, this process does produce attractive and serviceable furniture. Veneered furniture should by all means be sold as such. In making furniture, by veneering a thin strip to another piece of the same wood, warping can be prevented. This is often done in mahogany and other good furniture. When selecting furniture, you should learn whether the veneer is used to make a cheap, attractive piece of furniture or if it is used to prevent the warping of the larger pieces.

Sometimes we are able to trade at a store whose labels and salesmen can be depended upon to describe honestly the merits of their wares, although not all stores are in this classification.

Getting Furniture Suited to its Purpose.

Before selecting any article of furniture, we should ask ourselves if it suits the purpose for which we need it.

If you are in need of a dresser for your room, for instance, it should serve two purposes, that of providing drawer space and a mirror. A chest of drawers is very convenient for wearing apparel and provides plenty of drawer space. However, if you can have but the one piece of furniture and it is necessary to provide a mirror and the dresser drawer space too, you no doubt will conclude to get the piece that will answer both purposes. A mirror over a chest of drawers is not of much use, but a long mirror can be hung elsewhere in the room and prove very useful.

If you lived in a small house with tiny rooms, and started out to furnish it, what kind of furniture would you consider? Would you ask to see the large massive pieces, which are intended primarily for mansions or large homes, or would you try to make your furniture conform to the house in which you must live? A small room with large pieces of furniture is not attractive. If you are selecting a desk or table, you should ascertain whether or not you have room for the knees and also whether or not the chair is high enough.

The family with small children should buy furniture which can be used by them without too much fear of spoiling its attractiveness. Harmonious family relationships are more important than expensive furniture, and the house whose furniture shows scratches or tears made by small hands or feet is more inviting than one whose gleaming furniture stands austere, lonely, and unmarked proclaiming a well appointed but childless home.

Groupings and Arrangement.

It is possible to have beautiful houses and exquisite furnishings and still have unattractive homes. How? By failing to apply the principles of art to the arrangement of the furnishings so as to produce a harmonious and pleasing atmosphere.

Articles of furniture which are used together should be placed together in groups. When we place articles together, we should consider especially harmony and balance. It is better to have too few than too many accessories. With too few the room will be dull and uninteresting, while too many will give a sense of confusion and disorder.

The arrangement and placement of small pieces of furniture and decorative accessories will help either to make the rooms more homelike and beautiful or to give a feeling of unrest. One cannot say too often that the use of too many decorative objects is to be avoided, but on the other hand coldness, formality, and severity will prevail when too few accessories are used.

If possible, try this interesting experiment. Take everything out of a room and then proceed to refurnish it in accordance with your knowledge of the artistic, using for the most part the things which you have. This experiment will certainly afford you ample opportunity to apply the principles of design and color harmony and to some extent the other art principles such as balance and proportion.

Let comfort, convenience, and restfulness, as well as balance, proportion, rhythm, emphasis, harmony, and color influence your judgment as you joyfully carry out this problem. Study the rooms and homes of your friends and use your imagination. Stand in the middle of some room that attracts you. Do you get a sense of balance? Locate the center of interest. Study the color scheme you think the owner had in mind. Decide whether the walls, ceiling, woodwork, and floors make good backgrounds or attract too much attention. Find out how structural and decorative design are emphasized. Do you feel a sense of rhythm, good proportion, and harmony as you permit your eyes to survey the room? Is the room friendly? Is there a note of cheerfulness anywhere about? You might find in the answer to these and similar questions information that would help you to make practical use in everyday life of the various art principles involved in tasteful arrangement of furniture and furnishings.

The Living Room.

The living room should be the center of interest in the home. It belongs to the whole family and is likewise enjoyed by their friends. Beauty and convenience, comfort and restfulness should be the keynotes, but how can we secure them? Beauty should be obtained through definite obedience to the principles of art; convenience, through right grouping of furniture for reading, writing, serving, and receiving visitors; comfort through the selection of furniture proportionate to the needs of the family group, usefulness and suitability being the chief aim; and restfulness, through the selection of chairs and furniture to suit the ages and sizes of the members of the family. Restfulness also comes from the right color selection and from harmony in design and arrangement.

The fireplace is usually the center of interest in the living room and too often in our modern homes it is placed in one corner of a long room, thus making it impossible for all the family and friends to "gather 'round the open fire."

All living room furniture should be desirable in size and shape, firm, well made, and comfortable. Frail, delicate chairs, even though heirlooms, have no place in the living room where bodily comfort and security are desired. That furniture should always be suited to its purpose is especially applicable to furniture in the living room.

Arrangement or Placement of Furnishings in the House. - In arranging furniture and in its selection, we should think first of its structural design. Furniture should be arranged against the wall just as trees, hillsides, and flowers would be placed in a drawing by an artist. Place the larger pieces first and consider the interrelation of wall space available and the lines of each piece of furniture. Practically all furniture, as well as most rooms, is rectangular in shape which helps us to see that rugs and large articles of furniture belong parallel to the walls in order to emphasize the shape of the room. Smaller pieces of furniture may be placed diagonally for convenience and comfort or to give a more informal, friendly atmosphere. A large piece of furniture placed diagonally gives a crowded careless appearance but placed parallel to the walls it creates the impression of restfulness.

The basic principle of all house planning and furnishing is usefulness, and diagonally placed furniture violates this principle by its wastefulness of space. A chair may be placed diagonally to create informality and to keep the parallel lines from becoming too monotonous without violating the principle of usefulness if the space around it may be used. A chest of drawers, however, or a divan placed diagonally in a corner not only presents a poor appearance but makes it impossible to use the space behind it.

The chief characteristics of any room should be complete unity of effect, with walls, woodwork, and ceilings providing an ideal background for people, furniture, and furnishings. Rugs belong naturally under the feet and should not call unduly for attention; furniture should be suited in size, shape, color, and lines to the room; curtains, draperies, and shades should conform to the lines of the windows and give protection and privacy but permit the fresh air and sunshine to enter. Altogether a room should be comfortable, peaceful, beautiful, and friendly in its appointments.

The Dining Room.

Cheerfulness and hospitality should be the prevailing notes in the dining room. Outside of the living room, it is the place where members of the family gather more than in any other room. Mealtime in harmonious, pleasant surroundings not only is an enjoyable experience but is an aid to good digestion. Here the family should find complete relaxation.

In this room, as in all other rooms in the house, one dominant color tone such as grayed green, orange red, yellow or blue, should obtain. Other colors should be composed in part of the dominant color. Here as in other rooms, it is well to decide upon a general color scheme and choose all other furnishings for the room with this color in mind.

All that we have learned about finishes for woodwork, design for furniture, and simplicity in its relation to beauty applies to the dining room for here we want to create a harmonious effect without monotony. The walls, wood-work, ceiling, and rug should be simple and inconspicuous. The light should be sufficient to illuminate the table but soft so that it does not glare.

The Bedroom.

Since the primary purpose of the bed-room is rest, it should be simply furnished, with careful attention to color and design. Walls should be subdued; there should be no gaudy design to cause irritation. Rugs should be restful in design and color. The room should contain at least one comfortable chair, and the bed should be placed so as to let as much air as possible into the room.

This room particularly should reflect the personality of its occupant. The young girl's bedroom for this reason should reflect daintiness and refinement and the boy's bed-room should reflect vitality and ruggedness.

A Comfortable Bed.

When buying a bed for your room you should consider the mattress and the springs first. We hear people say, "Oh, what a comfortable bed." They probably have slept well in the bed by reason of the fact that the springs do not sag and the mattress is not lumpy but soft and even. It is injurious to sleep on a bed with old springs that sag, and it is uncomfortable to sleep on a mattress that has lumps.

Mattresses are usually filled with cotton-felt material made up in layers. This material makes a better mattress than one in which the cotton is merely stuffed into the ticking. The cotton-felt mattress, if made of a good quality of cotton, gives very good service and is very comfortable.

Some very comfortable mattresses are made with springs inside which keep them from being hard and matted. In such a mattress all materials should be of good quality, otherwise the springs may sag and the mattress become bumpy and uneven. Kapok, which is a soft, fluffy material, is sometimes used as filling for mattresses, although it is likely to mat down after use and become bumpy.

Pillows are usually filled with goose or duck feathers because they are light and soft. Chicken feathers are some- times used but they are heavy and do not make a very comfortable pillow.

Bed Coverings.

A few years ago the white bedspread was considered the only correct bed cover. Colored bed- spreads are now popular. The colored bed coverings used by our grandmothers were hand-woven and often very beautiful in design. Problems to consider in buying bed coverings include whether they wrinkle easily, soil easily, are of light weight so as to be easy in laundering, are too expensive, can be secured in colors, and will launder well.

Warm Bedclothes.

Blankets have a soft nap on the surface which holds warmth. Because air is a poor conductor of heat, bedclothes that enmesh the air and hold it serve to keep us warmer than heavy, bunglesome bed-clothes. A cotton blanket that has been washed often is not so warm as a blanket of the same quality that has not been laundered, because the nap of the new blanket catches the air and retains it. The nap of a blanket may be raised by brushing or scratching the surface of the blanket after it becomes worn. On a cold winter night we are all glad to resort to a woolen blanket for it is much warmer than a cotton blanket. Since woolen blankets are expensive and difficult to launder, they are not so desirable as part-cotton blankets.

Often quilts or comforters are used on beds instead of blankets. Comforters or comforts are made by covering a cotton or wool wadding with some soft material, such as sateen or silkaline. A wool filled comforter is warmer than one filled with cotton. Quilts are lighter in weight than comforters, but not so warm. They are made with cotton filling, but less cotton is used in a quilt than in a comforter. Many quilts are pieced from artistic designs.

Sheets and Pillow Cases.

Sheeting is always made with a plain weave and a smooth finish. The quality of sheeting is judged by the smoothness and evenness of its texture. Sheeting is classified all the way from coarse, unbleached muslin, up to a high grade of percale.

We use sheets to protect us from the roughness of the blankets and to protect the other bedclothes. Sheets are usually made ninety-nine inches long, but many prefer a length of 108 inches because sheets of that length can be turned back at least ten inches at the top. Some sheets are only ninety inches long, but these are very unsatisfactory.

Sheets and pillow cases must be laundered frequently, so it is desirable to have them of durable material. If you are buying bed linen, notice whether the weave is close and firm. An open weave will not wear well. When buying sheeting by the yard, you may determine whether or not it is made of strong yarn by raveling a thread and testing its breaking strength. Loosely woven sheeting is usually heavily sized or starched for the purpose of making it look firm. This sizing can be removed by taking a piece of goods in the hand and scratching the surface with the fingernail. It can also be tested by rubbing a small piece of the sheeting until all the sizing is rubbed out. If a sample is washed until the sizing is removed, the sample will then show whether the cloth is sleazy or firm.

The High School Girl's Bedroom.

Besides a comfortable bed, the girl needs a dresser, a desk or table, at least one chair, and a reading lamp in the room reserved for her private and personal use. Her room may be furnished to look like a studio or a living room while serving the purpose of a bedroom. In either instance, the bed may be a studio couch which can be converted into a bed. Pictures, books, lamps, pillows, and other intimate touches will add cheer to the room and express the girl's individual personality. It is in the choice of the minor things, such as bowls and vases, pictures and books, that the individual personality is indicated.

Her color scheme should be dainty and refined, perhaps ivory and old rose, orchid and green, or blue and pink. If she is an active girl, fond of sports and outdoor life, her color scheme may be golden brown and plum; red- yellow and gray; or green and brown. Decorative accessories may include a sewing basket, china, pottery vases, toilet articles, cushions, desk appointments, and perhaps a candy or stationery box.

The High School Boy's Room.

The boy's room can be made as interesting as the girl's by substituting articles of masculinity and convenience for the dainty articles found in the girl's room.

The floor covering in the boy's room may be rag rugs or linoleum, which will not soil easily. Besides a comfortable bed, which may have a wood or metal frame, his room should contain a highboy or chest of drawers in natural wood to match the bed, a mirror, preferably plain and square or oblong, which should be hung low enough for the convenience of the occupant, a low table, a sturdy desk, a lamp, bookshelves, tie rack, at least one chair, and pictures whose themes suggest the personality of the occupant.

Sun Room, Porches, and Gardens.

Attractive wicker and other informal furniture, gayly painted, with an inlaid linoleum floor covering for the enclosed sun room and Venetian blinds to carry out the color scheme, bring the out-of-doors to every member of the family. An oven in the back yard where steaks may be broiled and a table on which to serve outdoor meals give the family many pleasurable evenings that would otherwise be sacrificed. The back yard furnished for the purpose enables the family to serve themselves and their friends with refreshments, outdoor meals, and picnics and makes outings very convenient. The best food and ease in serving are possibilities in the home back yard that are not found in the usual outdoor meal.

A sun porch which is screened for the summer as a protection against flies and mosquitoes, and heated for winter use is enjoyed by many families.

Entrance Hallways.

The main entrance should be furnished in an attractive, hospitable manner to welcome visitors as they come into the house. This entrance is usually small and simplicity and cheerfulness are the keynotes to its furnishings.

A small table, over which is hung an oblong mirror, is both convenient and harmonious. A bright bowl or bit of pottery or a vase of flowers adds a note of intimacy. Here the warm colors may predominate, since the visitor is in the entrance but a short time, and warm colors suggest welcome and hospitality.

Window Decoration.

The design and color of window decorations are the important aspects of the window decoration problem. In fact, if the design and color are satisfactory, it is not necessary to have expensive decorations. Rayons and cottons in artistic patterns and weaves are inexpensive curtain materials. Curtains should furnish privacy and not exclude light. The purpose in having draperies is to give color and attractiveness. Curtains and draperies that are durable and easily cleaned are practical in homes where there are children.

We usually divide window hangings into two groups; namely, side draperies, which are in reality used only for decorative purposes, and glass curtains which are used to insure privacy and to shut off or soften light.

Draw curtains are made of material similar to side draperies and may be used instead of shades and side draperies. Sometimes draw curtains are the only form of decoration used on windows. In such cases glass curtains may not even be needed. This is true when the light is not too strong, provided curtains are not needed for privacy except when the draw curtains are pulled.

Venetian blinds of all colors are now being used much more extensively than formerly. These blinds often replace all other window decorations. However, draw curtains or inside draperies are often used to add color, to soften the lines of the window, and to help create a more unified appearance.

When you buy your curtains, it is absolutely necessary to think of them in conjunction with the other furnishings in the room. They must harmonize in color with the general color scheme of the room. You can select a figured curtain material that has a background in harmony with the wall. If you choose plain materials for your curtains do not get those which make a violent contrast. For example, if there were no other white in the room, then white curtains would be inharmonious. In such a case, the white curtains would seem literally to stare. If the bedroom has very light walls, with white woodwork, white curtains and white bedspreads are appropriate. Be careful about using figured curtain materials, such as cretonnes, if the wallpaper has a definite, clearly marked pattern. If your curtains and wallpaper both have definite patterns they "fight" with each other for attention. It is no more expressive of good taste to have roses and flying birds pictured on your curtains than it is on your walls.

Materials used principally for curtains include cretonne, dotted Swiss, scrim, marquisette, casement cloth, and net. When buying curtains, you must take into consideration the width of the windows and the width of the material, to see if it will cut to advantage.

When buying curtains ready-made, it is necessary to consider workmanship, the quality of the material, and the size and shape of the window you are buying them for. Curtains that do not fit and need to be altered become unsatisfactory because of the time that is required in making alterations.

Here are some things to be considered in buying curtain materials:

1. Appearance. Are the design and color suited to the room?

2. Quality. Is it of good quality, or cheap and sleazy?

3. Durability. If there are thin spots where the threads will break and holes appear, it is a waste of time and money to hang curtains of that material.

4. Laundering. Do not buy materials that stretch and pull out of shape.

5. Fading. Do curtains of the material fade when exposed to light?

6. Weight of the material. Does the weight of the material permit the right amount of light to enter?

Decorative Accessories.

We have learned that design is concerned with the selection and arrangement of color, lines, and shapes in order to produce beauty and harmony.

Good design is economical for it lives through the years.

Structural design relates to the size, shape, texture, and color of the object itself, permitting suitability and use to lead the way; while decorative design is applied to the completed structure to enhance its beauty. Decorative design should add interest or needed accents to the thing being decorated and strengthen the shape of the object, but simplicity and moderation should be placed foremost. The relationship between structural and decorative design should be kept uppermost in mind in selecting and in making decorative accessories such as sofa pillows, table covers, clocks, mirrors, and picture frames.

The needed touch of color in the home can be added by a beautiful piece of tapestry, a bowl, or a vase, and interest can be added to the room by some antique piece of furniture or an heirloom such as brass candlesticks or a piece of rare glass. Such things, however, should be in good design and add to the interest of the room in which they are used. Too many decorative objects tend to clutter up a room and give a sense of restlessness and disorder. "Rotating" the use of such things in different seasons or for special occasions adds variety and distinction to their use.

Faulty lines and proportions applied to these little things can mar the harmony of the whole house. For example, teapots and dishes that are inartistic in shape, form, or color, and vases that are out of proportion are as distasteful as wrong accessories in dress. In glassware as well as in vases, good structural design is essential to real beauty. The same rules in decoration and color that apply to the larger pieces of furniture can he applied also to the smaller pieces such as pottery, china, dishes, and vases. Plain, undecorated china can be beautiful because of its fine contour. The beauty of china, pottery, and glassware depends to a large extent upon their structural design or contour. It would be interesting to go window shopping or visit the houseware sections in department stores and study the different types of dishes, vases, and similar products. These wares are displayed for sale because of the demand for them, but some are artistic and some are not. It is only when people become sufficiently educated to ask for better lines and decorations that more artistic wares will appear in the stores.

Knives, forks, and teaspoons should have a design which conforms to their use and their natural shape. The finish of silver also affects its beauty. High polish is not only hard to care for but is not considered so beautiful and distinctive as the full, lustrous finish. No household articles are used more than china, glass, and silver. Consequently, the best knowledge that we have or can gain should be applied to the selection of these articles.

Vases and Candlesticks.

Two vases or two candlesticks of like design tend to give a feeling of balance or completeness. As a rule, we separate two vases or similar articles by something of contrasting height, such as a clock or a piece of pottery, when we use them on the mantle or on a desk.

Lamps.

A lamp is a useful article and naturally should be placed where it can be used readily. Desirable colors for lamp shades are maize, yellowish tan, and gold, which give natural light. Rose gives a warm light, but this is not a natural shade. Blue, purple, green, and gray absorb the light and thus make dull and uninteresting shades for a lamp. Sunny colors in lamp shades enhance the beauty of the lamp.

We learned that wallpaper should not have large designs. The same is true of lamp shades. Pictorial de- signs, either in the shade or applied, are not appropriate for reading lamps. Many women and girls are inclined to overdecorate lampshades with lace ruffles and other trimming. Overdecoration mars the appearance of an otherwise beautiful lampshade.

Two things to consider in selecting lamps are that they should be adequate for needs and that the color and design should add beauty to the room.

How do we know when there is adequate lighting? The only way to know exactly how much light is needed in a given room is by testing with a sight meter. Your local electrical company will make tests for you if requested to do so. Light should be located at the most convenient places, as for example, a lamp for each chair or davenport to give sufficient light for sewing and reading without straining the eyes. A lamp at the desk which throws light on the paper without glare relieves eye strain. The old type of light was too low and its heavy shade was twisted into all kinds of shapes. We are beginning to see the need for following the best rules of structural design in selecting the body of the lamp and the best type of decorative design in its shade. The modern indirect lighting system has proved satisfactory, in that there are no shadows, and a soft, natural light is distributed evenly.

There are places in the house where a small light is adequate, such as the night light in the hall or near the bed in the guest room for guests who arrive late.

The size of the room and the type of work to be done in the room should determine the number and kind of lights. Wall lights are replacing more and more the central light with its brilliant glare. There is nothing more inharmonious or disconcerting than a central light that is hard and strong. Portable lamps or side lights generally furnish better and more desirable lighting than central lighting systems or ceiling lights.

The arrangement of furniture should govern the placing of lamps. A lamp or two on the principal table or a floor or table lamp to the left of easy chairs, are generally pleasing. The home service department of your local gas or electric company will be glad to send a representative to your home to give advice and assistance in working out your own individual lighting problem, as well as suggestions for the arrangement of lamps, designs, and colors to harmonize with your furnishings.

Pictures.

What pictures do you most enjoy? What pictures hang on the walls of your home? And why have they been chosen? Are some pictures especially suitable for the living room? For the dining room? For the bed- room? Pictures should seem appropriate to the family and to the room in which they are used. There are many types to choose from but those which have some universal appeal and that grow in charm and loveliness with the years should form the basis of choice. The theme of the picture, its color, and its design should be in harmony with the house and furnishings. Pictures are expressive of the personalities and characters of the people who choose them. Therefore, knowing something to relate about the artist and the background of a picture creates new interest in us by giving our friends insight as to our ideals and our ability to appreciate art.

Well-chosen pictures add interest to the room. Pictures as well as other accessories may actually add the needed accents in color and design to a particular room. A well-chosen picture may be the center of interest with all decoration taking its note from this picture. Pictures may also create disorder and confusion in our homes, or they may add distinction and beauty. For example, one picture on the wall may be beautiful and artistic, when half a dozen give a feeling of confusion and irritability.

Among the rules for hanging pictures one usually finds a few useful "don'ts" such as "Don't use fussy cords and tassels," "Don't use misleading lines of wire" as for example when one wire is hung to a single hook thus forming a triangular shape. Hang pictures so that wires do not show if possible. Make the picture seem flat against the wall if at all possible. The most approved height for a picture is on a level with the eye. When a series of pictures is used, they should be placed in relation to each other. Consider also the shape and size of the space in relation to each picture.

In brief, the same rules apply to artistic arrangement of pictures, tapestry, and minor furnishings as apply to the arrangement of other furniture.

Flowers and Vases.

Vases of distinctive structural design, with decorative design conforming to structural contour may be beautiful in themselves. Vases may be so overly decorated that they are neither beautiful in themselves nor suitable as containers for flowers.

It is not always an easy problem to find vases of the right size, shape, and color to use for any given bouquet of flowers. A vase which is to be used for flowers should be modest in color, of good structural design, and not overly ornamented, so that the flowers themselves may mainly receive our attention.

The habit of gathering flowers and placing them in vases probably originated in Japan. It is indeed an art to be able to arrange flowers tastefully, an art that begs for attention and most careful thought. The rules of color harmony and design apply to this problem in the same way they are related to all other decorative problems.

Good balance in vases is first secured by arrangement in respect to the size and length of the flowers to be placed in the vase. Stiffness or formality does not belong here. Cut flowers in varying lengths, probably no two should be exactly the same length. From three to five lengths of the flower to be used usually make up well. When more than one type or color is to be used, it is better to permit one type of flower or one color to predominate.

Placing the finished bouquet in a suitable setting in the living room, dining room, bedroom, or hall is equally important.

As a hobby, what could be more interesting than a study of flowers and flower arrangement? Much can be learned from the Japanese for the Japanese flower arrangement is known throughout the world.

Beauty in flower arrangement comes not by accident but by most careful and thorough consideration of the problem. Simplicity here as elsewhere is the keynote to beauty. Things are beautiful only when they fit the purpose for which they were created.

Beauty exists in a myriad of fragile, evanescent things that break at the touch and vanish as a dewdrop before the sun. Also it exists in creations that we can use in our homes to meet and fulfill our more practical needs or satisfy our esthetic desires. "Beauty," said the poet Keats, "is its own excuse for being."

"He who would grow a rose garden must first have the love of roses in his heart." Most of us have that love. Behind the walls of our houses we are excluded from the beautiful outdoors and we become restless through our longing for the products of gardens, fields, and woods. Flowers in the home, if tastefully arranged, bring the outer world to us.

CHAPTER 17

THE EFFICIENT KITCHEN

Since it is estimated that about seventy percent of the housekeeper's day is spent in the kitchen, it is important that this part of the house be arranged as conveniently as possible in order that she may do the maximum amount of work with the minimum expenditure of energy and time. In the days when the kitchen was used as a work shop, laundry, sitting room, and dining room, it was necessarily much larger than it is today, when it is used solely as a place for the preparation of food. One hundred and twenty square feet usually make sufficient floor space. Besides saving the housekeeper many unnecessary steps, a small kitchen costs less to build than a large one. It should be almost square in shape in order that step-saving equipment may be arranged conveniently.

There should be plenty of light and ventilation in the kitchen; furnishings should be easily cared for; walls and floors should be sanitary and easily cleaned. Built-ins should be conveniently arranged and located so as to require the least possible amount of walking. The height of sinks and other working surfaces should be adjusted to the needs of workers.

The kitchen must be considered in relation to the dining room and the outside living room. There should not be much distance between the place where food is prepared and the place where it is eaten. Since so much time is spent in the kitchen, it should be a pleasant, harmonious place, and for that reason it is well to have it overlooking the flower garden or some other attractive view.

Since there are four essential steps in the preparation of food — collecting raw materials, preparing, cooking, and serving, and the same number of steps in the clearing away of food — removing, scraping, washing, and putting things away, equipment should be so arranged as to take care of these processes conveniently and in order, with the least possible expenditure of time and effort. Draw a picture of your kitchen as it is today, showing by dotted lines the steps taken in the process of preparing and clearing away food. Is equipment arranged so that no unnecessary step is taken? Or is it placed wherever there happens to be available space for an article of furniture? Rearrange your kitchen on paper with the idea in mind of saving all unnecessary steps. It is only by careful study that the housekeeper will be able to see how many of her methods and habits are wasted effort.

Kitchen Tools.

Let us consider the kitchen as a work shop for the preparation of food. Formerly when kitchens were used partly as sitting rooms, all cooking utensils were kept hidden, but now with our gas and electric fuel and our attractive utensils, they may be kept in a convenient place in the kitchen. For instance, each utensil and tool should have its definite place on a hook or shelf near the surface where it will be used. Knives and other utensils which are often thrown carelessly into drawers become dulled and dented. By having such things on hooks, or in a special place, undue wear is prevented. A sanitary cabinet specially designed for this purpose is a very useful convenience.

Floors, walls, and tables in the efficient kitchen should be easy to clean, and preferably surfaced with nonabsorbent materials. Inlaid linoleum is an ideal covering for the floor, since it is nonabsorbent and does not collect grease and dirt as wood does. Care should be taken in laying the linoleum that the baseboard joining is perfect. A metal strip may be used to cover the joining or the seams may be cemented.

Tile is sanitary and nonabsorbent but its hard surface is tiring to the feet and it is slightly slippery as well. Its ideal use is for an area of about two feet around the base of the stove as a protection against fire. If used on the entire surface of the floor, rubber mats should be placed around as a prevention against fatigue and slipping.

Tile is ideal for the wall covering, as it is particularly easy to clean and is attractive in appearance. Oil cloth wall fabric is another good wall covering that may be kept clean by wiping with a cloth. Plaster also makes a satisfactory wall covering. Paper is unsatisfactory as it loosens with heat and steam and for that reason its use is impractical on both walls and ceiling.

Color in the kitchen is as important as any other place in the house. Since, as before stated, approximately seventy percent of the housekeeper's day is spent here, the surroundings should be attractive, cheerful, and restful. Warm gray, light apple green and "putty" or pine birch or maple in their natural finish are particularly attractive in the kitchen. Walls and ceiling should also be in light tones.

Table tops should be of nonabsorbent, easily cleaned materials. Porcelain is particularly satisfactory for the preparing table.

Built-Ins.

Built-in features such as cabinets, shelves, etc. should be arranged so there is no waste space. Cup- board shelves should vary in width from six to fourteen inches, depending upon their use. They should be wide enough for only one article so that it will not be necessary to move several articles in order to reach the desired one. Shelves should be just deep enough to hold the articles placed upon them.

The insides of kitchen cupboards may be finished with light enamel paint to avoid the necessity of using paper on shelves, as well as for convenience in working. Drawers built in the lower part of cupboards should not be too long or too deep if expected to facilitate manipulation, and should have the same finish as the shelves. They should be kept neat and in order so that articles are easy to find.

Built-in cabinets and work tables should be located so that a good light falls on the working surface and should be at a height convenient for the worker. Shallow drawers in the work table, divided into compartments, are convenient for holding knives, spoons, and other small equipment needed in food preparation. Narrow shelves above the work table are convenient for holding supplies needed in the preparation of food, and pots and pans may be placed in a cupboard below the table.

The quantity and the kind of equipment to select are individual problems for each housekeeper. What to buy varies with the size of the family, size of the house, and the family's financial budget. An overstocked kitchen uses space that is needed for other things but adequate equipment, well selected and arranged, makes housework a pleasure. All labor-saving devices that can possibly be afforded should be included. The four important things to consider when buying kitchen equipment are (1) size; (2) price in relation to durability and need; (3) design, finish, and quality; and (4) ease of cleaning.

Kitchen Utensils.

Kitchen utensils fall into three distinct classifications: (1) those used in food preparation; (2) those used in cooking, serving, and storing; (3) those used in washing dishes. The efficiency of equipment is influenced by the character of its construction. Equipment for the kitchen may be made of aluminum, earthenware, glass, tin, wood, enameled steel, cast iron, etc. Earthenware and glass are ideal for baking utensils as the food may be served in the dish it is cooked in, thus retaining the heat longer, and also eliminating extra handling and washing. Utensils should be of the right size, easy to handle, well-constructed, of good grades of material, and should harmonize in color and design as much as possible with the other kitchen equipment and furnishings.

Stoves.

The kind of stove to select is dictated by the type of fuel that must be used. Gas ranges in towns and oil or wood stoves in rural districts are the most commonly used at present although electric ranges are becoming more widely used both in towns and on farms that have their own lighting units. Electric stoves are easy to clean and give excellent service; gas stoves should be constructed so they may be taken apart and easily cleaned. The ideal cooking stove is the one in which fuel is used only during the actual cooking process and may be cut off instantly when food is not cooking.

When equipping the kitchen, it is a wise plan to make a list of all the articles needed and price them at various stores before purchasing.

Garbage should be drained carefully and kept as dry as possible. Waxed paper bags, or even newspaper bags, used inside of the garbage pail, keep the pail clean and facilitate easy and sanitary handling.

Good Times in the Kitchen.

Although much can be said for the small, efficient, time saving kitchen, it has its disadvantages as well, the greatest of which is that it does not permit the happy gatherings of groups that are possible in the larger kitchen. Fortunate are the inmates of the house with a large kitchen, wherein a table is set with a gay cloth, into which the high school boy and girl may invite their friends after a show, a dance, or a hike to scramble eggs and fry bacon; or the whole family may gather on a rainy evening to make taffy, popcorn, or have a waffle supper. Since the housekeeper must use so much of her day there, it is convenient, too, sometimes to have her more intimate friends or neighbors visit her in the kitchen during the preparation of a meal. Some of the happiest memories of childhood are bound up with the fascinating scents which come from a busy kitchen, such as the incense from fresh oven-baked rolls and cookies and the poignant odors from boiling coffee, bacon sizzling in an iron skillet, the preparation of roast turkey and dressing, or other delicacies in special holiday dinners.

The livable kitchen may be a very useful agency in bringing the family together in closer bonds of union and understanding. In such an instance, the sacrifice in loss of efficiency that comes from having an unnecessarily large kitchen is more than compensated for in the opportunity the large kitchen makes for the enjoyment of impromptu feasts and suppers in this most livable of rooms.

DOMESTIC

"No lofty sonnet flows from pen of mine,
No worship of the sun — of dawn — of light;
A silver moon to me reveals no sign,
No romance fills the mystic black of night.
The stars, which twinkle secrets to all others,
A lonely cloud, the rainbow's pastel hues,
The tender sighs and words of youthful lovers,
For me their poignant meaning seem to lose.
My thoughts all run to unpoetic things
Like rent, and food, and clothes, and bills for same.
And when my pen aspires, the doorbell rings,
Or neighbors tap upon my window frame.
My Muse inspires no pretty words or phrases —
My sonnet's in the way my bread dough "raises."

— Bee Miller

CHAPTER 18

CARE OF HOUSEHOLD FURNISHINGS

The Importance of Care.

When new, your house may be the acme of taste in architectural design; the beauty of its landscaping may escape challenge from the most discriminating art critics; the floor plan may represent all that efficiency and attractiveness could dictate; and the furnishings may be suggestful in every detail of harmony — by balance, proportion, and color. Yet unless it is well cared for inside and out, it will not remain the restful, engaging home it once was. The touches of decadence are more tragic, more discernible, and more repulsive amid scenes of former order and com- fort than is disorder where order and comfort never existed. Rundown, unkept houses suggest more than crumbling cement and rotting wood; to the observer's mind they carry farther and lead to mental speculations that are not flattering to the inmates of such abodes.

Magnificence and luxury have little significance in themselves but order, cleanliness, and taste do have significance. They suggest a place to which you enjoy bringing your friends; a place where you enjoy your leisure time; a home that provides the mental and spiritual benefits that home life should give.

The Cleaning Schedule.

Formerly there was an annual housecleaning day, usually in the spring, when everything in the house from garret to cellar was given a thorough cleaning. On these occasions, everyone was tired and cross and everyone found trouble in staying out of someone's way; but today, those tasks are distributed throughout each day and week and housecleaning has a definite place in the schedule which allows for rest and leisure time and yet serves to keep the house in good order. Every member of the family has a part in the daily or weekly care of the house, and through a spirit of willingness and cooperation, each takes his own responsibility and no one is overworked.

In making a schedule, special and weekly tasks must be taken into consideration also, since only some of the tasks are done daily. The schedule should not be the same for any two days of the week since each day has its special duties. If Monday is wash day, most of Monday's cooking may be done on Sunday, or if wash day is on Tuesday, as it is in many homes, Tuesday's meal preparation may be partially taken care of on Monday.

Each day should have definite rest periods, a short one in the morning, a longer one in the afternoon. This makes for greater efficiency, a better mental attitude, and less physical fatigue. The important thing in this as in other schedules is that once having been made, it should be strictly adhered to.

An adequate plan will provide for restoring cleanliness and order to home and furnishings and the maintenance of the house, furnishings, and equipment. Daily care of the house includes airing the rooms, making the beds, clearing away newspapers, magazines, and other accumulated materials, sweeping, dusting, emptying waste baskets, adjusting shades, rearranging furniture, etc. Weekly care includes laundering, general cleaning, and changing bed linens. Special care or that done at irregular intervals includes washing the bedding, waxing the floors, and ridding the household of ants, flies, mice, and other household pests.

Care of Bedrooms.

The bedroom should be thoroughly aired at least once a week, spreading the linens and covers over chairs near the open windows. Closet doors should be opened so that clothing may be aired. After airing the bedroom for about an hour, the bed should be made up. To make a bed properly, place the mattress pad straight on the mattress with a sheet over it; tuck the sheet in at the sides and ends, drawing tight to eliminate wrinkles; and fold in and miter the corners. The top sheet should be placed on the bed and tucked in firmly at the bottom. Blankets and other bedding should be placed over the top sheet and firmly tucked in at bottom, turning the top of the sheet back over the bedding at the head of the bed so the bedding may not become soiled. The pillows should be shaken, pressed into form, and placed on the bed as desired.

When the weekly change of linen is made, the bedroom should be cleaned thoroughly and the bedding should be given a thorough airing. Occasionally the springs should be cleaned by wiping them with a soft cloth. Windows should be given a thorough washing once a month and curtains washed whenever soiled. There are numerous good window cleansers that keep windows clean and bright.

However, they may be washed satisfactorily with soap suds and polished with a dry, soft cloth.

Bedrooms particularly should be clean, neat, and fresh. Furnishings may be simple or massive as the owner wishes, but cleanliness and freshness cannot be over-emphasized.

Care of Bathroom and Closets.

Bathrooms should be clean, sanitary, and odorless. Floor, tub, and bowl should be cleaned daily. Once a week the walls should be cleaned and the floor mopped and scrubbed thoroughly. Deodorants should be used in bowl or stool which should be scoured frequently.

Closets for clothes should be aired, dusted, cleaned, and kept in neat order. Shoe trees should be put in shoes and the shoes then placed on shelves or kept in a shoe bag which can be tacked on the inside of the closet door. Hats should be kept on stands or placed in boxes. Special closets such as cleaning closets, which contain mops, brooms, and cleaning preparations, and linen closets for all the household linens should be clean and well-arranged so that each mem- her of the household will have no trouble in finding the article he needs. care. Some floors need daily sweeping, which should be followed by use of a dust mop. Waxed floors should be cleaned with a mop moistened with turpentine and then polished with a dry mop. Waxed floors should not be oiled or washed. Varnished floors need daily mopping with a dust cloth, oil mop, or dry mop. Water will destroy varnish as well as coarsen the wood. Woodwork should be wiped frequently with a dry dust cloth and once a month given special attention.

Walls should be cleaned frequently; if papered, they should be wiped down with a soft cloth to keep from tearing or marring the paper; if painted, they should he washed with warm water and mild soap.

Care Prolongs the Usefulness of Furniture.

Whether or not a piece of furniture is liked influences the amount of use it will get. If one living room chair is much more comfortable than the others, everyone will want to use it, while a less comfortable chair may remain untouched for days. Chairs, sofas, car seats, etc. may be protected from climate, scratches, and dirt by covers. These may be made at home or bought ready-made. Many homemade covers are as attractive as the original covering. Other articles such as blankets, may be stored when not in use; table pads, rubber mats, etc. can be used to protect furniture and floors from undue wear. In climates where there is a great amount of sunshine, which is hard on furniture, furniture may be protected by slip covers or by lowering blinds. Rugs tend to fade when exposed to sunshine as do cretonne and other cloth chair covers.

In some homes, there is no respect for property. Dogs and other animals are allowed to jump upon nicely upholstered chairs and sofas, scratch them with their claws, and shed hairs on them; burning cigarettes are left on pianos or other furniture, making burns which are almost impossible to repair; tables are carelessly scratched by buttons on sleeves; lovely china and vases are handled carelessly and broken; children are not taught that they should not handle certain articles until they are old enough to do so properly; and mud and dust are tramped in on rugs because people neglect to clean their shoes before entering. Thus two identical pieces of furniture, placed in two different homes, would vary in length of beauty and usefulness. In a home where respect for property is taught, where beauty and harmony are appreciated, and where there is some knowledge and appreciation of the care and skill that are taken to create lovely articles of furniture, a charming home may be maintained for generations; while in a home of the opposite kind the charm of lovely furnishings may be destroyed in months.

Household Pests and Their Extermination.

One important item in the care of furniture and rugs, linen, and clothes, is the prevention and extermination of household pests, such as ants, cockroaches, flies, mosquitoes, and moths. Cleanliness is the most effective means of preventing the invasion of our homes by household pests, but even the cleanest of houses occasionally may become infested. Some of the approved methods of ridding the household of pests are denying entrance by closing runways and cracks with putty or plaster of paris, using poisonous powders which may be sprinkled in cracks and on shelves and drawers, poisoning with strychnine and arsenic, mixed with a flour and water paste and placed on strips of paper and laid on tables or in closets, and exterminating with fumes, which should be used with care to prevent the possibility of fires. Every precaution should be taken where poisoning methods are used to protect children and pets.

Ants.

Ants sometimes seem to appear suddenly in our sinks and cabinets without the slightest or apparent cause. Washing with strong soap suds is a very effective method by which to check such an invasion. Borax may be spread on shelves as another effective measure. Sponges may be soaked in sweetened water, and after ants crawl into them, plunged into boiling water. If it is possible to discover the ant hill, inject kerosene into it and close it tightly with cotton soaked in kerosene. Ants may be killed by sponges soaked in syrup and poisoned with arsenate of soda. Ants thus poisoned will carry the poison to larvae in their nests.

Bed Bugs.

To destroy bed bugs, inject benzine or kerosene into all crevices of beds and walls. Two other effective ways of exterminating bed bugs are using turpentine oil on the beds and scalding the beds with hot water.

Carpet Beetles.

Thoroughly clean the carpet and spray with benzine. Floors should then be washed with hot water, the cracks thoroughly cleaned, and kerosene or benzine then poured into them and under the baseboards. Fill the cracks with plaster of paris. Before replacing the carpet, lay tarred paper over the floor.

Fleas.

Fleas are carried into the house by household pets, and thrive in carpets, rugs, and floors. Carpets should be swept and taken up often, the floors washed with strong soap suds, and cracks in the floors filled up. Sprinkle carpets with benzine, gasoline, naphthalene, or alum.

The House Fly.

This is the most common of household pests and its extermination is almost a perpetual requirement. The most common and effective method is that of using the fly swatter. Sticky flypaper may be placed around, but this is both unattractive and mussy. Some of the most effective poisons which may be placed about the house in saucers are pyrethrum, made from Persian insect powder and bulach, which may be sprinkled liberally at night but in unused rooms; formaldehyde solution, made by combining one part of formaldehyde with ten parts of water, and placed in saucers; and bichromate of potash solution, which is made from one part of bichromate and two parts of water, and placed in saucers.

Mosquitoes.

Anything that will make a dense smoke will drive away mosquitoes. Pyrethrum powder made into paste and burned is effective but should not be used where people will inhale the fumes.

Moths.

Moths are ruthless destroyers of clothing and rugs. Clothing should be taken to the sunlight and brushed thoroughly and the clothes closet should then be washed thoroughly with strong soap suds. After washing the closet, the walls, shelves, and boxes should be sprayed with oil of cedar, gasoline, or benzine. Burning a sulphur candle is an effective, but not popular, method of exterminating moths, as it creates an unpleasant odor.

Rats and Mice.

If yours is a family which likes cats, having a cat is one of the most effective ways of keeping the home free from rats and mice. Otherwise, traps set near possible entrances are effective instruments of destruction. Take care to scald the traps before setting them in order to remove any odor that might make the prospective victim too wary to be entrapped. There are various poisonous preparations on the market, but using them is dangerous particularly if there are pet animals about.

Roaches.

Roaches can often be caught in a pan well lined with grease, as it is impossible for them to crawl through grease. Plunge the grease trap into very hot water to kill the roaches. Poison paste spread on bits of card- board and placed in runways is effective. The most commonly used dusting powders to destroy roaches are powdered borax, pyrethrum powder, sodium fluoride, and sulphur flowers. These may be sprinkled on shelves, bookcases, or any other place inhabited by the pests.

CHAPTER 19

REMODELING AND REFINISHING

Why Remodeling is Necessary.

After we have lived in a house for varying periods of time, we often find that many improvements could be made to make it more convenient, efficient, or attractive. Sometimes the size of the family has grown and the house does not conveniently accommodate that growth; sometimes there is a decrease in size which leaves space that could be converted into apartments; and perhaps styles in architecture or furniture and conveniences have so changed that the house is not modern or convenient.

Regardless of the reason for changing, however, the first thing to do when considering remodeling is to determine carefully the state of repair the house is in. In many instances it would cost so much to remodel an old house that it would be cheaper in the long run to build a new one.

The rehabilitation and conversion of an old house that was lacking in modern conveniences and architectural beauty, into a comfortable, and even a beautiful building has been accomplished to the delight of many families. Such improvements as new paint, shutters, a new entrance, flowers and shrubbery, a trellis, minor changes in porches, windows, and doors, have been known to change completely the exterior of a home without hurt to any sentiment or tradition connected with it.

The Importance of Plans.

Before making changes, the plan of the house should be studied carefully and its good points noted as well as its bad ones. Then on the old plan, in dotted lines, the desired changes should be drawn. Will there be sufficient window space? Are the walls so cut up with doors and windows that no room is left in which to accommodate the furniture properly? Answers to these questions may be found by studying similar features in the house of someone else.

When an additional room or porch is to be built on the old house, it should conform to the original design and consist of the materials previously used in order that it may appear as a part of the original house and not just as something "tacked on." The appearance of many homes has been ruined because these details were not carefully studied before remodeling took place. Proposed plans should be gone over by a good architect, one who will not only give helpful advice regarding the desirability of changes but furnish an estimate of the costs. He should also make suggestions for the correction of faults in the original design.

The services of an architect are almost a necessity if extensive changes are to be made.

If the ceilings of the old house are too high, it is possible to build in false ceilings at whatever height is desired. Unattractive windows and doors are made less noticeable if the walls and woodwork are painted the same color. After paper has been removed from old walls, the walls may be thoroughly cleaned and painted. Floors may be improved by refinishing them in harmony with the rugs or woodwork. The changes in windows, doors, and walls should all be considered in relation to the exterior before making definite changes.

Interior Changes and Additions.

Additions most commonly made in the interiors of houses are closets, cabinets, and bookcases. One of the most important of these fixtures, the cabinet closet, is a strong sales factor in selling or renting houses and apartments. Closets should not be built too deep, or so narrow and long that the contents in front must be brushed against or removed to reach those in the back. The most convenient type is the oblong closet with the door in one side. Shelves in all closets should be so constructed that front articles do not have to be removed in order to reach the ones in the back. Shelves should be of a height convenient to reach and not too far apart. High shelves are suitable for storage but not for common use.

The linen closet should be placed in a general hall rather than in the bathroom, so it may be easily accessible at all times. The medicine closet should be a "recess" built in the wall, the door even with the surface. A light should, of course, be directly above to make things readily distinguishable at any time of day or night. Built-in cupboards and cabinets are ideal fixtures of the small kitchen.

Walls.

In reconditioning the walls, every particle of the old finish should be removed. In the case of cracks or breaks in the plaster, remove any loose plaster with the edge of a broad knife; wet the new edges from which it was removed and pack plaster of paris into the cracks and holes. Smooth the cracks even with the wall before the plaster hardens. After all paper or paint has been removed and cracks and holes filled, the new plaster in the holes should be allowed to dry thoroughly. Then the wall should be sandpapered and coated with painters' glue water which should be brushed in thoroughly and evenly. Wipe off any surplus glutinous size before it dries, using a damp cloth or sponge. When the glue is thoroughly dry, the wall is then ready for refinishing.

Since there are so many available materials for wall covering, the choice may depend upon the kind of home you have. Wallpaper, plaster, tile, and wood paneling are the most commonly used materials. Wallpaper can be chosen in almost unlimited colors and designs. The choice of color and design can either make or mar the appearance of a room. It may conform to the interior pattern, color, and period characteristics or conflict with them. Modern decoration calls for patterns that are delicate in coloring and unconventional in design. Another attractive feature is the wide price range, which is from sixty cents a roll to $3.50 and up.

For best results in papering a painted wall, go over the entire wall with No. 2 sandpaper, then apply soda water. This procedure breaks the hard smooth surface of the paint. Then wash the surface of the wall with vinegar water. After it is thoroughly dry, go over the wall with glue size thoroughly and evenly. Test before papering by covering a small piece of wallpaper with paste, pressing it against the wall and leaving the corners free. Remove after a few minutes; if it sticks tight, the glue is of proper consistency; if it pulls off easily and without tearing, more glue should be added.

Plaster may be used with a variety of finishes. It is available in many colors and can be secured in various finishes from semi-smooth to as rough a texture as you wish. With good plaster work as a base, glazed tiles have become increasingly popular. These are available in a wide range of colors and patterns.

Paneling with wood is a very effective wall treatment, which requires little wall decoration. This process is particularly suitable for the living room, giving it an air of intimacy and warmth. Dignity is also lent by the variation of texture produced by the grain of the wood. Paneling is suitable in cooler climates as it not only looks warm but is warm, especially if a coat of plaster has been put on before the paneling is applied. Home owners often hesitate to have wood paneling because they think of it as being too expensive, when actually it is possible to select beautiful types of paneling that can be put on by an ordinary carpenter at a very reasonable price.

Painting.

For best results in painting, the newly plastered wall should be allowed to dry for six months before painting. If the wall must be painted before that time, however, wash the plastered wall with strong vinegar water.

Refinishing Woodwork.

Another method of remodeling is by refinishing the woodwork. The usual finishes may be divided into two main parts: natural and painted. In the first, the native beauty is strengthened by the use of transparent finishes such as stain and varnish or stain, shellac, and wax. In the second method the surface of the wood is entirely covered.

All woods do not take finish equally well; soft woods, such as whitewood or poplar do not take the natural finish so well, as do cypress, birch, oak, gumwood, and spruce. Pine usually looks better painted. The artificial graining of soft woods to represent hardwoods seems a shameful imitation, since there is so much beauty and charm in their natural finish. As in architecture, there should be simple honesty and charm in the refinishing of woodwork in our homes.

If soft wood has been used for trim, the woodwork should be painted. Dark rooms may be brightened with light woodwork, however, it requires much cleaning, particularly where there are children.

Woodwork may be in almost any color, the most common being white, ivory, tan, sand, putty, and various shades of gray. Many of our best decorators paint all woodwork, including the doors, the same color as the walls, although it is very effective to paint the woodwork a shade darker than the walls. The following factors must be considered in choosing the wall color: exposure and number of windows since rooms with fewer windows need more light, use of the room, size of the room, design of furniture, and dominant color of furnishings.

Staining and Finishing.

Both the quality and the grain of the wood may be enriched by staining. The steps in the proper finishing of natural woodwork are:

1. A priming coat of raw linseed oil and turpentine stain of the color required.

2. When dry, sandpaper with the grain with No. 2 sandpaper.

3. Coat of white shellac.

4. Paste wax, rubbed in, or

5. After stain, two coats of interior varnish, preferably dull finish. Varnish should be lightly rubbed with No. 2 sandpaper between coats.

Floors.

The process for refinishing floors depends upon the kind of wood that is used, its former treatment, and the new finish decided upon. Each finish has its own special problem of daily care and renewal.

If the old covering of paint or varnish is in too bad a condition to permit satisfactory "touching up," all paint or varnish must be removed. This can be done by an electric planing machine, which will leave the floor in almost the state of new wood ; a workman may be employed to scrape off all the old paint or varnish with a sharp edged tool and sandpaper the surface until it is smooth; or we may use prepared paint and varnish remover in accordance with the directions on the package.

Waxed Floors.

Waxed floors may be refinished in accordance with individual preference, if there is no conflict between the choice of finish and the kind of wood in the floors. The best materials should be used for the sake of economy. Stain, filler, oil, paint, varnish, shellac, and wax or a combination of some of these may be used. Before applying any finish, however, the floor should be planed and sandpapered parallel with the grain of the wood, then swept and dusted with a soft cloth.

Stains are used to bring out the grain of the wood and to harmonize in color with other furnishings or woodwork. Stains are applied thinly with a clean brush and allowed to dry for at least twenty-four hours, after which the floors are polished with a weighted brush covered with carpet. They are then ready for the filler and wax or varnish.

Waxed floors may be renewed by going over the surface with a clean, soft cloth, moistened with turpentine or kerosene. Waxing is one of the most practical, as well as attractive finishes for hardwood floors, preserving the natural color of the wood and bringing out the beauty of the grain. With proper care, waxed floors improve with age. Perhaps their only disadvantages are the amount of labor required to polish them and the fact that water turns the finish white, although water spots may be quickly removed by rubbing on a little wax with a woolen cloth or weighted brush.

Wax may be applied to floors that have been stained, painted, or varnished, or directly on the bare wood. Many hardwood floors are given a coating of shellac before being waxed, but they will be less slippery if shellacking is omitted. Success in waxing the floor is attained by applying the wax in a thin coating and rubbing thoroughly the surface it covers.

Paint is commonly used on softwood floors. It is not durable but is easy to clean and reduces to simplicity the problem of matching or harmonizing woodwork and furnishings. If the floor is to be repainted, it should be carefully washed, rinsed, and allowed to dry. Retouch worn spots with paint as near the color of the rest of the floor as possible and allow them to dry. Then sandpaper adjoining edges until smooth, dust thoroughly, and give the entire floor a coat of paint a shade darker than the original coat. A second coat may be added if desired.

If the floor is to be revarnished, a similar procedure should be followed. Varnish gives the floor a hard, smooth, and glossy finish; is easy to apply and easy to clean. Its disadvantages are that it has a tendency to wear off and leave patches of bare wood. More satisfaction results if varnish is warmed before using because, when warm, it flows more easily and does not leave dark lines.

Other common ways of refinishing old floors are by re-oiling and by covering with linoleum. The latter is particularly good for badly worn and splintered floors.

Durability, ease in cleaning, and economy are the factors to be most considered in refinishing floors.

Furniture Refinishing.

To refinish an article of furniture, it is first advisable to have any needed repair work done. Then, remove all ornaments, such as carvings which are glued onto the article. Scrape off the varnish or paint with a sharp instrument or remove it by sandpapering.

Varnish may be softened by the use of a commercial varnish remover, or by turpentine and alcohol.

After stains have been removed by oxalic acid, the wood should be allowed to dry thoroughly. Then the surface should be smoothed by the use of sandpaper, steel wool or steel scraper, always working with the grain of the wood so that the surface will be absolutely smooth. The article may be stained any color desired or left its natural color.

If stain is used, it should first be tried on an inconspicuous part of the article. Stain should be applied with a brush or cloth and rubbed until there is a luster. It may require several coats to get the desired color, but one should allow each coat to dry thoroughly before applying the next.

There are several kinds of furniture finish such as wax, varnish, and oil. Choice should be determined by the kind of wood, the use of the article, and, of course, personal preference. The three essentials of good furniture are good wood, good construction, and good lines. If the article possesses these points, refinishing is worthwhile.

Unit 5

FAMILY LIFE

CHAPTER 20

SOCIAL GROUPS

The Family Group.

Long before the dawn of civilization, family life existed as a social agency. It has remained steadfast and basically unchanged in a world of change, losing in part its fundamental privileges and prerogatives when political governments took autocratic and despotic form or fell into corruption and decay, only to reclaim them later. To this time, no law has ever been successfully imposed that had for its purpose the bringing of family life under the supervision of an external authority. For over three hundred years the inhabitants of Serbia and Montenegro were subjected to the political rule of Turkey. But with unwavering fidelity, the people remained steadfast in allegiance to their family customs, traditions, and religious ideals without surrender either to the assimilating forces of an opposing culture and religion or to the force of laws aimed at conforming their civilization to that of Turkey.

Family Stability and Cohesiveness.

Stability, always a pronounced characteristic of the human family, is strikingly shown in the face of disaster or misfortune. In a crisis all of the centripetal forces of family life unite to prevent dismemberment through the encroachment of sickness, poverty, or the influence of external causes, regardless of whether they are social, political, or economic. This attribute of cohesiveness is further shown in the predisposition of the family to resist the inroads of a culture and religion foreign to its own racial, cultural, and religious patterns. The invading Normans who conquered England were never able to uproot and supplant the poorer language and simpler family customs of the Anglo-Saxons with theirs. Instead, the Normans adopted the language and religion of the people they had lately conquered and in time forgot the language they had brought from France. It is not to be inferred, however, that Anglo-Saxon culture was not modified to an appreciable extent by the culture patterns of the Normans. The language was enriched by the absorption of many Norman-French words. Also the social customs of France which had been introduced and used in court ceremonials became patterns and standards in social etiquette for many walks of life.

CHAPTER 21

HISTORICAL BACKGROUND OF THE AMERICAN FAMILY

The First American Settlers.

The first white American inhabitants of the area now comprising the United States were people who came from England, Spain, France, Holland, and Sweden. Each settlement that was founded was in miniature a reproduction of the country from which its population came — in language, family customs, and the application of civil law.

As individuals the settlers had sought new homes in the American wilderness from vastly different motives. Some longed for greater religious freedom, some were adventurous treasure seekers, some were political refugees, some religious exiles, others debt ridden and oppressed, were seeking relief from their economic burdens. It was destined that the differing hopes, desires, and ambitions of these first settlers would exert a powerful influence upon thought and opinion and finally find realization in the establishment of a democratic form of government under which home life was enabled to break loose from the shackles of custom and build a new pattern.

English Supremacy.

After England gained political ascendency over the thirteen original colonies the laws, traditions, and customs of that country became predominant in colonial civil and domestic life. English law was harsh and cruel in many aspects and especially so as applied to the rights and privileges of women. The husband was lord of the household with powers practically as absolute as those of a monarch. The laws passed by the colonial legislatures related to affairs in which men almost solely were interested and therefore gave scant attention to woman's rights and privileges. The Revolutionary War period was reached with woman still occupying a position so inferior that she could own nothing in her own right. Her personal effects, clothing, jewelry, were subject to forfeiture in payment of her husband's debts. Unless she was widowed, a woman could not own land, cattle, horses, or other chattels. When George Washington married the rich widow, Martha Custis, some unfriendly critics accused him of taking this particular bride because under the prevailing law, title and ownership of her vast estates would pass to him. In the home, women were subject to discipline similar in many respects to that imposed upon children. If a beating was due a wife for scolding or other obnoxious behavior, it was within the lordly right of her husband to administer it. Plans for the education and marriage of children were arranged by the husband. Such influence as the wife had in arranging these affairs was achieved by indirection rather than through forthright cooperation.

Education in Colonial America.

Education as we view it was not held in public esteem to any great extent. Therefore, the training that children received was obtained at home except in the few progressive centers where community schools had been established. The discipline of children was stern and exacting and the course of instruction little suited to the nature of youthful interests. The books were equally ill adapted, the reading course being confined to religious literature or lectures on behavior standards at home, at the table, and at church.

Influences Working Toward Change.

It is not to be assumed that the picture of domestic life as above presented embraced in perspective a true representation of every feature. Influences were at work which would ultimately so change the picture as to make it almost unrecognizable.

For one thing, the country was sparsely populated and land was to be had on easy terms and in such vastness of area as the owner could till and defend. Under these conditions there was no economic barrier to large families. In fact, the large family was an economic asset from the standpoint of supplying the population needs of the colony as well as that of adding more workers to the individual family. Socially, also, there were distinct advantages connected with the large family. Companionship, ever a boon to human need, the large family supplied in the absence of near neighbors. In family gatherings on long winter evenings a new spirit of cooperation and mutual understanding arose. In this atmosphere was born a sense of deference towards womanhood that was definitely a departure from tradition in family relations.

In the beginning of colonization, food and shelter needs were not only acute but predominant over all others. The former was supplied by the flesh of game from the forests, fish from the numerous streams, and native vegetable products such as corn, squash, and potatoes. The problem of shelter was more difficult of solution. There were forests of timber and mountainous masses of stone but few tools with which to convert the raw products into finished building materials. As a consequence, the first houses were crude log structures insufficient in room space and deficient in shelter capacity. Under the hardships imposed by these conditions, sickness was as inevitable as night after day. It came, and without medical resources the battle was unfalteringly waged against its relentless rush with women in the forefront fighting for the lives of their families and neighbors. Although not inured by previous experience or training for life in their new environment, these women faced the situation as unflinchingly as did their husbands. No work was too hard, no privation too severe for their endurance.

In New England the women dried fish, the flesh of game, and other foodstuffs for winter use, tilled the gardens, and with the thrift characteristic of that section until this day, fashioned clothes from the skins of animals or from cloth they had spun and woven by hand.

Farther south and westward along the outer fringe of the constantly expanding frontier, the story of heroism was repeated in the experiences of countless other women who shared work with their husbands, tended the sick, and stood guard with guns over the thresholds of their homes. Here again we see the evidence of a definite break with European customs and traditions in the rise of womanhood to a position of influence and leadership through the collapse of formality and the development of a spiritual comradeship among those who day after day shared work and danger on a basis of equality. It was impossible for men and women to go hand in hand through the rigors of these struggles clinging to theories of man and woman relationships that were proved false and unfitting in every emergency.

Growth in Woman's Initiative.

The English common law principles had their basis in the theory that when a man and woman married there was a union of the two into one individuality. Therefore, being the stronger physically, man would take the lead in all matters affecting the interest of his wife and himself and bear the brunt of all burdens. This conception could not live in the face of American conditions. Often the pioneer wife was left alone and compelled to act in her own defense and the protection of her children. In experience after experience self-dependence was forced upon her by the necessity of circumstances. And as you have previously learned, the wife stood on an equal footing with her husband in the work that she did. Men could not be witnesses to the glory of her accomplishments without undergoing a definite change in their attitudes toward all women.

Primitive Nature of the Colonists' Struggles.

These women and men had been reared under a system of culture that at the time marked man's highest progress in civilization. The atmosphere into which the system had moved was entirely primitive. It could not survive except by subduing again the same forces and overcoming the same obstacles against which primitive man had fought in the beginning of civilization. Unfortunately, they were not equipped for the struggle with the hardihood and endurance of primitive people. And so the softening effects of civilized living had to give way to the hardening of mind, body, and purpose or these people would have perished from the face of the earth. Thus men became hard and fought back with a grimness that on the surface appeared as a reversion to savagery. But that was not the case. The pioneer met savagery with savagery in his fighting methods but in his home relations there were a tenderness of manner and a solicitude that bespoke the knight of old rather than the rough-hewn adventurer.

American Folk Ways.

From the force of necessity during the colonial period people were compelled to adopt new modes of living to meet emergencies as occasions demanded. Their first homes were barren of the comfort that homes provided in Europe but the people never forgot the ties that bound them to the culture systems of that continent. Denials and repressions made them all the more eager for the things that would make life more enjoyable. Beginning with huts that were not the equals in providing shelter of the Indian teepees and wigwams, they improvised substitutes for the bureaus they could not have from goods boxes and skins; made rugs and carpets from rags, native grass, or skins; and strove in every way possible to make convenience take the place of the luxury they were denied. Thus, under the exigencies of this new environment, new "folk ways" developed which were so distinctly original as to resemble nothing but themselves, and could, therefore, be called "American."

As time went on, the new culture pattern grew in scope and dimensions by the addition of characteristics that were entirely lacking in the domestic picture of any other people.

For example, thought was freed to the extent that men could practice their own religious beliefs and voice their political convictions. Women were casting off the fetters of custom and finding equality in right and privilege with men; a more chivalrous attitude towards women and children was in process of growth; homes were growing in comforts and conveniences; and autocratic family rule was giving way to the forces of sympathy and understanding.

CHAPTER 22

THE TWENTIETH CENTURY AMERICAN FAMILY

American Standards of Living.

The customs of American family life were in a state of transition from the beginning of the colonial period until about the dawn of the nineteenth century. At that point in our history, family life became fairly well stabilized in an essentially original pattern in which living standards were elevated far above the European level. On the average, we had more com- forts and more conveniences than any other people. The few cases of indigence and want that occurred were easily cared for by community charity. The acquisition of wealth enabled us to retain the culture patterns of the old world and at the same time, by the introduction of democracy in the conduct of home affairs, women and children secured liberty of action, opportunity for self-expression, and complete release from the thralldom of oppressive customs.

Home Life, Aspects of.

During the period of change that had its beginning in the introduction and use of machine labor, the stability of home life in America received its most grueling tests. Never before in our national life was hardship so generally prevalent. The means of self- sustenance were lacking in thousands and thousands of homes. More and more women went outside the home for employment. In the period from 1880 to 1930, the number of women employed in work outside their own homes increased from 2,000,000 to 10,000,000. In business offices alone, during this period, the employment of women and girls rose from less than one thousand to nearly two million. In many instances, women were forced to seek outside work in order to supplement the family income; in others, girls took employment because it enabled them to have clothes and luxuries for which the home budget could not provide.

In this critical period divorce actions grew in number, the birth rate decreased, infant mortality grew by leaps and bounds, and fewer marriage licenses were issued in proportion to population than in any previous period. That the institution of family life survived under the stress to which it was subjected is eternal proof of its value to society. It bent under the pressure of need for food, shelter, medicine, and hospital care but not to the point of breaking. The home was a rallying point at night for those who had met disappointment during the day, a place where morale was restored and courage was renewed for the battles of the morrow.

CHAPTER 23

LEISURE AND RECREATION

History of Leisure.

Long ago, leisure for those who toiled meant only surcease from the day's labor because the working day was so much longer than it is now. The work week was broken only occasionally by holidays, hence the working man had little recreation. For the most part, therefore, recreation was for the wealthy class of people. Women also had to put in equally long hours at home because they had little equipment. Modern methods of canning were unknown. Food for the winter was dried or put up in brine or preserved with sugar, spices, and vinegar. Vegetables and fruits were kept fresh in cellars and caves for a limited time. Clothing was made in the home; ready-made garments were for the few people who were well to do and could be secured only in the larger cities. Today we recognize the value of devoting a part of the time at our disposal to the building up of our bodies and our minds so that we may live our lives fully and live them well. We think of leisure as being "spare" time that is not used in the pursuit of a dominant objective in life. For instance, for the high school boy or girl whose dominant objective is getting an education, the hours out- side of school are leisure hours; for the adult who earns a living for himself and family, leisure is the time he has aside from the requirements of his job. The homemaker whose definite objective in life is making a home for her family, thinks of her leisure as time not definitely devoted to home management.

People today are realizing the value of a balanced diet of work, play, and rest almost as much as the value of a balanced diet of protein, carbohydrates, and fats. So we have better facilities for using leisure time today, and more leisure time to use. Families with moderate or even low incomes can purchase ready-made clothes, buy canned food, and secure many of the modern labor-saving devices at reasonable prices, which were not available in the past except to wealthy families. The hours of working for both men and women have been somewhat reduced, hence our use of leisure has had to be revised and in reality we have had to look for new ways of using our leisure. Sewing bees, quilting bees, box parties, hayrides, sleigh parties, and candy pulls have given way to dances, bridge parties, and automobile drives. Some people think the old method of using leisure was superior to that of today, and criticize the modern automobile, cinema, and radio for disrupting family unity; others are equally vehement in their criticism of the "old days" and look upon the more modern inventions as a means of bringing the family members closer together. It is up to each age, however, to use its own available tools for creating family harmony. Could you give three examples of family enjoyment that are possible today that were not possible when your parents were your age?

By using the automobile, picnics, Sunday drives, and vacation trips are a means of bringing the family into a closer union. Summer vacations particularly, which may be shared by the family, were often prohibitive in cost when the family was dependent upon the train for transportation, and prohibitive in time when the family was dependent upon the horse and buggy for transportation. Now the entire family can get in the car and enjoy their vacation together for practically what it would cost one person on the train, and can cover as much territory in the car in two weeks as the horse and buggy could have covered in six months. The cinema and radio too can be made instrumental in cementing family ties. In a family where interests are shared, there are several radio programs that all the members like and listen to together, with mutually enjoyed comments and discussions. In some families, one person makes it a point to keep well informed on the current screen productions so as to select one which would be enjoyable to the whole family and thus make a pleasant "family night" entertainment. Even if we do not like to listen to the baseball scores, we are glad to let some one member of the family listen to them in peace because a little later our favorite program will be on the air and we want no objection raised while we listen.

Leisure in the Home.

Families are beginning to recognize the need for planned recreation, just as for other essential things, such as food and clothing. Leisure should not be considered a waste of time; it should not be planned accidentally or haphazardly but should be planned with as much consideration as the daily menu.

Leisure should be planned to contrast with daily work. A person who is with people all day wants to have a little solitude in the evening, while a person who works alone all day wants company and gaiety. That psychological principle presents a serious difficulty in family relations. The father is with people all day and wants to be alone in the evening, while the mother is at home all day and in the evening wants the society of others. This may also be true of other members of the family. To meet this situation, an understanding relationship within the family must be promoted and this requires tact and patience.

In order to get the most enjoyment from your leisure time, your plan must, of course, be flexible. You can plan to do those things which give you most pleasure and lasting enjoyment without detriment to the happiness of others. For this reason, you will want a variety of interests. If you have only one interest in life and become too absorbed in that, you are not so interesting to other people. When they have caught that one interest from you, there is nothing left to draw upon and they soon tire of you. A boy who likes to read should also have outdoor exercise; the girl who likes to dance misses much enjoyment and pleasure if that is her only type of activity during her leisure hours. Leisure should give us an opportunity to build healthy bodies and alert minds.

Again, you will want a balance between your work and your play. Your leisure should give you an opportunity to provide what is lacking in your work time.

You, of course, want to get genuine satisfaction and pleasure from your leisure time. You would not want to go to an opera merely because your favorite friend liked classical music if your own taste ran in an opposing direction. Nor would you want to attend an educational lecture on a subject you were not interested in when down the street was a motion picture you had been waiting impatiently to see.

You also want to plan your leisure interests with your future in view. Are your leisure activities now those which will add to your happiness in later years? It is in the days of youth that we form our habits for later years, and so part of our leisure should be devoted to interests which will give us permanent pleasure. For that reason, everyone needs a hobby.

Hobbies.

We think of a hobby as a definite interest which we pursue voluntarily, aside from our dominant objective in life. It is during our leisure hours that we have the opportunity to devote ourselves to our hobbies. They are then a means of rest and relaxation. The high school boy comes home from school mentally and physically tired, rushes to his shop, and spends all available time before dinner rigging up a radio. Then he comes to his meal rested and refreshed.

No one can decide upon your hobby for you; it must be something in which you are interested and turn to voluntarily. Hobbies usually fall into one of three classes; those of collecting, such as collecting stamps, shells, books, butterflies, and furniture; those of doing, such as the activities of hiking, swimming, and skiing; and those of creating, such as modeling, painting and cabinet work. Collecting seems to be the most common hobby.

Gardening is a popular and useful hobby. Growing things seem to appeal to everyone. We enjoy getting close to the soil and to nature. Also we can use the vegetables on our table and help the family finances by supplying part of the groceries; or if we prefer a flower garden, we can provide the table centerpieces, and the lovely yard. Related hobbies might include flower arrangement or collecting vases.

Some people choose the art of conversation as a hobby. Conversation provides a medium for the exchange of ideas and thoughts and therefore is an art worth cultivating. It is seldom that we devote an entire evening to conversation, although there is nothing which gives more enjoyment and pleasure than an informative, sparkling, witty conversation.

Games as a form of family recreation may teach good sportsmanship which is the ability to win or lose gracefully. It should be easier to learn the lessons of good sportsmanship with the people who really love you and care for you than to learn the same lessons among comparative strangers.

Individual and Shared Interests.

Every family should have at least one interest in common which all the members would be really happy in sharing together. If all members like to go mountain climbing or swimming or fishing, it gives the individual greater pleasure because it is shared with the others. Even if it is but listening to a certain radio program, it affords greater pleasure if the family as a whole enjoys it.

One of the reasons for teaching family relationships in school is to show how plans that will enable every member of the family to have his own recreation with his own group may be made possible. The family members can have enjoyable times in going together to the library to read, by each selecting his own particular type of magazine and literature; or they can go to concerts and picture shows together where there is mutual interest in the program. Sometimes families need time to rest, relax, and enjoy each other more than anything else.

The age of children, age of parents, and the health of family members have both a direct and an indirect influence on the way the family should use its leisure. As children grow older and have their own interests, there should be an understanding among the members of the family of that fact.

Leisure should provide time for rest and relaxation, as well as active exercise. Each individual should be allowed to use a part of his leisure for his own private enjoyment. We do not want to plan leisure to the extent that no one has his own privacy; privacy, too, should be planned for. If we go too far and plan every minute of the leisure time, it will be just as bad as not having enough.

Individual preferences in leisure are as apparent as they are in other activities of life. Sometimes a lack of interest in any one type of recreation is due to a lack of knowledge or familiarity with it. For example, a lack of appreciation of music or the drama and lack of interest in games and sports may be because we do not understand them.

Those who have learned really to enjoy a good sport, good books, or a hobby, will not have much difficulty in filling their leisure hours.

The Home Library.

Reading is perhaps the most usual form of relaxation enjoyed in the home. It would be well if we would take advantage of this to bring the family closer together. A "home library" where both books and magazines that appeal to the various members of the family are to be had does much to stimulate interest not only in reading but in family life. Since a good biography is enjoyed by people of almost every age, part of the family recreation might be secured through reading aloud. Some families enjoy assigning certain books to different members of the family and having a report given, since the family members who really enjoy reading find it difficult to find time to read all the books in which they have an interest. Thus, several of the modern "best sellers" might be enjoyed by the whole family in the length of time it would take to read only one book.

Leisure time may be used in relaxation and rest, in developing hobbies, in cultural education and advancement, or in active exercise. A well-balanced leisure includes time used alone in pursuit of some objective, time shared with the family, and time shared with the community. More leisure hours entail more responsibility on the family in planning for the individual members, for the family itself, and for the community of which the family is a part.

Leisure Outside the Family.

There is need as children grow older for group activities. In a family of several ages of children, each age has a different interest. Some part of the recreation of this family should be planned to take place outside the family so that children may meet with groups of the same age and interests. An eleven-year-old girl whose brother is sixteen and whose sister is eight, will obviously need recreation other than that secured in her own family.

In reality, hospitality is the spirit in which you entertain. It is not what you have to entertain with, but the way you entertain and the joy you get from sharing what you have with others that count.

The family may share in the recreation of the community and may help in making community recreation possible. Programs put on by organizations and schools should be enjoyed and appreciated. Programs and plays produced by high school clubs, bands, and music clubs should be supported by the family. Children and those much older get pleasure out of learning to act but they must have an audience. Unless their plays are attended, the joy and enthusiasm of the people who planned them are killed.

Today we have organizations interested in promoting recreation for the whole community. We have public parks, supervised playgrounds, and swimming pools. Such organizations as the Y.M.C.A., Y.W.C.A., Boy and Girl Scouts, and Campfire Girls are providing for the leisure of children and youth. A healthy body and a clean mind have been emphasized by these youth organizations. The study of bird and animal life, of trees and flowers, and of all outdoor life, together with hiking, camping, and cooking over the open fire are encouraged and have added much to the pleasure and education of the young people who make up these organizations. Summer or vacation camps and hiking trips and week-end retreats are enjoyed by the youth of today.

The interest of churches in planned recreation has created new interest in church and social activities. Many business and industrial enterprises have made it possible for their employees to have "get-togethers" thus encouraging group relationships and planned leisure.

Special Days

Family holidays, such as Thanksgiving and Christmas, really enrich family life and add to its enjoyment. Other days commemorate events of concern to the community or church, such as Easter, which concerns primarily the church and the Fourth of July, Halloween, Decoration Day, and Labor Day, which the family members share with other families and with the community. In the family there are birthdays that belong to the family alone. Some families plan a "Family Night" and take turns in making programs for the evening. Sometimes they stay at home and read aloud, or discuss current topics, or have music; other nights they may go to a concert or see a picture but it matters little what they do, if it is something they enjoy doing together.

Advancement.

Much of our leisure time should be used in planning for personal advancement, which might include attending lectures, reading good books, hearing good music, or doing anything that would enrich our personal lives and give us a more cultural background. Magazines, books, music, travel, and the like should be provided for in the budget just as food and clothing. Perhaps your home is near a public library and you can enjoy reading without much expense to your family; perhaps your love for music is satisfied by a band concert in a nearby park instead of a radio in your home, or instead of opera. The cost for advancement may be negligible or it may be large, depending upon the tastes of the members of the family, but it should never be neglected. Public libraries, museums, and art galleries in many communities offer opportunities for educational advancement. With all these facilities and others at hand, there is small excuse for anyone to remain uneducated.

It has never been more apparent than it is today that families cannot live to themselves. The members of the family, at certain ages particularly, are influenced more by community activities than by those of the family. When there was little leisure time, there was little need of community activities. Today we need recreation that recreates. What is your own definition of recreation? Of leisure? Of a hobby? Some people define recreation as the use of one's time to re-create or to renew interest. Can you think of a better one?

CHAPTER 24

PERSONAL AND SOCIAL RELATIONSHIPS

Personality.

To have a charming personality is the innate wish of every normal boy or girl, man or woman because all want attention and friendship. Each of us has an individual personality that, be it pleasing or disagreeable, strong or weak, may be improved or even changed. Personality is in essence spiritual, physical, and mental. It comprises poise, good grooming, carriage, voice, conduct, and all the various character traits and emotional attitudes that go to make up "charm."

Charm, of course, cannot be developed overnight. There are many fundamental traits to develop within our own selves which require patience and an honest and sincere effort. Some people seem to be born with the ability to win people to them effortlessly, but the majority of us have to acquire such an ability.

Perhaps we have difficulty because due to our egoistic natures, the most interesting thing to us is self. When we can get to the point that our first thought is of the other person rather than of ourselves, we will have gone far, if not all the way, toward the development of a winning personality; hut it is not a simple thing to do or something that can be affected or pretended.

There must, of course, be a supply of mental force for others to draw upon. We cannot merely be interested in people and have them continue to enjoy us unless we constantly supply the stimulus. We also must have our own interests and hobbies for we cannot be dependent upon the society of others for our happiness. So, for our own mental poise, which is essential in a charming personality, we should have varied interests, obtain new knowledge, and develop a more cultural background. Mastering some extra hobby or subject increases our self-respect and the respect others have for us.

Poise.

Poise is both a physical and mental attribute. Physically, we should possess good health, to insure us against irritability and nervousness. Therefore, we should exercise daily in the open air in order to gain the physical balance without which poise cannot exist. Fencing is an exercise that is particularly good for balance, but in swimming, dancing, horseback riding, golf, tennis, and other sports there are more opportunities for matching talent and skill with congenial companions and opponents. Companionship in all games and sports is the element that supplies interest and vitality.

The most important feature of mental poise is the attitude we have toward ourselves. We must know ourselves intimately and respect ourselves; poise comes from being at ease with ourselves and it follows that if we are at ease with ourselves, we are at ease before other people. Outside distractions cannot confuse us if within our minds we are serene and confident. The tenseness of mind which creates friction in personal relations usually springs from the lack of self-confidence.

To have respect for ourselves, there are certain physical as well as spiritual factors to take into consideration. We cannot admire our bodies if they have a poor carriage, so we must stand straight and tall. We must have well balanced meals so that our bodies will not become scrawny or overweight. Our voices should be low and well modulated. To have pleasing voices, correct breathing and proper carriage are necessary.

Carriage.

A firm, erect, and graceful carriage adds as much to personality and poise as any other one thing. Correct posture is only attained through practice so constant that the proper habits result and correct posture becomes automatic.

Stand as tall as possible, hips, abdomen, and chin in, head up, shoulders erect but not stiff. When walking, swing from your hips, toes pointed straight forward rather than out, stepping with the weight on the heel and then shifting weight to the ball of the foot. This gives you correct balance, keeps the body in a straight line, and enables you to breathe freely. Hands should be allowed to hang completely relaxed and swing freely at your sides. When sitting, posture is just as important as when standing. Keep the abdomen well in, rest your back against the back of the chair, and keep your knees together. Do not slide down on the base of the spine.

Voice.

The voice with character and personality is low, well-modulated, resonant, clear, and is distinguished by careful but not stilted enunciation. The basis of a pleasing speaking voice is correct breathing. The throat, tongue, jaws, and lips should be relaxed. Breath controlled by the throat instead of the breathing muscles produces harsh, unpleasant sounds. Careful enunciation includes pronouncing the syllables of a word that have stress — as dictionary, not dic-tion-ry, sep-a-rate, not seprit — and eliminating mumbling and nasalizing. A lovely speaking voice, although rare, is possible for all of us.

Manners and Conventions.

An important element in smooth personal and social relationships is the knowledge and practice of the accepted manners and conventions. These conventions make for harmonious relationships; with a little study and practice their use becomes as easy and natural as applying the brakes of an automobile to avoid jars in riding over rough ground. There are certain fundamentals of etiquette to observe at home, at school, in public places, and in business that should be learned by each of us in an effort to live with others agreeably and harmoniously. Conventions have been agreed upon both as to the general principles of behavior and the establishment of moral standards. They must, of course, to be valuable, have a logical purpose behind them and for that reason they change from time to time. Thus some of the practices which are conventional now were perhaps at one time frowned upon. Not so many years ago a girl who bobbed her hair was considered immoral, now that has become accepted as a conventional manner of hairdress.

Good manners are simply an expression of character, unselfishness, and thoughtful consideration for others.

Outward forms change with the social customs of society, but the real obligations of boys and girls to their families, to their neighbors, and to the communities in which they live never change. Good manners are almost as necessary to civilized man as the knowledge of how to earn a living. To know and obey the accepted standards of conduct at home, at school, and elsewhere, gives one self-assurance and charm.

The rules of good manners can easily be learned, but charming manners come only by habitual use. These rules change, as does everything else in the world.

Reading a new book occasionally and observing the manners of well-bred people help to keep one informed of changes in social usage.

People who live together at home or in the same com- munity soon have similar manners, ideas, and ideals.

In the same way, nations over a long period of years develop their manners, their distinctive customs, their styles of dress, and rules of conduct at home and elsewhere. These developments grow out of what seems to be the best way of doing things and become general through the force of imitation and habit. We have learned that imitation and habit are powerful forces in determining human behavior and that habits very largely control the character and personality of every individual. We imitate the manners of the people in the community in which we live in their ways of doing things until their ways become habits with us. Thus our friends and associates are powerful influences in the habits we build. The entire problem of people living together, in mannerly and righteous conduct, resolves itself into a problem of forming the right kind of habits and avoiding bad associations. Therefore, we should choose our community, our friends, and associates carefully because they are likely to influence the habits we are building for life.

Good manners and good taste are very closely akin. Personal cleanliness and daintiness are matters of good taste and also reflect good breeding and good behavior. A well-mannered person is never conspicuous in clothes, manners, or voice.

Are you forming the habit of being courteous? Good manners should be practiced constantly. To build a habit, continued practice is necessary. Practice courtesy in your school and in your home, and you will soon find that being courteous is easy and natural.

Since one of the essentials of a good personality is self- respect, increase yours by keeping yourself in good physical condition by eating and sleeping regularly, by taking plenty of exercise, and by obeying other health rules. Keep yourself clean with frequent bathing, and dress in good taste so that others may be in your presence without noticing what you are wearing.

Remember that natural charm and courtesy win lasting friendships. Remember that consideration for others is the basis of all true courtesy and of true charm. Forget yourself and think of others at home, at school, and in public.

At Home.

Are you courteous to your family? Is your home the place where you are treated the best but grumble the most? Is "please" a strange word in your home? Do you always thank members of your family for favors? Do you forget to introduce your mother and your father to your friends when they call at home? If you cannot avoid passing in front of members of your family do you say "I am sorry," or "I beg your pardon"? When you accidentally slam the door do you come back and say "I am sorry" and close the door carefully? Do you respect the privacy of the members of your family? Are you as careful to keep promises at home as elsewhere? ' Do you borrow without per- mission? Remember that other people judge you largely by the way you treat your parents and other members of your own family.

Boys and girls can be courteous at home by helping with household tasks, by helping to meet emergencies such as that caused by a case of sudden illness, by helping to celebrate family birthdays and other important events, by learning to entertain their own friends and friends of others in the family, and by consideration for the rights and preferences of others.

Your attitude at home should be one of respect and consideration for those who are responsible for giving you the privileges of a good home. Taking care of your own belongings and helping generally with the household tasks should be a part of your everyday duties. Leaving the house without saying goodbye to your parents is discourteous. Changing your plans about coming home at mealtime or in the evening without notifying those at home who are expecting you is another way of showing discourtesy. How can you show your love and appreciation for a good home?

At School.

The success of any school depends to a large extent upon loyalty — loyalty of groups and loyalty of the individual. There must be teamwork and all groups must pull together for the good of the whole school. One who is loyal to his school does nothing that will lower the standing of his school in the community or in the state. He considers that the success and welfare of the school are his responsibilities. He prepares his lessons faithfully; he is studious and attentive in the classroom; he is quiet in the library; and he is polite and courteous at all times. He does not scar school furniture by marking it with a pencil or defacing it with a penknife. He is quiet and orderly in the halls and does not require constant watching during intermissions. He is a good sportsman on the playground. He endeavors to observe the rules of good manners at the lunch table, in the library, and on the grounds.

In the classroom, as well as everywhere else, it pays to be pleasant and courteous. Usually the best liked boys and girls are those who meet others with a cheerful greeting and are polite and agreeable. Courtesy will prevent a student from interrupting while another pupil is reciting; restrain him from making fun of the mistakes of others, from answering questions addressed to others, and from asking a question before one previously asked has been answered. Speaking distinctly, keeping the voice modulated, and standing erect are other courteous habits that should be practiced in the classroom.

In passing to and from in the halls and classrooms, it is wise to observe traffic rules, which means that you should turn to the right in meeting people, but if you find it necessary to pass a person, keep to the left in doing so. One should walk and talk quietly. The conduct of pupils in the corridors and halls reflects the discipline and character of the school. Pupils who observe the best rules of conduct do not run, sing, or whistle in the corridors.

It is just as important to observe good manners in the lunch room at school as in the dining room at home. Crowding is discourteous. Talk as you would in private or public dining halls, remain seated until the others at your table are through, and do not ran from table to table talking to everyone. Leave the table as you would like to find it. Remember that the evidence of good breeding, or the opposite, is more quickly noticed at the table than any other place.

Do you belong to any organizations or clubs in your school? When you become a member of any organization you assume new responsibilities. It is better not to join unless you are willing and able to do your part. Being an officer of a club, a class president or an officer of any organization, is a responsibility of which one should be proud. It gives an opportunity to train for leadership and for the duties and responsibilities of citizenship. Remember that being a good citizen, or a good leader, in school activities is the very best way of preparing yourself for future leadership and world citizenship. What are the qualities that make for good leadership?

In Public.

Good manners in public are just as notice- able as they are at home and at school. A safe rule to follow is to make one's self as inconspicuous as possible both in dress and action.

Calling to friends or whistling to attract attention should be avoided. Do not stop to visit with friends on the street. When friends and acquaintances meet who want to talk with each other, they should walk in the same direction, preferably in groups of two and never more than three abreast. Avoid talking to strangers on the street except to answer when spoken to in a courteous manner. Congregating on street corners and lounging against store windows are evidences of carelessness and bad manners.

A boy should always walk on the outside of the street rather than between two girls, although one girl should walk between two boys. Boys are expected to raise their hats in greeting or parting with girls or women. A boy should never take the arm of a girl when walking on the street. He may place his hand under her elbow to assist her into an automobile or other conveyance, or he may offer his arm to an elderly lady or an invalid, for support.

Girls and women enter cars before boys and men, but boys and men alight first in order to assist girls from the car. The boy pays a girl's fare only when she is his guest.

Boys should remove their hats upon entering the vestibule of a church. Whispering during service, rattling papers, twisting around in the seat, and other signs of inattention during the service should be avoided. Reverence and respect should characterize one's attitude toward all church services.

Real courtesy and thoughtfulness for others is important in public buildings. In most public buildings there are certain rules which should be obeyed. A boy should hold the door open for girls and allow them to pass through first even though they are strangers to him. In return, girls should not neglect to say "thank you." In passing through a doorway, boys and girls should wait until older people have passed through. Always hold the door open for the person directly behind you and never let it fly back in his face.

When shopping, be courteous and considerate in all your dealings. Do not block traffic by visiting with your friends in the aisle. Be courteous to the clerks and do not waste their time. Whenever possible, find out what you want to buy before you go to the store. Do not rap on the tables or counters to attract the attention of clerks.

Respect for public property is one of the most important of all civic habits. Good citizens protect public property even as they protect and care for their own private property. What care should be given to library books or other books belonging to school or state?

Public wash bowls should be left as clean as possible. Who wants to use a dirty, unsanitary wash bowl such as we often see on trains and in public buildings?

Manners Everywhere.

A happy greeting in the morning and a pleasant "good night" help in spreading good cheer everywhere. Upon entering a classroom, or a business office, or when meeting friends on the street or in other public places, a cheerful "good morning" helps in creating the right kind of atmosphere and starts the day right. A courteous, well-bred person is especially thoughtful of older people, takes time to greet them, and when- ever possible speaks a word of cheer to them. "A happy smile is always welcome." introductions. When a boy and girl are introduced to each other, the boy is presented to the girl, which means that the girl's name is spoken first — for example, Miss Blank, may I present Mr. Blank? or simply speak the name of each with a little emphasis on the girl's name. A boy is introduced to the girl, the girl never to the boy. A boy rises to his feet when introduced to anyone. A girl rises only when greeting her guests or older people. She does not rise when a boy is presented to her unless she is the hostess or unless the introductions are being made by an older man or woman whom she wishes to honor.

In all introductions, it is a safe rule to present young people to older people; less distinguished people to distinguished people. A man is always presented to a woman, a boy to a girl. Rise if you are being introduced to an older person and remain standing until the older person is seated. In acknowledging an introduction, smile and say, "How do you do, Miss Blank," never "Pleased to meet you."

In Conversation.

To be able to talk of things that interest your listener is a worthwhile art. To converse well, one must be interested in what interests other people. The way to make yourself pleasing to others is to show that you care for them, that you are really interested in their affairs. Be a good listener, but don't allow yourself to be so mentally lazy and so selfish that you fail to do your part in the conversation. One who does not listen care- fully is apt to make out-of-place remarks or irrelevant interruptions. One who talks too much may monopolize the conversation. Avoid talking "forever" on one topic. Do not exaggerate, but be definite and clear in your statements, and do not contradict. Be willing for others to have their opinions and do not try to force yours upon any- one.

When you telephone, avoid long conversations. Do not annoy your friends by calling too frequently and do not call at meal time or late at night. Ask directly for the person with whom you wish to speak. Never open a telephone conversation with "Who is that," or "Guess who this is." When answering the telephone, you may announce who you are or the telephone number instead of saying "Hello." If you are inclined to be impatient and speak irritably when you do not get a connection quickly, or when you get the wrong connection, remember the slogan of the telephone company, "The voice with the smile wins."

The Dining Room and Table Service.

Nowhere are beautiful manners more to be desired than in the dining room. Knowing how to set a table correctly and attractively, how to serve a meal correctly and graciously, and how to be charming and entertaining while unconsciously observing good table manners are among the finer and more worthwhile attainments in social life. Authorities differ as to some of the minor amenities, but all agree on those founded on good taste, common sense, and simplicity. Doing the thing that seems most natural, most convenient, and most considerate of others usually means that one is acting correctly.

Being Seated.

It is customary to stand behind the chair until the hostess or your mother starts to sit down, then move to the left of the chair and be seated. When the meal is over, rise from the left of the chair also, if convenient. Sit straight in your chair with your feet on the floor. Crossing the feet is permissible, but the knees should not be crossed nor should the feet rest on the rungs of the chair.

When boys and girls are present at the table, each boy may adjust the chair for the girl at his right, as she seats herself. He may also assist her in rising by pulling the chair out. Chairs need little or no adjusting if properly placed.

In the average home, each member of the family has a definite place to sit. The father and mother, who are really the host and hostess in the home, sit opposite each other. When there are guests at the informal meal, your mother will indicate where they are to sit.

At the informal meal, the hostess leads the way into the dining room and the ladies in the party follow, while the men enter last. But at the formal meal, the host, with the lady guest of honor, leads the way, the other guests follow in couples, while the hostess and the gentleman guest of honor enter last. The hostess usually tells each gentleman in the party whom he is to escort into the dining room. At formal meals or at all large parties, place cards are convenient to use to indicate where each guest is to sit. These cards may be placed on the napkin or behind the plate. When there is a lady guest of honor, she should be seated at the right of the host. When there is a man guest of honor, he is seated at the right of the hostess.

How to Use the Napkin.

Unfold the napkin before beginning to eat. If it is a very small one, unfold it completely; if large, unfold it in half. The napkin is placed on the lap to protect the clothing. It may also be used occasionally to wipe the lips before drinking water or after eating meat. Fold the napkin at the close of the meal if you are at home or if you intend to use the napkin the next meal. If you are a guest for only one meal, leave the napkin unfolded at the side of your cover.

How to Use the Fork.

If the fork is used with the knife, as in eating meat, it is used in the left hand, but when used without the knife, it is held in the right hand. Forks are used in eating cream toast, vegetables, pie, and salads. Such foods are cut with the edge of the fork and then raised to the mouth with the tines of the fork pointed up. When food is too soft to be eaten with the fork, it should be eaten with a spoon. Some desserts can be eaten either with the fork or the spoon. A fork can be used for firm desserts, while a spoon should be used for soft desserts. Always use the fork to cut food when possible and sensible. The fork should not be used to take bread or baked potato from the serving dish. Bread should be taken with the fingers. Potatoes and all other vegetables should be served with a tablespoon.

How to Use the Knife.

The knife is used for cutting only those foods which cannot be cut with the fork, or for spreading butter, unless a butter knife is provided. Bread should be broken into small pieces and buttered; spreading the whole slice of bread is bad taste. When the knife is not in use, it should be placed on the back side of the plate with the cutting edge toward you. Both the blade and the handle should rest on the plate; resting only the blade on the plate is not good usage.

Using the Knife and Fork Together.

When cutting meat, the fork is held in the left hand to hold the food in place. After the meat is cut by using both the knife and fork, the knife in the right hand and the fork in the left, the knife may be laid on the side of the plate while the food is lifted to the mouth with the fork still in the left hand with the tines down, or the fork may be transferred to the right hand and then used to lift the food to the mouth. Use the method most convenient and natural to you.

When passing a plate for a second helping and when the meal is completed, the knife and the fork, with prongs up, should be placed in the center of the plate. At one time they were placed on the side of the plate, but are less apt to slip off if placed in the center.

How to Use the Spoon.

Since it is awkward to put the whole bowl of a spoon into the mouth, it is not considered good usage to do so. In using either a teaspoon or soup-spoon, put only the side of the spoon into the mouth. When eating soup from a bowl or soup dish, move the spoon away from you and not toward you. Soup served in a cup may be drunk as a beverage. Use the teaspoon only for stirring beverages and for testing to determine whether they are sweet enough or cool enough. Place the spoon in the saucer and lift the cup by the handle to your lips.

Using the Fingers.

Bread, cookies, and any dry food that does not soil the fingers may be removed from the serving plate with the fingers. In eating bread and dry sandwiches, break off a small piece with the fingers. Club sandwiches are often eaten with a fork. Radishes, celery, artichokes, firm cheese, nuts, candy, crackers, cookies, firm pickles, olives, and the like are eaten with the fingers.

Table Service.

Customs in table service vary in different sections of the country as well as at different times in the same country, so definite rules about all phases cannot be set down. Fundamentally, propriety in table service should be governed by convenience and simplicity, just as in other phases of correct etiquette.

Types of Table Service.

The kind of table service that is used varies with the formality of the occasion and the preference of the family with regard to formality. When boys and girls are learning to serve, they take the place of a waiter, a maid, or a butler, and in this discussion it should be understood that "waiter" refers to anyone who waits on the table, and that father and mother are the host and hostess in your home while the guests are friends and relatives who come only occasionally.

English Style.

This type is used most extensively where there is no maid service and is commonly called "family style." The main foods are put on the table in serving dishes and served to the individual plates by the host or some other member of the family. Salads, and desserts may be served in individual dishes. Sometimes the entire meal is served without anyone's rising from the table. Tea carts and wagons are a great convenience and save many steps. Of course, hot foods are usually best if left on the stove until ready to be eaten. Some cold foods served are better if left in the refrigerator until the course is ready to be eaten. Extra bread, silver, and dishes can be placed on the tea wagon. Salad dishes can be removed from the table and placed on the tea cart if there is room. This type of service is hospitable and informal and preferred in many homes, even where servants are available.

Russian Style.

In the Russian style, all food is served from the kitchen or serving tables, the host or hostess taking no part in the service. The maid or waiter places the plates in front of each person or else the empty plates are placed before each person and the serving dishes passed to the left of each guest. All dishes are passed, placed, and removed from the left of the guest except the beverages, which are placed at the right, because most people use the right hand in drinking beverages. If beverages were placed from the left it would be necessary to reach in front of the guest and of course this should be avoided. One waiter can usually give good service to about six people in this type of service. This is the type of service that is customarily used at high-priced cafes, clubs, and hotels. It should be used in the home only when adequate help is provided.

Compromise Style.

This, as the name implies, is a compromise between the English and Russian types. The method has some of the hospitality of the English type and some of the formality of the Russian. The first course is usually on the table when the meal begins. Such foods as soup, salads, and desserts are served Russian style from the kitchen and the main dishes are served by the host or hostess. The main course is served by the host, while the coffee, the dessert, and sometimes the salad are served by the hostess. This method is used in a home where maid service is available.

For Family Use.

Any combination or modification of these types of service that suits the needs and conveniences of the individual family may be used. Common sense and convenience are usually found to be in line with the best usage. Some kind of informal service is preferred by most families, which usually means a slight modification of the English type. For example, if there is a first course, such as fruit or soup, it is usually on the table when the family is seated. The dessert may be on the side table or tea cart in individual dishes, ready to be served. The salad is often placed on the table before the meal begins.

Some families prefer to bring all the food from the kitchen in general serving dishes. Then the food is divided into portions by those seated at the table or the dishes may be passed at the table. If the food is to be passed, each person is expected to pass the article of food nearest him. All the dishes should start in the same direction, for instance, each person who passes food when sitting at the table should pass the dish to his right, with his right hand, so that the person next to him may receive the dish in the left hand, and serve himself with his right hand.

Setting the Table.

A table cloth, luncheon cloth, or runners may be used as covering for the table. The important thing is its cleanliness. No one enjoys eating off a soiled table covering.

The centerpiece should be low enough that people may see each other and converse with one another without having to deflect the body from a natural position.

Glassware, china, and silver should be gleaming and should be placed so as to balance the table properly.

At least twenty-four inches and preferably thirty inches should be allowed for each individual place. The plate should be one inch from the edge of the table. Silver is placed in the order of its use, the forks on the left of the plate, the knives and spoons on the right. The cutting edge of the knife should face the plate. The bread and butter plate is set at the left, just above the forks, the butter spreader resting on the side of the plate parallel with other silver with its spreading edge toward the center of the plate. The glass is placed at the tip of the knife, on the right side of the plate. The folded napkin is placed on the plate, except when food is already on the table when guests are seated, then on the left of forks, with the open edges toward the plate. Individual salt and pepper containers may be placed in front of the plate or between two covers in line with the water glass. Salad plates are usually placed at the tip of the forks, but if a bread and butter plate is used, the salad may be placed at the left of the forks, or above the plate to the right of the bread and butter plate, or at the right of the spoons in case a beverage is not served with the salad course. cups and saucers are placed at the right with handles of cups turned toward the edge of the table for convenience in lifting.

Chairs are placed even with the edge of the table to enable the guest to be seated without moving the chair, as well as to prevent crushing the hanging cloth.

In correct table service, everything is placed, served, passed, and removed from the left, with the exception of the beverage and extra silver which are placed at the right with the right hand, and removed with the left hand. When offering dishes to others, hold them low and as near as possible to the person to be served. Never rest them on the table. At both formal and informal service, guests are served first, although in formal service in first class restaurants each dish is first presented to the host for approval, then the person on the right of the host is served. The host is always served last.

Duties of Host and Hostess.

When you plan a dinner party, choose guests whom you believe to be congenial. Avoid all last minute hurry and late preparations by mentally visualizing every detail in advance. Imagine yourself a guest and see your party from the guest's viewpoint.

When the hostess has no assistance in serving a meal, she sits at the end of the table near the kitchen door. With a maid she sits at the opposite end of the table where she can signal to the maid. The host sits opposite the hostess.

If a member of the family is serving, her seat should be near the kitchen door. Guests are always seated where they will be most comfortable. Usually a woman guest is seated at the host's right and a man at the right of the hostess.

The hostess, with or without a maid's service, is largely responsible for the success of the meal. She feels responsible for the conversation and for everything that pertains to the happiness and comfort of her guests. Guests watch the hostess to know when to be seated, when to begin eating, and when to rise from the table. Both the host and hostess eat until all the guests finish.

When the host serves the main course, he should make a special study of carving for this is perhaps the most difficult of his duties. Carving is not so general as it once was but it is indeed an art that is appreciated. Men who carve well really enjoy it and it gives a spirit of hospitality to the meal not present when the dishes are brought ready to serve from the kitchen. The thoughtful hostess directs the attention of her guests by interesting conversation away from the host who carves to avoid confusion or self-consciousness on his part. The carving equipment consists of a good steel knife with a sharp edge, and a platter large enough to allow for the servings as they are cut or an extra plate on which servings may be placed. The platter is placed directly in front of the host and the plates piled either at his left or in front of him. Enough meat should be carved to serve all guests before any part of it is placed on the plate. Servings should be about the same size.

When the host finishes a plate, he may tell the maid to whom it is to be served or if there is no maid, he passes the plate to his right, and states for whom it is intended. He himself may serve the vegetables with the meat or have the plate passed to the hostess for the remaining servings.

The host assists the hostess in every way possible in making the guests happy and comfortable.

Lest You Forget.

Manners at the table, as elsewhere, are based on consideration for others.

Place the used silver on your plate when the course is finished to facilitate easy removal.

Seeds are removed from the mouth by use of the fingers rather than with a fork or spoon.

Cocktails are eaten with a fork when a cocktail fork is provided, otherwise with a spoon.

Salads are eaten with forks.

Butter one small piece of bread or roll at a time, never the whole slice.

Don't put your elbows on the table.

Don't talk with food in your mouth.

Don't reach across the table.

Don't leave your spoon in your cup. Lay it on the saucer.

Invitations.

Invitations to informal parties may be given in writing, by telephone, or in person. They should be given from five to seven days before the event. Replies should be explicit, repeating the date, time, and nature of the party so that if a mistake was made the hostess would have an opportunity to correct it. Acceptances or regrets should be given immediately upon receipt of the invitation.

Formal invitations are always worded in the third person. They may be written or engraved. Example:

Miss Jane Andrews
requests the pleasure of
Miss Ann Richardson's
company at tea
on Friday, the tenth of April

at four o'clock.

The formal acceptance should be on note paper and written in the third person. Example:

Miss Ann Richardson
accepts with pleasure
Miss Jane Andrew's
kind invitation to tea
on Friday, the tenth of April.

Formal regrets should also be written in the third person on note paper. Example:

Miss Ann Richardson
regrets that she is unable to accept
Miss Jane Andrew's
kind invitation to tea
on Friday, the tenth of April.

Invitations by school clubs and similar organizations are engraved or written and worded substantially as in the following example:

FULTON HIGH SCHOOL
requests the pleasure of your company
on Wednesday, the tenth of January
at four o'clock

The use of visiting cards is the most popular form of extending invitations to teas, bridge parties, informal dances, and to meet a guest. Cards of the girl's mother are generally used but if the guest list includes only friends of the girl herself, she may use her own cards. A boy of high school age is expected to use his mother's cards. Answers to visiting card invitations should be worded in the third person on note paper or on a visiting card

Correspondence.

Just as in choosing furniture for the house, suitability should guide us in selecting writing paper. Large writing is more suited to a larger sized paper than small writing. Paper should never be ruled or perfumed. The most satisfactory color for all occasions is plain white or cream. Oblong shaped envelopes are best for business; square ones for social use. Paper should be neatly folded; twice for business letters with their oblong envelopes, and once or not at all for social letters, depending of course upon the size of envelope and paper. Much paper for social use is cut the same size of the envelope and slipped in without folding.

The date and address are placed in the upper right hand corner; the salutation varies from the very formal "My dear Mr. Jones" to the very informal "Dear Joe."

The body of a business letter should be clear, concise, and to the point. Personal letters are longer and may include any detail of interest.

A formal note usually closes "Sincerely," "Sincerely yours," or "Very truly yours." The informal letter closing depends upon the degree of intimacy between the writer and the addressee.

At the Office.

The efficient, well ordered office places courtesy at a distinct value and if you are planning to work in an office during the summer or when you graduate, you would do well to study office etiquette. Simple tailored clothes and neat, trim shoes with medium heels are worn. The hands should be well groomed and if liquid polish is used, of a very conservative color.

An employee does not issue invitations of any sort to his employer.

Personalities should not enter into office relationships. You are a part of a large and important machine and your duty is to give loyal, efficient service.

Under no circumstances call office employees by their given names while you are at the office. "Miss Brown" or "Mr. Jones" sound much better than "Mary" or "Joe." Addressing others by only their last names without the prefix "Miss" or "Mr." is equally in bad taste.

When You Travel.

When traveling, as when staying at home, the best rule to follow is to take into consideration the other person and "do as you would be done by." The first concern of course is your luggage, which should be durable and neat. Do not take any more baggage than you absolutely need; it is troublesome, expensive, and in the way. Baggage may be checked in the baggage room at a station.

On the train, do not wear the heavy perfumes that are in- variably disagreeable to others; do not eat in the Pullman or chair car, particularly food with strong odors.

Do not seek acquaintanceship with fellow passengers but on the other hand do not be rude if their friendship is proffered. A restrained conversation about topics of the day or other topics not involving personalities is permissible and helps the time to go more quickly.

The best and most convenient way to carry your money when traveling is in the form of traveler's checks.

Before you travel, read literature about the place you intend to visit so you can look for the most interesting things.

Behavior in the dining car should be the same as in a first-class restaurant.

If you are to travel in the sleeper at night, you will be given the number of your berth and section when you purchase your ticket. There is a dressing room at the end of the car, in which you will find hot and cold water, drinking water, towels, mirrors, and chairs. Berths are usually made up around 9:30 or 10:00 o'clock, although the porter will be glad to make yours whenever requested to do so. You will need slippers and a dark simple dressing gown for your trips to and from the dressing room.

A hanger on the inside of your berth will accommodate your outer clothes ; a hammock and shelf your shoes, hats, hose, and under clothes. If your shoes need shining, place them outside the berth and the porter will take care of them during the night.

If you have an upper berth, the porter will bring a ladder to facilitate your getting into it. When you are ready to rise the next morning, ring for him to bring the ladder.

The porter should be tipped twenty-five cents a day for each day you are on the train and ten cents extra for each additional service.

The "Travelers Aid" will give you advice and information on any point so it is never necessary to ask questions of strangers.

On a boat, tailored and sports clothes are best, with one evening dress, or a tuxedo for a boy of high school age. A robe and slippers are also needed. On a slow cruise or on a boat with a few passengers, one usually gets acquainted with his fellow passengers but on a fast liner, the same formality is observed as at large hotels.

Tipping.

Though tipping is prohibited in some places it has become so generally the custom that it is done automatically by most people. In restaurants, the tip is ten per cent of the total bill, but never less than twenty-five cents when the table has a cloth on it.

At a hotel, the bell boy who carries your baggage to the room expects to receive a twenty-five cent tip. A ten cent tip is given for ice water, packages, or telegrams. Tipping is almost necessary to obtain good service, so if you do not tip or cannot afford to do so, avoid the expensive places where service is expected to be rewarded with tips.

"Dates."

Many high school boys go through agonies wanting to ask a girl for a date and not being sure how to go about it. If you know the girl, the simplest thing would be to plan a definite thing to do which you think she would enjoy, such as seeing a certain moving picture, going to a play, or going to some other form of entertainment, then to tell her you would enjoy having her go with you. If the girl with whom you want the date is unknown to you, the only thing to do is to get a mutual friend to introduce you. Most girls prefer that the first date with a boy they have not known very long be in company with another couple who are friends. This arrangement makes for easier conversation and a smoother evening in every way.

Football Games.

Although football games are perhaps the most informal entertainment conceived, propriety is observed here as elsewhere. Wear durable sports clothes to football games so you and your escort will not have to worry about your best hat getting rained on or your coat getting soiled from sitting in the stadium. Wear flat-heeled shoes so that you can climb steps and wade mud if necessary. Try not to jump up so often in your enthusiasm as to make it necessary for those behind you to stand in order to see. Learn the rules of football in order that you may not need to ask your escort for explanations. Do not put on make-up while the game is in progress. If you are not interested in football, stay away from the game.

At the Theater.

When an usher shows a couple to their seats, the girl precedes the boy; if there is no usher, the boy walks in front to find a satisfactory seat and then lets the girl precede him and be seated, so that he may sit on the outside. Girls with large hats should remove them so that the person behind will not have difficulty in seeing. It is disconcerting to those near for you to talk or eat during the performance. Be as quiet as possible out of consideration for others. After going home from the theater or other entertainment, the girl may invite the boy in if it is not too late, or may tell him goodnight at the door, and thank him for a pleasant evening. She should not say "When will I see you again?" If the boy desires to see her again, he will ask for the opportunity to do so. The easiest way to hold people you like is by not making their escape from you too difficult.

At the Dance.

If you are not a good dancer, take some lessons. It is the good dancers who are the most popular on the ballroom floor. When a boy asks a girl to dance, he says "May I have this dance?" or "May I have a part of this dance?" or "Would you care to dance?" The girl may reply in the affirmative or merely smile and nod.

In taking the correct position for dancing, the partners face each other, the boy's left hand at the back of the girl's waist, firmly but not tight, to facilitate leading; her left hand is on the back of his right shoulder, her right hand resting in his extended left hand.

At break dances, the boy who breaks in touches the girl's partner on the shoulder and he immediately surrenders the girl to her new partner. If she is a clever girl and likes the partner who is relinquishing her, she says "sorry" in a voice audible only to him.

The girl dances at least the first and last dance with her escort for the evening.

A boy should not leave a girl alone on the dance floor. He should escort her to her seat. However, if the boy does not extend this deference there is no need for the girl to be any more panic stricken at having to spend a minute alone on a dance floor than in any other public place. In case her partner for the next dance does not appear, she may go to the dressing room.

A well-bred boy does not continually try different steps with his partner if she does not readily follow. Once you have tried a step which has proved too difficult for your partner, do not attempt it again with her; instead of its displaying your superior dancing ability to advantage, trying a difficult step only shows your lack of courtesy and makes both you. and your partner appear ridiculous.

Before leaving the dance, tell your hostess or chaperon that you have enjoyed the evening.

Teas.

Teas are informal and friendly. Perhaps no other entertainment is so popular during high school days as "The Tea" or affords a better opportunity for gaining knowledge of social usage. All through your life you will be invited to teas and will be inviting others to your teas, so let us attend one today.

Your invitation has read:

Mrs. John Richlieu
requests the honor of
Miss Jane Doe's
presence at tea
on Saturday, February 8
at four o'clock.

Invitations to a large tea are usually mailed from ten to fourteen days before the date set. After accepting the invitation, your first concern of course is one of dress. You may appropriately wear a neat street dress if you are a girl; a street suit if a boy; but do not wear sports clothes.

Your nails, of course, are clean, your hair is clean and attractively arranged, your shoes are polished; in short, you are well groomed.

When you have arrived at the house of your hostess, a maid or a friend of the hostess will open the door for you.

Boys are expected to remove hats, overcoats, and gloves and hand them to the maid or leave them where indicated. Girls do not remove their hats or gloves or, unless indicated, even their wraps. A girl removes her gloves just before she is served and holds them with her purse.

Your hostess will be standing near the door. You must go directly to her and say, "How do you do." She may say, "Fine so glad you could come, Jane" and will probably guide you toward the other guests. If you do not know them, she may say, for example:

"Jane, this is Roy Burk, who is over for the week-end from Center. He played fullback on the Center High team last year. Roy, Miss Doe is guard on our basketball team this year."

Each must acknowledge the introduction, you by saying "How do you do, Mr. Burk"; he by saying "How do you do, Miss Doe."

When making introductions, the popular hostess always supplies some note of interest to give her guests a topic with which to start the conversation.

You may say "I see that Center won their game with State last week" or "Does this indulgence in tea mean that you are not in training this year?" Roy may explain that he is working — and thus an interesting conversation is off to a good start.

A boy always rises when presented to a guest; a girl remains seated. A girl does not extend her hand when introduced but does not refuse to shake hands when someone offers his hand. Formal introductions are not necessary in a friend's home, since the fact that guests are together in a mutual friend's home is recommendation enough for them to engage in conversation.

If you feel self-conscious or ill at ease, remember that no doubt most of the other guests feel the same way, so try to set them at their ease. Remember also that the hostess asked you because she thought you would be an asset to her tea and she is depending upon your help in making it a successful and enjoyable affair. Try to help her by seeing that the other guests enjoy themselves. If you are left alone, try to appear as if you are enjoying yourself and you will not be alone long. A person who enjoys his own company makes enjoyable company for others.

When you wish tea, do not hesitate about what to do but go directly to the table where it is poured and say pleasantly "May I have a cup of tea?"

A boy may obtain tea for a girl or woman and take the cup, on the saucer or the plate, to her. Girls may take plates to older women.

The person who pours will ask if you would like sugar and cream or lemon. You reply, "Lemon, thank you" or "Cream, please." Do not take both lemon and cream. Help yourself to sandwiches, cakes, or whatever refreshments are provided. Refreshments should be simple.

Napkins always are placed in a pile in a convenient place. The napkin which you take should not be completely unfolded. When you have finished, you are expected to hand it with the plate to the maid or assisting hostess, but if there are no assistants, you should place your plate on the buffet.

You may leave a tea whenever you wish after you have stayed long enough to chat with a few guests and thanked your hostess; but you should not stay until the time limit is up unless for exceptional reasons.

Showers and Weddings.

Showers are a popular form of entertainment from the time we give our favorite teacher a "fruit shower" to that which seems to be the most popular form today, the shower given the bride-to-be. Showers, however, may be given to new house owners, to someone who is going away, to a newcomer, particularly a clergy- man, or in behalf of the new or expected baby. Sometimes they are specified on the invitations as "Lingerie Shower" and the like; at other times the gifts may be miscellaneous in nature.

Invitations may be telephoned, written, or given in person, and may be given at any time during the day.

When showers are given by a group of intimate friends, each member contributes a specified sum for the purchase of a present of greater value than the collective value their individual presents would represent.

Weddings.

Invitations to weddings are mailed about three weeks before the date set for the ceremony. They are mailed to friends of the bride and groom and to their families and their friends.

Weddings are usually held at high noon, four o'clock, or eight o'clock in the evening. At a simple wedding the bride may wear traveling clothes; at a church wedding she wears a wedding dress and veil. The groom's apparel is governed by that of the bride. If she wears traveling clothes, he wears a business suit, if she wears a wedding dress, he dresses formally.

Formal attire for the groom includes a black cutaway coat, dark gray striped trousers, white or black waistcoat, black tie, wing collar, white buckskin or light gray suede gloves, a boutonniere, and black shoes. The best man dresses in the same manner as the groom.

Bridesmaids are dressed alike and the style of their costumes is suggested by the bride. The maid or matron of honor dresses like the bridesmaids but reverses the colors; for instance, if they wear pink dresses with blue hats, she wears a blue dress with a pink hat.

At a church wedding, the groom's family sits in the right front pew, the bride's to the left in the front pew. Guests are shown to their places by ushers.

The bride's family pays for the wedding invitations, announcements, music, and other expense incident to the bride's part in the wedding, such as gifts for the bridesmaids. The groom's expenses include the license fee, wedding ring, gift for the bride, bride's bouquet, clergyman's fee, gifts and boutonnieres for ushers, and the traveling expense.

Announcements are mailed the day of the wedding. Announcements require no gift or acknowledgment.

Wedding gifts may be shown or not as the bride chooses. Should she show them, she should be careful to group them so as to exhibit each one to its best advantage. Duplicate gifts should not be placed together and valuable presents should not be placed so close to those of much less value as to call attention to the contrast. Cards may be left with the gifts or removed.

At the bridal table, the bride sits at the right of the groom with the best man on her right and the maid or matron of honor at the left of the groom. Other attendants sit at the bridal table. The mothers and fathers of the couple sit at a special table with the clergyman and other distinguished guests.

Light refreshments may be served or an elaborate meal, as the bride prefers. The bride cuts the first piece of the bridal cake, then it is taken out, cut, and brought back to the guests.

After leaving the bridal table, the party joins in the dancing in the reception room. After most of the guests have left, the bride and groom change into traveling clothes and leave.

Meaning and Value of Friendship.

Everyone wants to have friends. Today more than ever before, friendship and the personality that wins friends are being emphasized not only as highly desirable characteristics but as assets necessary to a successful life. The person who has friends enjoys life more, is happier, and better balanced mentally than the one without friends.

Traits that encourage friendship are good nature, a sense of humor, tact, courtesy, thoughtfulness, enthusiasm, cheerfulness, sincerity, sympathy, poise, dependability. What other traits can you add? Do you have many friends? What traits do you have that discourage friendship? That encourage friendship?

There are numerous books that tell how to make people like you and how to develop your personality. Many correspondence courses on a charming personality, as well as books relating to the subject, are sold each year. It is well that we become frank enough to admit to ourselves that the desire for love and admiration is something normal and to be worked toward. By making a conscientious effort we can all have likable, interesting personalities and yet retain individuality.

Doesn't it make you glow to meet someone who greets you with enthusiasm and warmth and listens attentively while you tell him of the wonderful week-end you have just enjoyed? Occasionally your listener may interrupt but always with a question or remark to show you he is not only listening but enjoying your narrative. One of the principal traits of winsomeness is the capacity to be a good listener. In the three people you like best, what are the outstanding traits of character that draw you to them?

Do you possess these same traits? Could you develop them? To develop socially among friends, you must first develop socially among the members of your own family. A person who can be agreeable with the members of his family almost invariably can get along well with other people, for those who are closest to us are most critical of us. It is perhaps harder to be agreeable at home than outside because we can be hurt most by those we love most. We do not bother to hurt those for whom we do not care.

To live in harmony with the members of our family, we must respect their rights, we must cooperate in the family's enterprises and problems, we must accept our share of responsibility without shirking or complaining, and we must keep ourselves as attractive as possible both mentally and physically.

Generosity, unselfishness, and affection form the basis of true friendship. Fortunately, we do not need to be perfect to enjoy friendships. Our friends see our faults and may even scold us for them but they love us in spite of them. Those friends with whom we can be natural call out the best that is in us. We do not have to hide things from them. They may not agree with us, but they listen to us and try not to misunderstand.

Disloyalty spoils friendship.

To betray confidences is one of the worst things we can do. We should be loyal to our friends of both sexes. If it is impossible to be loyal to certain people, then we should not have those people as friends.

Friendship is reciprocal; our friends want sympathy, understanding, and encouragement from us. When we reciprocate a feeling of friendliness, confidence in themselves is imparted to our friends and security, courage, and happiness supplant discouragement in their minds.

Personal and Social Relationships with members of the same sex or the opposite sex is based on a common interest. The general appearance of people may be attractive and encourage attention but if there are no mutual interests to sustain the attraction, friendship does not materialize. All happy friendships as well as happy marriages are based on congeniality, that is, on the same basic likes and dislikes. A boy who enjoys outdoor life will not long enjoy as a comrade the girl who prefers staying inside and reading to the pleasures of a hike in the woods. The girl who goes in for social welfare will not like as a comrade the boy who derives his pleasure in life from a continual round of parties and dances.

Once we have made new friends, we cannot leave those friendships to take care of themselves. Friendships must be well tended and cared for. On the other hand, many people spoil a friendship that has started beautifully by getting too possessive. All of us like freedom too much to give ourselves over entirely to other persons. While a small degree of jealousy among members of the opposite sex is expected in friendships, intense jealousy not only makes the jealous person miserable but makes the object of his jealousy miserable as well as everyone else around them. We like most those who make us happiest and while an occasional misunderstanding may not affect a friendship, continued bickering and frequent misunderstandings destroy the foundations upon which any friendship must be built — sympathy, understanding, and congeniality.

Gossip and inquisitiveness are as much the enemies of a perfect friendship as jealousy. We value our individual freedom and our right to privacy and we all resent the prying of other people into our affairs, although we may be glad to confide in them voluntarily. It is human nature to shy away from anything that threatens our contentment; the perfect friendship never threatens.

Unit 6

HOME MANAGEMENT AND COMMUNITY RELATIONS

CHAPTER 25

MANAGEMENT, FAMILY FINANCE AND CONSUMER EDUCATION

What do we mean when we speak of management? Of family economics? Of family income, family budgets, and consumer problems? Should the world at large be concerned with the meager expenditures of the average and less than average family income? Who is the consumer and why bother about him?

Management is currently defined either as "The judicious use of means to accomplish an end" or "Conduct directed by art and skill." Neither definition is inclusive enough when applied to home management. In this special sphere the successful home manager must not only possess art and skill but must choose worthy means to accomplish her purposes and must apply them with tact and under- standing of the "human equation."

Economics is the term generally used in speaking of man's wants and the methods by which these wants are gratified. The meaning of family economics is not so definite. In fact, its meaning is so nebulous as to suggest that the value of housework is just being discovered. Is the house wife a producer or is she merely a consumer? Is woman's work a trade, a profession, a vocation, or an occupation? A panel discussion by members of your class on thoughts raised by these questions would undoubtedly elicit some interesting comments.

The Home Management Division of the United States Department of Agriculture, through the efforts of their research workers, found that the annual value of the average house wife's labor ranges from $1400.00 to $1500.00. Other studies have shown the value of her work to amount to considerably more. No one would expect the wage earner to pay that amount to his wife, but the work of women should be recognized and placed on a much higher plane than it has ever been. A change in attitude with respect to the value of woman's home work would do much toward stabilizing the home by giving women a feeling of equality instead of the sense of inferiority which has been altogether too prevalent.

What is wealth? Is all wealth material? Or do we have a right to classify the intangible things which satisfy human wants as wealth? The home of today has been called the home of consumption while that of yesterday, which was practically self-sufficient, has been called the home of production. In thinking entirely of material things one is forced to admit that the home of today has become a great consuming station, for some authorities say that women spend approximately ninety percent of all money earned in all the other vocations. Although admitting the truthfulness of this statistical fact, recognition of the unseen values that are produced in the homes of today would show that they are worth more than the things formerly produced in homes but now made outside.

The real foundation for happiness in the home is not in material things but in love, respect, tolerance, and under- standing between family members. Then who would deny to the members of the family who produce these values the claim of being the greatest of all producers! Good food and clothing, attractive homes, good health, and a harmonious home atmosphere all depend largely on good management. What is the value of the home manager's contribution in managing the home as a whole and in pro- viding for the happiness of every individual within the home?

Surveys of homemakers' duties all point to the significant fact that in the homes of today, the managerial duties are increasing although house work is decreasing. What does this mean? It means that much of the work of the former home has been taken out of the home by business and industry, but the business of the household has actually increased.

Good housekeeping is only a part of home making which includes both work and managerial activities. Wherever there is a job to be done, there lies close by a management problem. The relationship that results is one of leader and follower.

The responsibility and opportunity for service of the home manager have to do with problems relating to food, clothes, shelter, money income, home labor and services, conservation of time and energy, spiritual values, and character building.

If we are to have the maximum of personal growth and development, good management must be in evidence with- out taking itself too seriously. Good intentions and the best business management will not make the house livable unless good humor, freedom, and relaxation are enjoyed in the household. The efficient home must not be too obviously efficient, neither must good housekeeping be so good that the family deserts the house for more comfortable quarters!

The home manager should have a portion of some room as an "office" even if it is only a table in the kitchen, where she can keep her records, plan her menus, file recipes and receipts, and keep track of the household finances and family schedules. By arranging her work beforehand and devoting special hours to certain tasks, she will find that she can eliminate many unnecessary steps and have a definite rest period. For instance, she can conveniently attend to a part of the cooking of the next meal while she is in the kitchen washing dishes.

The health of the wife, who is mother, companion, nurse, cook, seamstress, laundress, and collaborator in all home activities, is the first consideration. All the scientific studies that have been made, and experience itself, point to the need for labor saving, time saving, and energy saving devices for the relief of this woman in the home.

The importance of right heights in working surfaces, labor saving devices, the right arrangement of furniture, equipment, and utensils have been mentioned in other chapters but too much emphasis cannot be given to values which mean so much to the tired, overworked mother in the average home who has no household assistant.

The Value of Planning.

A study of plans and sensible schedules for the house wife is certainly worthwhile. Someone has said "Plan your work and then work the plan." Interruptions in the form of unexpected company or from broken and worn-out equipment will occur in any household, no matter how well planned, but surely such interruptions can be cared for more advantageously with an organized background than with a background of disorder and confusion. Routine may be made to contribute rhythm, and even harmony, to the progress of the everyday activities.

The Family Council.

How does the average homemaker use her day? Would it be worthwhile if she would stop long enough to give her average day a critical analysis? Is there any help for her? Will a time schedule help? How can other members of the family help? The family council, no matter how informal, is the answer. The work of the home is the responsibility of every member. It is unfair to expect the wife and mother to carry the whole burden; in fact, no matter how willing, she is unable to carry it all. The family council is a clearing house for the interchange of opinion and the discussion of personal problems. It is as important to have freedom of speech in the family circle as in the nation; it establishes a sense of democracy and fair play, allows for relief of pent-up emotions, and paves the way for smoothing personal grudges. People who are mentally and emotionally healthy are willing to listen to differences of opinion and submit to criticisms of themselves and their work.

Every new invention, every new technical process has touched the home. Accompanying changes have widened the walls of the home and thrown open the doors. The mother is only one member of the family circle. The father, too, needs help and encouragement. The younger children and those who are older must lend their assistance. Together they must find the way, all striving for a better home and a finer community.

Domestic Labor.

Is there need for a new viewpoint concerning our domestic servant problem? Do household assistants receive the right kind of treatment? Are their wages sufficient to keep them in good health and permit them to save a little for the proverbial "rainy day"? Do household assistants actually need training and education better to fit them for their work? The answer to most of these questions is obvious. Some of the questions might give rise to debate, for here, as elsewhere, there are "two sides to the question."

If the work of the wife and mother is too heavy, as we have pointed out, what can be done? Usually the members of the household can assist her but this is not always practical nor is it always adequate. Frankly, a new attitude toward those who work in homes and do manual labor about the house is needed, even more than higher wages. As we plead for higher regard for "mother's work," for the home and its place in the community and nation, we must frankly face the difficult problem created by having the wrong attitude toward maids, cooks, and household assistants. Space here does not permit a discussion of the problem in all its phases but frank and open discussion would help us on our way to the right solution.

Family Finance

One of the chief responsibilities of the home is the management of money. A portion of the money income of the family is used for necessities, part of it for comforts and luxuries, some part for recreation and social pleasure, and some is wasted or spent foolishly. We consider money well used when it is expended for the necessities and things that bring real pleasure and happiness to the family.

Money is spent foolishly when it is used recklessly for pleasure at the expense of the real needs of the members of the family. The family income should furnish the members of the family with the wholesome satisfactions of life but of course these vary with different families. When an individual or a family as a group learns to face the money problem squarely and with determination, half the battle is won and the road to a happy solution lies open.

Since the manner of using the family income is one of the major determinations of the family council, the plans which are adopted should provide for the satisfactions of life, gifts to worthy causes, and savings for the future against the day when the earning capacity of some member of the family will be cut off through old age, illness, or an accident. Security is one of the basic needs of the family and financial competency is the best form of security.

What determines how much money shall be spent? Upon what basis do we make our choices? What is considered a necessity in one family may be called a luxury in another, and for this reason each family must necessarily plan the expenditure of its income to suit its own individual needs, wants, and wishes. So the family must set its own standard of living. Personal choices, likes, dislikes, and ideals of life enter into this spending problem. Some families prefer to save for special occasions such as a grand vacation in the summer with all the family together, even though it means a limited number of picture shows, less candy, and fewer soda fountain drinks.

Every member of the family should share in the responsibility of living within the income. When necessary to make sacrifices, all should have a part and when such needs are known to the whole family, they usually meet the problem with high courage.

For what does the family spend most of its money? Most of the money that is provided for the family is spent for daily living and not enough is saved. Sometimes this represents poor management, sometimes it is because the money income is too low to meet the standard of living which has been chosen or forced upon the family. Modern methods of living and today's social customs are not always in keeping with the money income. So much work has gone out of the home through the activities of modern business and industry that women have been forced to follow their work out of the home. Hence we find women, even mothers with small children, contributing to the money income of the family.

Keeping household accounts has been found helpful in many homes where their accounts were studied and used to promote better business methods. Such accounts have revealed discrepancies and deviations from sound methods such as the experience of families which spend too much for clothing and then find it impossible to buy milk for the growing children. In one instance, a family found money available for the picture show each week but had nothing for donation to church activities, not even pennies for the children's Sunday School!

Most families desire to save money and to be business-like, so they should welcome an opportunity to study spending policies through the medium of accurate systems of household accounting. Household accounts often reveal wasteful habits in the personal expenditures of an individual member; again, some piece of household equipment found to be too expensive, for instance a rug, may cost more than it is worth.

Some items in the accounts will be the same from month to month, others will vary. For instance, if you are renting, the rent will probably be the same month after month; but the gas and light bills will be much larger in the winter than in the summer. In the case of illness, there will be doctors' bills which, of course, do not come every month. Long distance telephone calls, when emergencies arise, also make the telephone bill larger some months than others.

Budgets.

It is important that a plan for spending be made, just as for other household problems. The plan for spending is called a budget. Keeping accounts gives information upon which to base the budget. Budgets help individuals and homes as well as business concerns. Banks and other business institutions have recognized the value of family budgets and accounts and have prepared helpful books and bulletins for the education and convenience of home makers.

The first step in making out a budget is to keep accurate accounts over a certain length of time. These accounts should be carefully analyzed to see if money has been spent unwisely or wasted and where it could have been saved for some useful purpose. Generally, budgets fall under the following headings: food, clothing, shelter, operating expenses, savings, recreation and improvement. The next step lies in finding out how much money should be set aside for each item in the budget. Whenever possible, at least ten percent for saving should be deducted from the income even before it is divided for other items. The income tax should also be deducted.

The size of the income determines the amount to be used, but in general the percentage of distribution among the various items is as follows:

Food.

Approximately 25% should be set aside for food purchases in the moderate-income group. As the income increases, the percentage for the food budget decreases. In the low-income group as much as 50% is sometimes required for food.

Clothing.

Clothing usually gets 15% of the income except in lower incomes, when it sometimes falls as low as 10 %. The proper selection and care of clothing assist materially in keeping this item within the allowance. The apportionment of the money for clothing for each member of the family will necessarily be one to be decided by each family but surely no one member should be permitted to impose upon the others.

Shelter.

Shelter for the family should not exceed 20% of the income. The location in regard to school, to work, and to other centers, as well as the appearance of the neighborhood should be taken into consideration.

Operating Expenses.

These will vary considerably but should always be kept at the minimum. When the cost of operation goes above 12%, a careful check should be made and every effort put forth to check the waste.

Recreation and Improvement.

Recreation, education, health, travel, church and club membership are items included under the last heading in the budget. These expenses vary greatly. Some families plan to use 25% of the income for this purpose but even that amount scarcely takes care of expenses when a big dentist's or doctor's bill is presented; hence too much emphasis cannot be placed on the desirability of saving for these unexpected emergencies.

With each estimated budget there should be kept a statement of actual expenditures. A comparison of the two, from month to month, will indicate whether the estimated budget was at fault, whether the home manager did not get best value for the money, whether the members of the family failed to cooperate, or whether the cost of emergencies increased income expenditures. The comparison will insure a better budget for the next period. It will tell the family what it can afford and show how to get the maximum of benefits from the income.

Children and Money

Unwise spenders are usually those who have no sense of money values and such persons need help. Children should learn early in life how to use money. In fact, every member of the family should know the source of the family income and what expenditures it must cover. Children need to have some money of their own, for it is only by actual experience in handling money that we fully learn its value. Whenever possible, children should be permitted to handle money even before they are old enough to earn money. Opportunity for earning a little money should be provided even though it is not a necessity in the family. This opportunity will not only add to a child's education but it will give him a certain joy in the accomplishment of things which others all about him are experiencing.

The chief uses of money are spending, saving, and giving. Usually the first money a child spends is upon himself to satisfy a want. Soon he should learn that his wants must not exceed his "income" and when he learns this, he begins to see the relation between saving and spending.

Opportunity to give should be provided at an early age. Giving something to a playmate, bought with the giver's own money, or giving something to some worthy cause such as the Community Chest or Red Cross should be encouraged.

How can the child be taught to save? Perhaps he will see a book or a toy that he very much desires but which costs more than he possesses. Saving for a few weeks to buy this desired toy would be a fine way to learn the value and satisfaction derived in saving for the future.

High school boys and girls are interested in the needs of the family for food, clothing, shelter, operating expenses, health and advancement. They are of course old enough to know about unexpected expenses such as those for emergency surgical operations, accidents, and the purchase of a new car. Saving for these special things means careful planning or budgeting.

Charge accounts encourage all of us to buy more than is necessary. It is so much easier to spend than to save. Installment buying is another thing that leads many of us into trouble. Some form of systematic saving is an indispensable help in the habit-forming years of life because when one sees money accumulating it lends encouragement to make additional savings, even at some sacrifice.

Savings and Investments.

Saving is just as important as earning and spending. Saving makes provision for future needs and security against privation and want. Savings buy homes, educate children, provide for unexpected illness or accidents, and provide for old age when earning capacity necessarily decreases.

Savings may be invested in a home or other real estate. Though these are considered reasonably safe investments, they do not bring big financial returns. But to many people, owning their own homes brings satisfactions which cannot be measured in terms of dollars and cents.

Life Insurance.

Life insurance is considered a safe in- vestment and surely part of everyone's income should be invested in insurance. Perhaps nothing else gives the same measure of security, in proportion to the amount of the investment. Reliable companies will be recommended by your state life insurance office. A study of life insurance policies of various types is most worthwhile.

Stocks and Bonds.

Stocks and bonds afford satisfactory investments and often the interest on these is more than that from most other forms of investment. Bonds are perhaps a better investment than stocks for the majority of people because they are safe and often non-taxable.

Summary.

A financial program for the business management of the home is a family affair which depends for success upon the mutual understanding, confidence, and cooperation, not only of the two heads of the household, but also of the children.

In the homes of yesterday, there was less need for education of the family in money management because less money was handled. Through the years, the home has gradually changed from a producing unit into a consuming institution. Thus, the home of today buys and pays for most of its products with money.

This condition increases the need of a definite plan for spending; and in addition, it demands that the whole family critically analyze its own needs, desires, and wishes in relation to its own money income, its natural resources, and the social income (the things which the community gives to the home and to the individual.

When children and older boys and girls budget at home, they know how to make plans at school and elsewhere in so far as money is concerned. This knowledge tends to give a feeling of security, self-respect, and economic independence to all those who possess it.

Business men all run their affairs on the budget plan. Experts are often employed to study where mistakes are being made or where money is being wasted. Large business concerns take inventories to determine needs and improvements. In the light of what they disclose, some practices are discontinued, new methods are recommended, and new equipment is added.

What can be done by similar methods to make home and family life more effective and pleasant? Applying exact business methods to each individual home is difficult, if not impossible, but all homemakers can make effective use of business methods in the conduct of their affairs.

Though we are living in an age in which most of the actual "production" has been taken out of the home, there is still much opportunity to add to the family income by making over garments, canning foodstuffs, growing a garden, and raising chickens. We can add to the family in- come by the use of thrifty habits such as extending the life of garments through proper care, keeping lights turned off when not in use, and devising countless other ways to conserve the resources already in the home.

Consumer Education

Who is the consumer? Why should he need education? What is meant by consumer buying? The consumer is everyone. His needs begin at birth and keep increasing until he reaches his maturity at full manhood or womanhood and continue as long as he lives. Sometimes the needs of the consumer adolescent exceed the capacity of the pocketbooks of his parents for holding money and through lack of frankness and understanding all members of the family suffer the consequences. Here again we see the need for the family council and its democratic, frank procedures. Consumer education is receiving new emphasis in home economics education today, and rightly so, for the home economist has much to contribute in the new yet old field of consumer buying— new because the public is showing a keen interest in better buymanship and old because the problem of supply and demand is as old as the human race.

In order to be clearly understood, let us use the term "consumer" when we refer to everyone who uses commodities in any way. "Consumer buyer" refers to the one who purchases goods from others, and this term applies to the child with a few pennies to spend as well as the house wife on her marketing expeditions.

The consumer is asking manufacturers to tell him about their products and to be truthful, definite, and informative. The consumer realizes that, as an individual, he is helpless; but that with other consumers en masse, he has a right to attention, even from the government, and from state colleges and universities, as well as from the manufacturer.

The consumer today wants to know that he is getting value received and he has a right to this knowledge and the protection it gives. The consumer's needs are largely met through provision for the general needs of his family. In fact, his standard of living is set by the family. There are over 29,000,000 families in the United States. What these families spend, how they save, and how they give, determine to a large extent the financial security and happiness of the nation.

The amount of money that can be spent is the first consideration because in using this allotment the individual family must decide between necessities and desires. What others in the neighborhood or the same social group are using exerts a powerful influence, but often there is folly in submitting to it. More and more people are realizing that it is silly to try to keep step in social pace with the family that makes a display of its superior standards when other families in the same neighborhood live well but in keeping with their incomes.

The home, as has been said, has changed from the home of production to the home of consumption and in general this is true but much production is still carried on in the home of today. Production in the home of today is in reality a carry-over from that of former years. Commodities are changed or made over; food is still prepared attractively; clothing is mended, repaired, and remodeled; furniture is re-upholstered; and curtains and draperies continue to be made.

The best products and commodities that are used widely in homes can now be secured in stores but it is difficult to secure reliable information concerning those products which are used in small quantities in the individual home. Large concerns buy by specification and can employ experts; the home maker cannot do this as an individual and so home makers must ask for assistance from stores and manufacturers in buying.

The methods used in buying have a very definite bearing on the successful use of the family income. Cash purchases are usually wisest for experience seems to indicate that those who pay cash spend less and consequently are able to save more. Personal marketing is also better than marketing by telephone but this is not always possible, especially when there are all ages of children in the family and when the mother's strength is already overtaxed. Charge accounts are a convenience but they seem to encourage too much buying. Then, too, the stores must necessarily charge more in order to take care of losses through unpaid debts and the cost of collections. Extra bookkeeping is also expensive and must be paid for by someone. Installment buying has caused many people to overtax their ability to pay. The amounts of furniture and household equipment which are reclaimed by stores when only "half paid for" should sound a warning to those who are considering the "small down payment" method.

In addition to losses caused by poor buying methods, much money is wasted by thoughtless buying, overbuying, and the lack of proper care of furnishings after they are purchased.

Learning to be an Intelligent Buyer.

The change from producer to consumer buyer has brought many new problems to the home. When products were made in the homes, their quality was known; today the consumer must study if he is to become informed. For this reason, consumer education is now finding a definite place in the educational world and in women's clubs and study groups where in- creased attention is being given to consumer buying.

Who shall decide what the family needs, the family itself or those who have things to sell? A few pertinent questions put directly to himself by the purchaser will be found helpful. Do I need this article? Will this article fill the particular need? How much use will it give? How long will it last? What will be the cost of upkeep? And finally, am I buying it because I need it or through pressure by a salesman or through social pressure? These and other questions which will occur to you will help you in making decisions.

Buying and selling today are involved and complicated. There is so much competition that salesmen have been forced to use high-pressure methods in a sort of "survival of the fittest" battle to sell consumers. Consumers are human and find these sales efforts hard to resist, but they are often unreasonable in their demands on both the manufacturer and the distributor, and sometimes the consumer buyer is not willing to pay for the services which he demands. The habit of returning goods, for example, has been greatly abused by consumers who in that way take an unfair advantage of stores. It is alleged that forty per cent of women's wearing apparel is returned and that much of this has been worn at least once! Furniture and household equipment are also sent out on approval and used for special functions and then returned.

The credit system is a convenience to the consumer but has been greatly abused by the belated payment of accounts. Abuse of this system should be avoided for the protection of stores ; and for the best interests of the average consumer, the credit system should be abolished.

The conditions under which goods are produced is of interest to the consumer. Firms that employ workers at too low wages and make them work under unsanitary conditions should not be patronized. The Federal Government is helping here and rightly so.

Courtesy and consideration should be shown to clerks for they are not mind readers and it should be remembered that time is money to them. Reliable information concerning goods should be given by them. The consumer should depend upon reliable labels, grades, and brands.

The consumer needs reliable information giving correct and adequate facts concerning all products. Consumers as a group should demand such specifications.

The standardization of products would be of great assistance if the consumer had sufficient education to appreciate standards. Through high-pressure sales methods many consumers are led to waste money on products they would not buy if they had better information.

Since practically all advertising is directed at the poor consumer, he is practically helpless unless armed with all available information.

Fairness to the consumer and dealer alike is desirable, and to bring this about government agencies are needed. Consumers need to work together to secure information and protection from the government. More adequate laws protecting food and drugs should be passed and enforced, and market inspection should be provided universally.

CHAPTER 26

HOME AND THE COMMUNITY

The home and community are dependent upon each other; the community looks to the home for support of its projects, the home expects organized service and protection from the community. The combined forces of the home and community work to serve the individual citizen's interests, activities, and happiness.

Home makers are becoming increasingly conscious that the home is primarily responsible for the training which develops desirable citizens. It is the training we receive as children that governs our conduct as adults. The home being the center of interest around which everything else revolves, the community standards obviously represent the cumulative sum of home standards. Thus, attractive homes make an attractive community because the community reflects the interests of its homes.

YOUTH AND THE FUTURE

Building Future Homes. - Regardless of whether you go to college after high school or enter the business world, it is probable that eventually you will establish your own home and be among the 29,000,000 American home makers of this generation. Not all of us stop to realize that home making, too, is an occupation and one which requires both ability and skill. It calls for training and study too, and you cannot become a good home maker merely by setting up housekeeping in a "hit or miss" fashion.

The woman who is a home maker must be many other things as well; namely, hostess, cook, maid, seamstress, nurse, economist, and companion. Most husbands who are homemakers are also gardeners, plumbers, mechanics, electricians, and carpenters after their regular office hours are over.

The importance of home making as an occupation is being given more and more recognition and a large number of men as well as women are asking for training and study in this occupation. Home economics courses for boys have been formulated in high schools and also in colleges. These courses are not considered at all effeminate but as pathways leading to the possession of enviable accomplishments and invaluable knowledge.

The internal characteristics of the good home are sound standards, creative and intelligent leadership, family cooperation, and group unity. These worthy home virtues are reflected in worthy conduct in all external affairs. Their influence is lastingly felt not only in our local community life but also in our national life. That the time-honored institution of home life is more worthy of preservation than any other social agency is the verdict of history. When a breakdown comes in the character of the family organization, man's noblest social creation, well may we inquire as to the nature of the calamity that is soon to follow.

Armed with the knowledge that successful home life is necessary to the home's organic existence as well as the continuance of civilization, farsighted home makers are demanding for themselves and their children training commensurate with the responsibilities they must assume and on which so much depends. Their demands will not be satisfied by any course of training short of the provisions that have been made for training those who expect to follow other vocations.

THE END

If you enjoyed this book or received value from it in any way, then I'd like to ask you a favor: would you be kind enough to leave a review for this book? It would be greatly appreciated! Thank you for your support!